The Butterflies of Iowa

The Butterflies

Dennis W. Schlicht
John C. Downey
Jeffrey C. Nekola

A BUR OAK GUIDE

# of Iowa

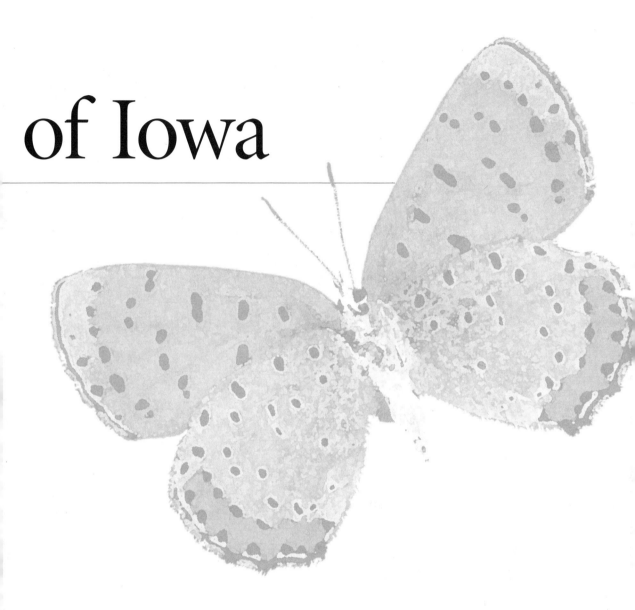

UNIVERSITY OF IOWA PRESS | IOWA CITY

University of Iowa Press, Iowa City 52242
Copyright © 2007 by the University of Iowa Press
www.uiowapress.org
All rights reserved
Printed in the United States of America

Design by April Leidig-Higgins

The University of Iowa Press is a member of Green
Press Initiative and is committed to preserving natural
resources.

Printed on acid-free paper

ISBN-10: 1-58729-532-6 cloth, 1-58729-533-4 paper
ISBN-13: 978-1-58729-532-4 cloth, 978-1-58729-533-1 paper
LCCN: 2006932734

07 08 09 10 11 C 5 4 3 2 1
07 08 09 10 11 P 5 4 3 2 1

This book is dedicated to our families,
for their support through many decades
of butterfly studies, and to all students of
Iowa butterflies, whose contributions have
made our work much more complete

The butterfly counts not months but
moments, and has time enough.
—Rabindranath Tagore

Contents

Preface and Acknowledgments

THIS BOOK DEALS SPECIFICALLY with the butterflies of Iowa. Along with more comprehensive texts and field guides (Glassberg 1999; Opler and Malikul 1998; Pyle 1981; Scott 1986; and Winter 2000), it can be used as a manual for the identification of all butterflies known to occur in Iowa as well as 90 percent of the butterflies in the Plains states.

In the first part of the book, we provide information on the natural communities of Iowa, with special attention to butterfly habitat and distribution. We follow this with a history of lepidopteran research in Iowa, from J. A. Allen in 1867 to today's researchers and enthusiasts. Next we present a chapter on creating a habitat — whether in your backyard or on a larger scale — that will attract and nurture butterflies. Finally, we set out the challenging questions and issues relevant to the study of butterfly populations in Iowa.

The second part of this book contains the species accounts, organized by family. Each account includes the common and scientific names for each species as well as its Opler and Warren (2003) number, status in Iowa, adult flight times and number of broods per season, distinguishing features, distribution and habitat, and natural history information, such as behavior and food-plant preferences.

Following the species accounts are the illustrations in part III: color photographs of all the butterflies known to occur in Iowa along with detailed range maps and flight diagrams for each species.

We end the book with a checklist of Iowa butterflies, collection information specific to the photographs, a glossary, a list of plant names used in the text, references, an index of butterfly names, and the hope that our readers will enjoy and appreciate the butterflies of Iowa as much as we do.

JOHN DOWNEY BEGAN this study in 1968, when he moved to the University of Northern Iowa in Cedar Falls from southern Illinois. John was joined in 1969 by graduate student Michael C. Christenson, who brought together distributional data on Iowa butterflies for a master's thesis completed in 1971. Dennis Schlicht continued to add distributional records from that time until 1988, when he was asked to become a coauthor. Dennis was also instrumental in stimulating other avid naturalists in the state, including John Fleckenstein, R. W. Howe, Jeff Nekola, Frank Olsen, Ray Hamilton, David Cuthrell, Tim Orwig, Jerry Selby, John Nehnevaj, Mike Saunders, Doug Nauman, Mark Leoschke, and Ron Harms, to add their expertise and records to this study. Lee Miller contributed to the project from 1975 to 1978. Although Lee left Iowa in 1961, he continued his interest and field observations during annual visits.

In recent years Jeff Nekola, Tim Orwig, and Frank Olsen enthusiastically helped us with field records and data. Jeff's knowledge of plants and ecological associations disclosed many interesting distributional finds in uncollected habitats. Author of the chapter on natural communities of Iowa, Jeff is responsible for parts of the chapter on the history of collecting and for major additions to the species accounts. His habitat records also extend throughout the distribution maps. Jeff's contributions resulted in his addition as a coauthor in 2000.

Before 1988 the only recent information regarding Loess Hills butterflies was collected during the two weeks of the 1980 Loess Hills Lepidoptera Foray. Tim Orwig was our official ambassador of the Loess Hills, extending our knowledge from this brief flight period to the entire growing season. In the process, he has added greatly to our knowledge of many of our rarest species. Tim had the great fortune to be inspired by working at Arthur Lindsey's Morningside College campus and surely collecting on his pathways.

Since 1989 Frank Olsen has undertaken several essential projects to accumulate temporal data on our butterfly fauna. He visited five Linn County nature preserves every three or four days each season and compiled a wealth of data on flight times and brood numbers. Frank, a dedicated worker, has also kept the records up to date in our database.

During the spring of 1995 a database of Iowa butterfly records was made reality by the invaluable assistance of twelve of Jeff Nekola's students from the University of Wisconsin at Green Bay. The approximately 11,000 records entered by Eric Damkot, Katie Steele, Jennifer Smits, Diana Dudley, Gerald Wicker, Charles Pickering, Joe Corson, Neila Bobb, Megan Hoffmann, Lisa Davie, Noel Versch, Rob Bradley, and Jay Mueller (over 500 hours of work!) made possible the up-to-date distribution maps and flight graphs for each species in this book.

Special thanks are also due to Dorothy Dillon and Linda Schlicht, who painstakingly typed and retyped drafts of this book, converting our scrawled comments into the first drafts. Tim Orwig traversed the state several times to give us invaluable editorial assistance and moral support. Thanks also to Nancy Goodlove, Jane McConaughy, Jim Messina, Ronald Royer, and Frank Olsen for editorial assistance.

John Downey died on February 20, 2005. His enthusiasm for the wonders of life touched everyone who knew him.

Part One. An Introduction to Iowa Butterflies

The Natural Communities of Iowa and Their Butterflies

B utterfly species are not randomly distributed in Iowa. They live only where their requirements for life are met. These include places where egg-laying, larval feeding, pupation, mate selection, and adult nectaring can occur. While some common species, including the Cabbage White, Sachem, Clouded Sulphur, Silver-spotted Skipper, Common Sootywing, Pearl Crescent, and Eastern Tiger Swallowtail, can undertake these activities in a wide variety of habitats, others are much more selective. For those species, only a very limited number of places will provide habitat through all the stages of their life cycle.

For example, Sleepy Duskywing adults are most commonly seen in xeric glade prairies of northeastern Iowa, where they search for mates and find nectar sources. The larvae, however, feed on oaks in the surrounding woodlands. Without both of these habitats, populations of the Sleepy Duskywing could not survive. In species with limited habitat requirements such as this, populations are restricted to areas in which the proper association of vegetation types is present. Potential sites for these uncommon species can be located by identifying such areas of suitable habitat.

Geologists have divided Iowa into eight landscape regions (Prior 1976): the Paleozoic Plateau, Iowan Surface, Southern Iowa Drift Plain, Des Moines Lobe, Northwest Iowa Plains, Loess Hills, Missouri Alluvial Plain, and Mississippi Alluvial Plain. Within each of these distinctive landscapes a number of unique habitats occur. Just as each habitat supports a characteristic flora (see Eilers 1982, for instance), each has also been found to harbor distinctive butterfly faunas.

In this chapter, the butterfly faunas of the important natural habitats within Iowa's landscape regions are briefly discussed. Only species considered to be naturally reproducing in Iowa are included; migrant species generally show few habitat preferences. Generally, the Iowan Surface, Paleozoic Plateau, and northwestern section of the Des Moines Lobe have been fairly well biologically documented. Other landform regions of the state have a much less well known lepidopteran fauna, however. More intensive sampling will undoubtedly uncover many additional species and associations from the habitats found in these regions.

Paleozoic Plateau

The northeastern corner of Iowa is well known for its rugged topography. This region was once termed the driftless area by early Iowa geologists, who believed no glaciers had covered the area. With the discovery of pre-Illinoian drift deposits on this landscape, however, it is now clear that the Paleozoic Plateau was glaciated at the same time as the surrounding terrain (Prior et al. 1982). The rugged nature of this region was apparently caused both by permafrost action and by Mississippi River down-cutting within the last twenty thousand years (Hallberg et al. 1984). The removal of glacial till by these erosive factors has allowed development of the only completely bedrock-controlled landform region in Iowa (Prior 1976). A number of interesting habitats are found within this landscape.

WOODLANDS

Woodlands are the most common native habitat remaining within the Paleozoic Plateau. They are primarily found on the steep, rocky land adjacent to streams and rivers. Limestone cliffs are frequently present. Many of the remaining woodland areas have been severely disturbed by grazing.

A relatively large amount of woodland habitat remains throughout the state, not just in the Paleozoic Plateau, so most of the butterflies associated with it are widespread. These include the Juvenal's Duskywing, Hobomok Skipper, Silver-spotted Skipper, Dun Skipper, Banded Hairstreak, Eastern Comma, Question Mark, Mourning Cloak, Red Admiral, Red-spotted Purple, Hackberry Emperor, Tawny Emperor, and Little Wood-satyr.

Some of the uncommon or rare species of woodlands include the Sleepy Duskywing, Harvester, Hickory Hairstreak, and Columbine Duskywing. The Columbine Duskywing may be limited to Paleozoic Plateau woodlands. These rarer species seem to be restricted to only the largest and most undisturbed woodlands. One of the rarest resident butterflies in the state, the Compton Tortoiseshell, may be observed in a few areas of Allamakee and Dubuque counties where large groves of paper birch are present. Adults seem particularly fond of trails or roadsides near streams.

Most of Iowa's woodland butterflies exhibit an affinity for openings and edges, probably because mate location is easier due to the higher light levels and visibility. At times literally hundreds of individuals may be seen along deserted stretches of gravel roads, often concentrated around puddles and moist places near woodlands. Particularly good examples of woodland habitat may be found at White Pine Hollow State Preserve in Dubuque County, Brush Creek Canyon State Preserve in Fayette County, Pike's Peak State Park in Clayton County, and the Yellow River State Forest in Allamakee County.

GLADE PRAIRIES

Steep, rocky, south- or southwest-facing hillsides in northeastern Iowa are not always covered by woodland. Prairie vegetation can be found on these dry slopes, particularly along the major river systems and their larger tributaries. Though glade prairies are dominated by prairie grasses and forbs, scattered paper birches, red cedars, and bur oaks are also present.

Glade prairies contain a diverse lepidopteran fauna that includes some of the most uncommon species in the state. The Common Roadside-skipper, Dusted Skipper, Wild Indigo Duskywing, Sleepy Duskywing, Columbine Duskywing, Olympia Marble, Silvery Blue, Reakirt's Blue, Ottoe Skipper, Juniper Hairstreak, Edwards' Hairstreak, and Striped Hairstreak have all been collected from these habitats. Other frequently observed glade prairie butterfly species include the Delaware Skipper, Coral Hairstreak, Crossline Skipper, Banded Hairstreak, and Northern Cloudywing.

The species composition of Paleozoic Plateau glade prairies is very similar to that of Loess Hills prairies in western Iowa. Few rare plant species occur in both glade prairies and Loess Hills prairies. Yet almost 60 percent of the rare glade prairie butterfly species are also found in the Loess Hills. Because of the similarity between their lepidopteran faunas and the presence of plant species with Great Plains affinities, it is likely that the glade prairies and the Loess Hills prairies both represent relics of a once more widespread xeric prairie community which flourished in Iowa some five thousand years ago during a time of warmer and drier climate (Prior et al. 1982).

Good examples of glade prairie may be observed along the Upper Iowa River, at Fish Farm Mounds State Preserve, and at Lansing's Mount Hosmer City Park in Allamakee County; at Turkey River Mounds State Preserve in Clayton County; and near Wadena in Fayette County.

SAND PRAIRIES AND SAVANNAS

Sand prairies are restricted in the Paleozoic Plateau to terraces along the Upper Iowa River and a few small tributaries of the Mississippi in Allamakee County. These areas mark a former elevation of the adjacent streams and rivers prior to late Pleistocene down-cutting by the Mississippi (Hallberg et al. 1984). Previously covered by dry, sandy prairie and black oak savanna, most of these areas are currently used as pasture. The sand prairie and savanna habitats are particularly interesting to botanists because some very rare Iowa plants, including poppy mallow, deep green sedge, huckleberry, wild lupine, spikemoss, rough-seeded fameflower, and blueberry, are known to grow on these sites.

Do rare lepidopteran species utilize these places as well? The only well-collected Paleozoic Plateau sand prairie and savanna site is at Fish Farm Mounds State Preserve in Allamakee County. Among the species observed there are the rare Columbine Duskywing and Pepper and Salt Skipper as well as the more common Juvenal's Duskywing, Gray Copper, and Bronze Copper. Sites containing wild lupine populations may also host populations of the nationally rare Karner Blue, which has been found in similar sandy habitats with lupine in nearby Minnesota and Wisconsin.

FENS

Any peatland area that has water enriched with minerals by passage through soil or bedrock is considered a fen (Moore and Bellamy 1974; Succow and Lange 1984). Such habitats are rare in the Paleozoic Plateau, developing where groundwater contained in shale-limestone contacts, glacial gravels, or sand terraces has been exposed through erosion. Such permanently saturated habitats are favorable for growth of wetland plants and animals. The dominant plant species of these habitats, often forming a dense turf, are sedges. In the late summer, fens become conspicuous for their showy displays of flat-topped aster and spotted Joe-pye-weed.

Butterflies present on Paleozoic Plateau fen sites include the Milbert's Tortoiseshell, Meadow Fritillary, Silver-bordered Fritillary, Black Dash, Bronze Copper, Eyed Brown, and rare Baltimore Checkerspot. The butterfly fauna of Paleozoic Plateau fens is essentially identical to that of fens on the surrounding Iowan Surface.

Fens occur near Postville in Clayton County, Freeport in Winneshiek County, Dorchester in Allamakee County, and St. Lucas in Fayette County.

MOIST VALLEY BOTTOMS

The majority of valley bottoms in the Paleozoic Plateau have been disturbed by humans through conversion to pasture, cropland, and towns. These bottomlands are now typically dominated by nonnative and weedy plant species. In wet areas, however, some native plant communities still exist. Most of the butterfly species found on these sites are those that favor human disturbance, although a few uncommon ones, such as the Milbert's Tortoiseshell, Meadow Fritillary, and Columbine Duskywing, may also be present.

Good examples of such habitats may be found along Grannis Creek and Bear Creek in Fayette County, Buck Creek and the Turkey River at Motor Mill in Clayton County, and French Creek in Allamakee County.

ALGIFIC TALUS SLOPES

In a few isolated areas of the Paleozoic Plateau, ice-age plant and animal communities have been maintained by cold-air drainage from adjacent ice caves. Many rare Iowa plants, including northern wild monkshood, Iowa golden saxifrage, twinflower, northern lungwort, one-sided shinleaf, rosy twisted stalk, and land snails like *Discus macclintocki*, *Catinella gelida*, and *Vertigo hubrichti* are found in such areas. After thorough survey work, no rare butterflies have been observed on these sites. Moth species do occur there, and more investigation will be necessary to determine whether or not species within this group are restricted to algific (cold-producing, from the Latin root *algus*, "cold") talus slopes.

Iowan Surface

The Iowan Surface, immediately south and west of the Paleozoic Plateau, was also exposed to harsh climatic conditions during the last ice age. Permafrost erosion into older glacial tills created the region's gently rolling topography and removed windblown silt (loess) as it was being deposited (Hallberg et al. 1978). The lack of an all-encompassing loess mantle on the Iowan Surface has exposed an older, more complex assortment of soil substrates in this region. Each substrate is associated with a unique plant and lepidopteran community.

At one time prairies covered most of the upland areas with a pre-Illinoian till substrate on the Iowan landscape. Plant species distribution in this habitat was influenced by water availability, which ranged from wet to mesic to dry. The deep, rich soil and gentle relief of these prairies have favored their conversion to cropland. Original plant and animal communities are present at only a very few places (such as Hayden Prairie State Preserve), with most of these being wet areas. Overzealous burning of the few remaining sites jeopardizes even these few remnant lepidopteran populations.

Because of the almost complete destruction and aggressive management of this community, the original butterfly fauna of the dry and mesic Iowan Surface tallgrass prairie will never be known. Small remnants of this habitat at Hayden Prairie State Preserve and Crossman Prairie State Preserve in Howard County are known to support populations of the Silvery Blue, Poweshiek Skipperling, and Regal Fritillary.

Wet prairie was not so easily converted to corn and soybeans. More such sites remain, so their butterfly fauna is more completely documented and is known to include the Meadow Fritillary, Silver-bordered Fritillary, Purplish Copper, Two-spotted Skipper, Black Dash, Dion Skipper, Coral Hairstreak, Broad-winged Skipper, Long Dash, Acadian Hairstreak, Eyed Brown, and Aphrodite Fritillary.

Wet prairie areas can be found in most protected prairie remnants of the Iowan Surface, such as Hayden Prairie and Crossman Prairie in Howard County, Split Rock Park in Chickasaw County, Brayton-Horsley Prairie in Bremer County, Randalia Prairie in Fayette County, Cedar Hills Sand Prairie State Preserve in Black Hawk County, and Blazing Star Prairie in Buchanan County.

LIMESTONE RIDGE PRAIRIES

Other Iowan Surface prairie habitats were located in areas with shallow (limestone ridge prairie) or dry (sand prairie) soil. Because these areas were not as productive for agriculture, they have experienced a lower destruction rate than adjacent prairie habitats. Limestone ridge prairies occur throughout the Iowan Surface where erosion has exposed underlying bedrock. These prairies are characterized by plant species with western affinities, such as pasque flower, silky aster, ground plum, yellow Indian paintbrush, downy gentian, and toothed evening primrose, which are more frequently encountered on glade prairies of the Paleozoic Plateau, the gravel prairies of the Des Moines Lobe, and the Loess Hills prairie along the Missouri River.

The butterfly fauna of limestone ridge prairies is very similar to the fauna of glade, gravel, and Loess Hills prairies. It includes the Delaware Skipper, Coral Hairstreak, Poweshiek Skipperling, Crossline Skipper, Tawny-edged Skipper, and Aphrodite Fritillary. Future work on the success of these species in this and other prairie types may disclose why they are restricted in their distribution.

Good examples of limestone ridge prairies may be found near Florenceville in Howard County, Austinville in Butler County, Raymond in Black Hawk County, Troy Mills in Linn County, and Earlville in Delaware County.

Sand prairies are found throughout the southern half of the Iowan Surface, wherever deep sands have accumulated from the action of wind, water, or a combination of both. Such areas are typically located along the east side of major river systems or the crest of paha ridges (capped with wind-blown sediments). These sandy areas have been subject to subsequent wind erosion, reworking the deposits to form dunes. Water readily drains off these sandy soils, making the habitat quite xeric, although some remain mesic throughout the year. Some small depressions within these sand deposits collect water during the spring. Because such areas are usually completely dry by early summer, they are termed vernal pools.

The plant community of these sites is characterized by many dry-adapted species, some of which, like the fragile prickly pear and big-rooted prickly pear, are typical of more western locations. Many of the plants associated with vernal pools, like pinweed, cross-leaved milkwort, lance-leaved violet, and yellow-eyed grass, are more characteristic of sand savannas of the Atlantic coastal plain.

The butterfly species found on Iowan Surface sand prairies include the Delaware Skipper, Gorgone Checkerspot, Little Yellow, Eastern Tailed-blue, Gray Copper, Coral Hairstreak, American Copper, Juniper Hairstreak, Crossline Skipper, Tawny-edged Skipper, Byssus Skipper, Banded Hairstreak, Striped Hairstreak, and Regal Fritillary.

Sand prairies and vernal pools can be found along the Cedar River from Bremer to Muscatine counties, the Wapsipinicon River from Buchanan to Clinton counties, and the Maquoketa River in Delaware and Jones counties. In addition, paha ridges and upland limestone outcrops in Benton, Linn, Buchanan, Delaware, and Jones counties are often blanketed by sand. Good examples of sand prairie on the Iowan Surface may be seen at the Cedar Hills Sand Prairie State Preserve in Black Hawk County, Hitaga Sand Ridge Prairie Preserve in Linn County, and Mockridge County Wildlife Preserve in Clinton County.

FENS

Fen habitats were first identified from the Iowan Surface by the state's earliest geological workers (White 1870; Calvin 1897, 1902). Conventional wisdom among Iowa biologists contended until recently that fens were found only in four northwestern Iowa counties (Lammers and Van der Valk 1979). Since the rediscovery of fens in eastern Iowa in 1984 (Nekola 1988a), over 170 sites have been located in twenty-eight eastern Iowa counties (Nekola 1988b, 1993). Most of these occur within the area of the Iowan Surface.

Fens were able to form on the Iowan Surface as gravel and bedrock were frequently exposed in the erosion of the landscape. Such gravel and bedrock exposures can contain groundwater aquifers and, if uncovered, will create a habitat with a cool, constant water supply. Many of Iowa's rarest plant species grow only in this special buffered habitat associated with groundwater discharge on these fens. Very rare land snails, some previously known only as fossils, have also been documented recently from these sites.

A number of Iowa's rarest butterfly species, including the Baltimore Checkerspot, also utilize these habitats. Other species seen in Iowan Surface fen communities include the

Milbert's Tortoiseshell, Meadow Fritillary, Silver-bordered Fritillary, Black Dash, Dion Skipper, Gray Copper, Bronze Copper, Broad-winged Skipper, Long Dash, Acadian Hairstreak, Aphrodite Fritillary, and Regal Fritillary.

Examples of fen communities on the Iowan Surface may be seen at the Brayton-Horsley Prairie and Northwoods Park in Bremer County, Cedar Hills Sand Prairie State Preserve in Black Hawk County, Cutshall Access Park in Buchanan County, Buffalo Slough in Cerro Gordo County, near Maynard in Fayette County, New Hartford in Grundy County, St. Ansgar in Mitchell County, Waubeek and Paris in Linn County, Manchester in Delaware County, Ionia in Chickasaw County, and Jackson Junction in Winneshiek County.

WOODLANDS

Woodlands occur along river systems and their tributaries throughout the Iowan Surface. Such woodland habitats were not originally as common as in the Paleozoic Plateau. Many of these woodland tracts still exist due to their shallow, rocky soils and steep slopes, which made them of poor agricultural quality. Grazing and repeated timber-cutting, however, have left most of these remaining sites in poor condition.

The butterfly fauna of these sites much resembles that of Paleozoic Plateau woodlands, although the species diversity is generally lower. Some species such as the Columbine Duskywing and Compton Tortoiseshell are absent.

Southern Iowa Drift Plain

The Southern Iowa Drift Plain covers approximately the southern half of the state. This area was not exposed to such intense permafrost erosion as were the former two land-forms, probably because the climate was somewhat more moderate during the last ice age. Thus loess mantle blankets most of the region, eliminating much of the substrate diversity seen in both the Paleozoic Plateau and the Iowan Surface. Streams have eroded the landscape of the Southern Iowa Drift Plain into the rolling hills made famous by Grant Wood (Prior et al. 1982). Old cemented glacial tills and bedrock are sometimes exposed along major streams and rivers. In the easternmost section of the Southern Iowa Drift Plain (Eastern Tabular Uplands of Roosa 1982), limestone is often close to the surface, creating woodland and prairie habitats similar to those of the surrounding Paleozoic Plateau and Iowan Surface. Because of the well-eroded nature of the plain, wetland areas are rare. Many species of plants and animals, including some butterflies, reach their northern range limit in this region.

Even though it is a large and diverse area, the Southern Iowa Drift Plain has been only cursorily surveyed for butterflies. More investigation will be necessary before the fauna of this landform can be considered well documented.

WOODLANDS

Woodlands once covered a significant portion of the Southern Iowa Drift Plain. Much of this forestland bordered major rivers and streams, following steep, protected slopes up ravines and tributaries. Shimek State Forest and Stephens State Forest lie within this region and contain the majority of Iowa's state forest land. Some preliminary survey work on the lepidoptera of the Lick Creek and Croton units of Shimek State Forest was recently undertaken. Both common and uncommon woodland species were collected. While some of these uncommon species, such as the Sleepy Duskywing, Juvenal's Duskywing, and Northern Cloudywing, are found throughout Iowa, most are southern species at the northern limit of their range. Among these are the Common Roadside-skipper, Ozark Baltimore Checkerspot, American Snout, White M Hairstreak, Zabulon Skipper, Hayhurst's Scallopwing, and Southern Cloudywing.

Some of these species may be restricted to southern Iowa woodlands due to the distribution of their larval host plants. Henry's Elfin larvae in Iowa are apparently restricted to the redbud, which as a native tree is limited to woodlands in the southern third of the state. Likewise, the Zebra Swallowtail and Pipevine Swallowtail larvae eat paw paw and Virginia snakeroot, respectively, both of which are very rare and restricted to Iowa's southern counties. Additional collecting in these woodlands may produce records of other new species for the state, such as the Falcate Orangetip, which has been located in only two counties to the south in Missouri.

Good examples of Southern Iowa Drift Plain woodlands may be observed in Shimek State Forest and Stephens State Forest in Appanoose, Clarke, Davis, Lee, Lucas, and Van Buren counties; Lacey-Keosauqua State Park in Van Buren County; and Starr's Cave State Preserve in Des Moines County.

LIMESTONE RIDGE PRAIRIES

Exposed ridges of limestone bedrock are occasionally encountered in the easternmost section of the Southern Iowa Drift Plain in Clinton, Dubuque, Jackson, and Jones counties. Just as in the Paleozoic Plateau and the Iowan Surface, such bedrock exposures are often covered by xeric prairie plants.

The lepidopteran fauna of these sites is quite similar to the fauna of limestone prairies and glades of other landforms. The Delaware Skipper, Columbine Duskywing, Gray Copper, Coral Hairstreak, Ottoe Skipper, Leonard's Skipper, Juniper Hairstreak, Crossline Skipper, Banded Hairstreak, Striped Hairstreak, and Regal Fritillary have been observed. It should be noted that these Southern Iowa Drift Plain limestone prairies have a richer lepidopteran fauna than those of the Iowan Surface, including the Ottoe Skipper and Columbine Duskywing. They are less rich than glade prairie sites in the Paleozoic Plateau, however, because the Sleepy Duskywing, Dusted Skipper, Common Roadside-skipper, and Silvery Blue are absent. Yet all these sites are similar in possessing strong affinities with Loess Hills and Great Plains prairie communities.

Examples of limestone ridge prairie have been observed on the Southern Iowa Drift Plain in Jones County near Temple Hill, Manikowski Prairie State Preserve in Clinton County, and Hamilton's Prairie in Jackson County.

TALLGRASS PRAIRIES AND SAVANNAS

The dry uplands, ridge tops, and south-facing slopes of the Southern Iowa Drift Plain were dominated by prairie and savanna habitats. Often such sites support plants typical of dry-mesic prairie, xeric prairie, and dry woodlands. Because little remains of this habitat, not much direct evidence can be accumulated regarding its original flora and fauna.

Some uncommon lepidopteran species, including the Common Roadside-skipper, Mottled Duskywing, Little Yellow, Dainty Sulphur, Melissa Blue, Zabulon Skipper, and Byssus Skipper, have been observed on remnants of this habitat.

Remaining Southern Iowa Drift Plain tallgrass prairie and savanna habitats may be observed in the Croton Unit of Shimek State Forest in Lee County, F. W. Kent Park in Johnson County, and southwest of Fairfield in Jefferson County.

Des Moines Lobe

At the close of Wisconsinan glaciation, a last surge of ice plunged south over central Iowa before the continental ice sheet wasted away in a warming climate (Prior et al. 1982). This last gasp of the Wisconsinan glacier has been named the Des Moines Lobe. During its brief tenure, the Des Moines Lobe completely changed the appearance of north-central Iowa, in some areas smoothing the surface by burying river valleys and in others making great ridges of glacial debris, termed moraines. In places where the ice stagnated, kettlehole depressions formed, creating basins conducive to development of wetland habitats. Rapid melting of the Des Moines Lobe from 14,000 to 12,500 years ago caused the rapid down-cutting of its outlet rivers. Much of the length of the Des Moines River is thus lined by steep hills and bedrock bluffs. Loess could not be deposited on the ice-covered surface, so the Des Moines Lobe resembles the Iowan Surface, with a great diversity of possible substrates upon which native plant and animal communities could develop.

TALLGRASS PRAIRIES

Much of the landscape of the Des Moines Lobe was covered by prairie vegetation at the time of settlement. These prairies ranged from the dry uplands to wet pothole bottoms. European settlers who broke the prairie sod and drained the marshes to create some of the most fertile farms in the world forever changed this complex community. Few acres of the original mosaic of native prairie remain. Pieces can be found not only in nature preserves but in some unlikely places (for example, in pioneer cemeteries and along railroad right-of-ways). These small scraps of prairie often still harbor unique butterfly faunas.

Dry to mesic prairies on the Des Moines Lobe support populations of the Arogos Skipper, Delaware Skipper, Common Wood-nymph, Horace's Duskywing, Reakirt's Blue, Poweshiek Skipperling, Crossline Skipper, Tawny-edged Skipper, Aphrodite Fritillary, and Regal Fritillary.

On wet-mesic to wet prairies and marshes, other uncommon lepidopteran species may be observed, including the Meadow Fritillary, Silver-bordered Fritillary, Two-spotted Skipper, Black Dash, Dion Skipper, Bronze Copper, Broad-winged Skipper, Acadian Hairstreak, Eyed Brown, and Aphrodite Fritillary.

Good examples of native Des Moines Lobe tallgrass prairie may be seen at Hoffman Prairie State Preserve in Cerro Gordo County; Kalsow Prairie State Preserve in Pocahontas County; Kirchner Prairie in Clay County; Ames High Prairie State Preserve in Story County; Moechley's Prairie in Polk County; Stinson Prairie State Preserve in Kossuth County; Anderson Prairie State Preserve in Emmet County; Cayler Prairie State Preserve in Dickinson County; and along U.S. Highway 18 from Cylinder to Garner in Palo Alto, Kossuth, and Hancock counties.

GRAVEL PRAIRIES

The receding glacier left behind large ridges of till and gravel in the form of terminal moraines. These exposed ridges have very shallow soils, often exceedingly dry. A unique xeric prairie flora is found on these gravel moraine prairies, including some very rare Iowa species such as wooly milkweed, eastern biscuitroot, kittentails, skeletonweed, milkwort, and buffalo berry.

The butterfly fauna of these areas also contains some of the rarest species in the state. The Dakota Skipper was last seen in Iowa on a xeric gravel hill in northwestern Iowa. This disappearance exemplifies the sensitive survival situation of some butterfly species. The loss may be attributed to management activities or to natural phenomena. It was, however, "protected" on a preserve managed by the Iowa Department of Natural Resources using methods prescribed for the maintenance of tallgrass prairie. Other species found at these sites (often in small populations) include the Arogos Skipper, Common Ringlet, Dun Skipper, Silvery Blue, Coral Hairstreak, Reakirt's Blue, Melissa Blue, Poweshiek Skipperling, Long Dash, Crossline Skipper, Aphrodite Fritillary, and Regal Fritillary.

Examples of moraine gravel prairie may be observed at Freda Haffner Kettlehole State Preserve and Cayler Prairie State Preserve in Dickinson County, at Fort Defiance State Park and Anderson Prairie State Preserve in Emmet County, and east of Ruthven in Palo Alto County.

FENS

Fen habitats have long been recognized by biologists on the Des Moines Lobe in Dickinson, Emmet, Clay, and Palo Alto counties (Lammers and Van der Valk 1979). These fens support a distinctive flora, which (like the flora of Iowan Surface fens) contains many state-endangered species. Some of the plant species restricted to fens include the small fringed gentian, Kalm's lobelia, grass of Parnassus, leafy northern green orchid, hooded ladies' tresses, common arrow-grass, small arrow-grass, and small bladderwort.

The unusual buffered habitat of these fens has permitted the occurrence of a distinctive lepidopteran fauna as well. None of these species are restricted to fen habitats; all have also been observed in wet prairie remnants. Fens remain the most important habitat, however, in both number of occurrences and total population size supported for some of these species, including the Silver-bordered Fritillary, Black Dash, Mulberry Wing, Eyed Brown, Aphrodite Fritillary, and Regal Fritillary.

WOODLANDS

Woodland areas occur infrequently throughout the Des Moines Lobe, being restricted to the steep land surrounding the major rivers. In some places bedrock is exposed. The cool, moist sandstone and limestone of these bluffs have maintained populations of some plants, such as the Canada mayflower, which are otherwise frequent only within the Paleozoic Plateau.

The butterfly fauna of these woodlands is much like that of eastern and northeastern Iowa and includes the Hackberry Emperor, Tawny Emperor, Silver-spotted Skipper, Coral Hairstreak, Hobomok Skipper, and Banded Hairstreak. Additionally, some uncommon Iowa woodland species, such as the Sleepy Duskywing, Columbine Duskywing, and American Snout, have been observed, particularly in woodlands bordering the Des Moines River.

Remaining woodland tracts in the Des Moines Lobe may be observed at Ledges State Park in Boone County, at Woodman Hollow State Preserve and Brushy Creek State Preserve in Webster County, at Fort Defiance State Park in Emmet County, and along West Lake Okoboji near Milford in Dickinson County.

Northwest Iowa Plains

To the west of the Des Moines Lobe the landscape is once again dominated by gently rolling hills. Unlike the similar-looking Iowan Surface, much of the area of the Northwest Iowa Plains is covered by a loess mantle, which gradually becomes thicker to the west. Because of this, the Northwest Iowa Plains are not as diverse in available substrates as the Iowan Surface or Des Moines Lobe. Some loess-free areas are present within this region, however, primarily on the eroded hills along the Little Sioux River. Another loess-free area is found in extreme northwestern Lyon County, where the Precambrian Sioux Quartzite is exposed. Most of the rare species found from within this region are restricted to such loess-free areas.

TALLGRASS PRAIRIES

This community once dominated the landscape of the Northwest Iowa Plains. The good soil and shallow slopes have doomed much of this area to become cropland. Only one sizable native tallgrass prairie tract is known to remain in this region: the two hundred–acre Steele Prairie State Preserve near Larrabee in Cherokee County. A few smaller tallgrass prairie remnants also exist in this region.

As with the other regions of tallgrass prairie in Iowa, the almost complete habitat destruction prevents an accurate assessment of the original diversity and composition of the lepidopteran fauna. The few remaining tracts are known to support populations of the Arogos Skipper, Delaware Skipper, Coral Hairstreak, Melissa Blue, Poweshiek Skipperling, Mulberry Wing, Crossline Skipper, Tawny-edged Skipper, and Regal Fritillary.

Besides Steele Prairie, examples of tallgrass prairie in the Northwest Iowa Plains may also be seen in Dog Creek County Park in O'Brien County and O'Brien Prairie in Plymouth County.

GRAVEL PRAIRIES

Erosion of the Little Sioux River valley at the close of the Wisconsinan exposed large amounts of gravel. The remaining steep gravel slopes are quite dry, which has allowed colonization by xeric prairie vegetation. Some very rare Iowa plants, including prairie sagewort, wooly milkweed, lotus-flowered milk vetch, eastern biscuitroot, biscuitroot, slender penstemon, and Pennsylvania cinquefoil have been found on these sites.

Few of these xeric prairie remnants have been surveyed for lepidopteran species. The Arogos Skipper, Delaware Skipper, Coral Hairstreak, Reakirt's Blue, Melissa Blue, Crossline Skipper, Aphrodite Fritillary, and Regal Fritillary have been located. With further investigation, populations of additional rare species will undoubtedly be found.

Examples of these gravel prairies can be seen along the Little Sioux River near Linn Grove and Sioux Rapids in Buena Vista County; in Spring, Cherokee, and Pilot townships in Cherokee County; east of Peterson in Clay County; and in Grant and Waterman townships in O'Brien County.

LOESS PRAIRIES

Adjacent to the Big Sioux River in extreme western Lyon and Sioux counties deep accumulations of loess were deposited during the Wisconsinan, much the same as in the Loess Hills (discussed later). Erosion has cut deeply into these deposits, leaving steep, dry slopes. Many of the plants found in these prairies, such as blue grama, dotted blazing star, and skeletonweed, are also found in the dry prairies of the Loess Hills region farther to the south.

A few of these prairie sites were visited during the 1980 Loess Hills Lepidoptera Foray, whose participants included specialists from all over the country. Tim Orwig of Sioux City has made additional observations since the late 1980s. Species located include the Variegated Fritillary, Gray Copper, Ottoe Skipper, Long Dash, and Striped Hairstreak. Given the similar habitats and plant species of these prairies and those in the Loess Hills, a more intensive survey of the lepidopteran fauna of these prairies will probably uncover additional species.

Loess prairie remnants may be observed along the Big Sioux River west of Inwood in Lyon County and northwest of Hawarden in Sioux County.

SIOUX QUARTZITE PRAIRIE

In extreme northwestern Lyon County, metamorphic rock over 1 billion years old has been exposed at the land surface (Anderson 1982). A unique flora requiring hot, dry conditions is found on these outcrops of Sioux Quartzite. Many of these plants, such as buffalo grass, hairy water-clover, fragile prickly pear, and fameflower, are species of the Great Plains and are very rare in Iowa.

Butterflies such as the Arogos Skipper, Common Ringlet, Melissa Blue, and Edwards' Hairstreak collected from these outcrops include some of Iowa's rarest species. Others observed on Sioux Quartzite prairie remnants include the Delaware Skipper, Dun Skipper, Variegated Fritillary, Gray Copper, Coral Hairstreak, Reakirt's Blue, Long Dash, Crossline Skipper, Tawny-edged Skipper, and Banded Hairstreak.

The primary example of Sioux Quartzite prairie is located within Gitchie Manitou State Preserve northwest of Granite in Lyon County. A few other sites are known from the immediate vicinity.

Fen habitats occur within gravel deposits along the Little Sioux River and its tributaries in Clay and O'Brien counties. Like the nearby sites on the Des Moines Lobe, they support populations of rare or endangered Iowa plants, including small fringed gentian, Kalm's lobelia, grass of Parnassus, beaked rush, nut sedge, shining willow, and arrow-grass.

The lepidopteran fauna is also similar to the fauna found on the adjacent Des Moines Lobe fens and includes the Silver-bordered Fritillary, Black Dash, and Mulberry Wing. Other rare species may eventually be documented from these sites, which are poorly studied.

Examples of this community may be found northwest and west of Gillett Grove in Clay County, southeast of Sutherland in O'Brien County, and northeast of Klondike in Lyon County.

WOODLANDS

The Northwest Iowa Plains, due to lack of rainfall, had the least forest cover of any landform region in the state (Roosa 1982). Today forest is still restricted to moist, protected slopes bordering the major rivers. Some of the most extensive forest tracts are found along the Little Sioux and Big Sioux rivers.

The butterfly fauna of these woodlands contains most of the familiar woodland species mentioned for other landforms. In addition, populations of the rare Hickory Hairstreak have been located in Northwest Iowa Plains woodland tracts.

Examples of woodland remnants may be seen in Wanata State Park south of Peterson in Clay County and in Oak Grove State Park north of Hawarden in Sioux County.

Loess Hills

During the last ice age the Missouri River was one of the primary outlet rivers for summer meltwater from glacial ice. The annual flood of meltwater carried quantities of silt created by the grinding action of the ice sheet as it overran bedrock. This silt was deposited in the river channel. When water flows decreased with cessation of ice melt in fall and winter, great expanses of silt were exposed to the wind. Every fall, winter, and spring, when the flow of the Missouri was low, great dust storms would blow across the valley. This wind-borne silt (termed loess) could be carried for miles until it once again fell to the ground; most of the southern half of Iowa is covered by some amount of loess. Most loess was deposited adjacent to the river, however, creating great drifts sometimes more than 200 feet thick (Prior 1976), burying the previous landscape. From Harrison and Monona counties southward, loess covered Pennsylvanian shales, sandstones, and limestones. In Woodbury and Plymouth counties, Cretaceous bedrock was covered. The highly erodible nature of loess enabled deep gullies to develop and grow in size until only steep, narrow ridges of deep loess remained.

Those steep loess slopes facing south or west were exposed to drying by the sun and winds blowing in from the arid west. These slopes were colonized by plants of the Great

Plains, such as eared milkweed, lotus-flowered milk vetch, wavy-leaved thistle, dotted blazing star, stiff flax, skeletonweed, sand lily, buffalo berry, and yucca.

Particularly in the south (Pottawattamie, Mills, and Fremont counties), forest communities developed on the shaded north- and east-facing slopes where drying was not as severe. These forests often contained southern plants, such as the paw paw, which are at the northern limit of their range. Prairie fires and natural grazing were suppressed after European settlement, so the amount of forest in the Loess Hills has increased at the expense of the prairie. Forest is now frequent and threatens many prairie areas. This region still supports most of the remaining prairie habitat in the state (Roosa 1982), however, because the very steep slopes and dry soils prevented cultivation and even grazing.

Unlike some of the preceding landform regions, the Loess Hills have a relatively well documented lepidopteran fauna. The 1980 Loess Hills Lepidoptera Foray was extensively surveyed during the midsummer flight period on this landform, but the spring, early summer, and fall flight periods have not been as well documented. Only recently, with the efforts of Tim Orwig, have these periods also been studied (Orwig 1992; Schlicht and Orwig 1992). His discovery, since 1987, of the Olympia Marble, Wild Indigo Duskywing, Dusted Skipper, and Pawnee (Leonard's) Skipper in Woodbury and Plymouth counties and the Leonard's Skipper in Mills and Pottawattamie counties suggests that we still have much to learn about the Loess Hills lepidopteran fauna.

PRAIRIES

The xeric midgrass prairie of the Loess Hills supports uncommon Iowa butterflies as well as plants. As with the plant species, some of the lepidoptera known from Loess Hills prairies are typically found farther west in the Great Plains. Among the species observed in this habitat are the Common Roadside-skipper, Arogos Skipper, Delaware Skipper, Dusted Skipper, Gorgone Checkerspot, Wild Indigo Duskywing, Mottled Duskywing, Olympia Marble, Gray Copper, Coral Hairstreak, Reakirt's Blue, Pawnee (Leonard's) Skipper, Ottoe Skipper, Juniper Hairstreak, Crossline Skipper, Tawny-edged Skipper, Regal Fritillary, Southern Cloudywing, Northern Cloudywing, and Southern Dogface.

Although the habitat of these species is being encroached upon by forest, they also ironically face a threat from human efforts to preserve their habitat. Fire is now considered the management of choice for prairie communities (Smith and Christiansen 1982), but it is known to kill adults, larvae, and eggs of some butterflies (Arnold 1983; Dana 1985, 1991). Recolonization of a burned area from nearby surrounding unburned prairie is possible in parts of the Loess Hills prairies. Many are isolated from similar habitats and must now be treated as islands of native habitat within a sea of agriculture. If a prairie butterfly species is extirpated from a site with no nearby populations present for recolonization, site extirpation in this context equals local extirpation. In our opinion such local population extirpations always precede or are concomitant with species extinction.

We believe that the burning of too-large patches on a prairie or burning at an inappropriate time in the life cycle of a species creates a higher risk that invertebrate populations may become locally extirpated from a site. Current prairie management practices advocated in the Midwest emphasize large burned patches in relation to total prairie size and a fire-return frequency of once every three or four years. Unless the size of burned patches is made smaller and the return time for fire on any particular spot is changed to a more natural occurrence, humans may well "love to death" the butterfly fauna of the Loess Hills and other native prairies in the state.

Prairie habitats may be seen throughout the Loess Hills landform, but protected examples may be observed within Waubonsie State Park in Fremont County; the Council Bluffs city parks in Pottawattamie County; Murray Hill Scenic Overlook in Harrison County; Loess Hills Wildlife Area, Loess Hills State Forest, Preparation Canyon State Park, and Turin Loess Hills State Preserve in Monona County; Sioux City Prairie in Woodbury County; Five Ridge Prairie State Preserve in Plymouth County; and Stone State Park in Woodbury and Plymouth counties.

WOODLANDS

Native woodlands were originally restricted in the Loess Hills to the southern counties, where average yearly rainfall was higher. Although the habitat is more abundant today, most of the interesting lepidopteran species of these woodlands are found in the original forest cover of Harrison, Pottawattamie, Mills, and Fremont counties. The intergradations of prairie and woodland habitats have made for some interesting captures, such as the Olympia Marble on a woodland site.

Only the woodland area at Waubonsie State Park in Fremont County has been well collected throughout the season. Many other woodland sites were surveyed in midsummer during the 1980 Lepidoptera Foray. The fauna of Loess Hills woodlands, containing the Hoary Edge, Sleepy Duskywing, Zebra Swallowtail, Harvester, Henry's Elfin, White M Hairstreak, Hickory Hairstreak, Edwards' Hairstreak, Striped Hairstreak, and Hayhurst's Scallopwing, includes some of the rarest species in the state. Other taxa observed in this habitat include the Little Wood-satyr, Hobomok Skipper, Little Glassywing, and Banded Hairstreak.

Besides Waubonsie State Park, Loess Hills woodland areas may be found throughout Harrison, Pottawattamie, Mills, and Fremont counties. Protected examples may be observed within Preparation Canyon State Park, Loess Hills State Forest, and the Loess Hills Wildlife Area in Monona County.

Missouri Alluvial Plain

Once Iowa's two major rivers were bordered by extensive communities of native vegetation that were dependent upon constant turnover in the community caused by the periodic floods that changed the river channel and deposited sand, silt, and gravel. The dynamic properties of this habitat have been totally altered by humans. The Army Corps of Engineers has diked, straightened, drained, and leveed both of the great alluvial areas of the state, modifying both the natural processes and the vegetation of the areas.

Unlike the Mississippi Alluvial Plain, in which a few native habitats remain (primarily from Jackson to Des Moines counties), the Missouri Alluvial Plain has been almost totally altered. Extensive riparian forests, lowland prairies, sand prairies, and wetlands once occurred in the floodplain. Now only a few scattered wetland areas persist within Lake Manawa State Park and DeSoto National Wildlife Refuge. The Long Dash, Dion Skipper, and Acadian Hairstreak have been located recently in such areas. In addition, some remnants of woodland and sand prairie also still exist. The sand prairie sites are known to support populations of prickly pear and early ladies'-tresses, as well as the ornate box turtle. No investigation of the lepidoptera of these sites seems to have been undertaken.

Mississippi Alluvial Plain

SAND PRAIRIES

Great deposits of sand have accumulated along the Mississippi River in Muscatine, Louisa, and Des Moines counties. The dry conditions present in the upland sandy areas have allowed xeric prairie plants, many with Great Plains affinities, to exist. Some of the rare plant species of these sites include flax-leaved aster, bent milk vetch, deep green sedge, golden aster, erect day-flower, false heather, dwarf dandelion, prickly pear, large-flowered penstemon, cleft phlox, sand cherry, spike moss, and Pickering's morning glory. It is not unusual to find active sand dunes and blowouts on these prairies.

One of the most famous sand prairie areas is the Big Sand Mound Preserve in Muscatine County. This site has a well-documented butterfly fauna. Among the species observed are the Common Roadside-skipper, American Copper, Juniper Hairstreak, Crossline Skipper, Regal Fritillary, Hayhurst's Scallopwing, and Northern and Southern Cloudywings.

Other Mississippi Alluvial Plain sand prairie sites may be observed near Bellevue and Sabula in Jackson County.

OTHER HABITATS

Riparian woodlands and wetlands also occur within the Mississippi Alluvial Plain. Some very rare plant species are known to occur in these places. However, no lepidoptera have been reported from these areas. This lack of information indicates that serious long-range collecting efforts from such habitats are necessary.

Conclusion

Many unique habitats occur on the eight major landforms of Iowa. While the great majority of these habitats have been destroyed or severely altered by humans in the last 150 years, a surprisingly large number of individual sites remain. The documentation of the lepidopteran fauna of these habitats began only recently. There is much we do not know about the native butterflies of these sites. By learning about the geologic conditions which create these habitats and their characteristic plant species, it is possible to locate areas that have not been collected for butterflies. In the search for these habitats and the documentation of their lepidopteran communities, our understanding of Iowa's rich natural heritage will be greatly expanded. New species for the state and populations for our rarest species undoubtedly await discovery. With those discoveries the plant/animal/

habitat relationships which underlie our understanding of these natural areas will be advanced considerably.

As more and more natural areas are destroyed by humans in the state, the knowledge of original lepidopteran diversity will become harder to decipher. It is up to us to locate, document, and help protect the remaining native lepidopteran communities of Iowa while they still exist. We must discover management techniques that will not jeopardize survival of lepidopteran species. The identification of the most important remaining sites for butterflies and the protection of these sites and the species restricted to them are a priceless gift to the future. Lepidopterists can make their biggest contribution to these larger questions, leading to the conservation of our natural heritage.

A History of Butterfly Collecting in Iowa

S ome of the earliest recorded collectors in Iowa were not residents. J. A. Allen collected in Crawford, Greene, and Dallas counties and made field observations during the summer of 1867 and brought forty-six species east to Samuel H. Scudder. The lack of inclusion of Iowa specimens in the rash of new U.S. species being described in the mid 1800s led Scudder to publish his untitled note (1868b), where he shared information on Allen's specimens with members of the Boston Natural History Society and indicated that three of the Iowa species were new. By the time he published on them (Scudder 1869), he had decided that four were new: *Chrysophanus dione* Scud. (now *Lycaena dione* [Scudder]), *Apatura Proserpina* Scud. (now *Asterocampa clyton* [Bdv. & LeC.] form *Proserpina* [Scud.]), *Nisoniades martialis* Scud. (now *Erynnis martialis* [Scud.]), and *Hesperia iowa* Scud. (now *Atrytone arogos iowa* [Scud.]). By this time he had also received 150 Iowa specimens from the vicinity of Des Moines through E. P. Austin. In 1887 Scudder described *Atrytone kumskaka* Scud. (now *Problema byssus* [Scud.]). According to contemporary corresponding members of the Davenport Academy of Science (see *Proceedings*, vol. 3, p. 62), both Allen and Austin were residents of Cambridge, Massachusetts. No doubt both contacted Scudder personally in Massachusetts after having collected in Iowa.

One of the first resident collectors was H. W. Parker, who also published. He taught in Grinnell and collected mostly in that vicinity, adding to Scudder's 1869 list. He first described *Hesperia poweshiek* (now *Oarisma poweshiek* [Parker]). He later moved to Ames.

Perhaps the most dynamic early collector was Joseph Duncan Putnam, who might have become even more prominent in the history of lepidopterology if not for his untimely death at age twenty-six from tuberculosis. During his short life he was the moving spirit behind the Davenport Academy of Sciences and published on a variety of insect topics from bark lice to butterflies (Putnam 1876). He was an acknowledged authority on Solpugidae, the sunspiders. Putnam corresponded with many of the giants of entomology, including several of the leading lepidopterists he had met on his various travels: H. H. Behr, J. Henry Comstock, W. H. Edwards, H. A. Hagen, R. Ostensacken, C. V. Riley, H. Strecker, and Scudder. At one time or another, all these men helped identify insects that Putnam collected in Iowa, Colorado, Utah, and Wyoming in particular. Strecker assisted in the determination of some of the difficult species in Putnam's (1876) list of the butterflies in the vicinity of Davenport. The few Iowa specimens in the Strecker collection (now on extended loan from the Field Museum of Natural History in Chicago to the Allyn Museum in Sarasota, Florida) do not appear to have been collected by Putnam. Much of the correspondence between Strecker and Putnam and other letters to Putnam are still preserved in the archives of his namesake, the Putnam Museum in Davenport.

Since the publications of Scudder (1868a, 1868b, 1869), Parker (1870b), and Putnam (1876), additional papers have shown that Iowa had several resident collectors, some of whom were active only in their youth. Alice B. Walton and her sister Lilly P. Walton accumulated a fine entomological collection from the vicinity of Muscatine, in the mid 1870s. Alice Walton published this list, perhaps at the urging of Putnam, in the *Proceedings* of the Davenport Academy of Science in 1880 as well as in a book on the history of Muscatine County (Walton 1879).

Other early authors followed at intervals, including A. W. Hoffmeister (1881) in Lee County and Herbert Osborn (1890, 1891) in Story County. Henry G. Willard (1892), like Parker before him, lived in Poweshiek County and reared specimens at his home in Grinnell. A. S. Van Winkle (1893a, 1893b) in Keokuk County also reared butterflies, as well as collecting the adults. Resident collectors communicated with out-of-state authorities, even sending them living material. Thus Willard sent a Gray Copper collected in Grinnell to Henry Skinner (1893, 1911), who first described *Pamphila sassacus dacotae* Skin. (now *Hesperia dacotae* [Skin.]). Dr. C. Hoeg of Decorah sent eggs of a Common Checkered-skipper to George H. French (1897), who first described its life history.

A. F. Porter (1908) is one of the last pre–twentieth century resident collectors who also published. In a sense he was a gentleman naturalist transplant (in spirit at least) from the nineteenth century. He lived in Decorah and accumulated a very large collection with many exotic forms by personal collecting, trading, and purchasing. It was particularly rich in *Morpho* butterflies, which he apparently also used in various art forms. He traveled widely in the United States, Central America, and South America. Porter was a writer and photographer and made extensive efforts to document his travels. His former residence in Decorah has been converted to a museum housing some of his material. The bulk of this material (66,000 specimens) was given to Upper Iowa College. Most of that collection did not survive the 1980s, and some of it found its way into private hands.

During the second decade of the twentieth century several resident collectors published county lists, including George Berry (1914), Frank Pellett (1915), and Arthur Lindsey (1915, 1917 [as Lindsay]). Lindsey (1921, 1922, 1931) became a leading authority on the Hesperiidae. Berry published such an incredible list for Linn County that some question his data. Several of his specimens survive at Coe College in Cedar Rapids. *Pamphila ogallala* Leussler (now *Hesperia ottoe* Edw. form *ogallala* [Leussler]) was first described in 1921.

Arthur Lindsey was a native of Council Bluffs and graduated from Morningside College in Sioux City in 1916. In 1915 he published "The Butterflies of Woodbury County." He worked with William Barns on moths, but his main interest was skipper butterflies. The hills of Sioux City and Council Bluffs were wonderfully populated with a seasonal parade of skippers. Lindsey published "The Hesperioidea of North America" (1931) and revised the taxonomy of the genus *Hesperia* in 1942. By 1959 he had collected 6,000 skippers, including specimens from 28 type localities. In 1930 W. J. Holland named a California skipper in Lindsey's honor, *Hesperia lindseyi* Holland (Orwig 1994).

Very little was published on Iowa butterflies during the late 1920s and early 1930s, except for a small note by Lulu M. Berry (1934). Berry is said to have communicated with Porter and other naturalists of the time and sent specimens from her home near Vinton in Benton County. A Porter scrapbook even contains a photograph of her home. She was locally known as "the bug lady" and seems to have led a somewhat tormented life. Her gravestone near Urbana reads "Like the Butterfly at Last Thank God I'm Free."

This dearth of publications on Iowa butterflies continued into the mid 1950s. Although papers dealing with taxonomic groups or geographic areas by out-of-state authors, such as William D. Field (1938) and R. W. Macy and H. H. Shepard (1941), may have contained references to the occurrence of a particular species in Iowa, these secondary sources may not be as reliable as the primary literature in many instances. Sometimes the butterfly records are contained within works on more general subjects, such as studies on the insect fauna of Iowa prairies by George O. Hendrickson (1928, 1930). During the 1950s and 1960s Lee Miller and Ron Royer studied butterflies in central Iowa, especially Polk County. Both have had renowned careers as lepidopterists.

Whether or not Iowa collectors published their observations, many of the collections have been invaluable sources of information. Recent authors Lee Miller (1961), Michael Christenson (1971), and Stephen Miller (1972) have profited greatly from these collections. Of course, the present volume depends heavily on records obtained from a wide variety of sources in both public and private collections.

Some insights on the numbers of lepidopterists in Iowa might be obtained from the biennial list of members of the Lepidopterists' Society. While not all collectors join such organizations, we can still use local membership as an index, even though the result might be much lower than the actual number. In the last two decades the membership has remained fairly constant (six to ten members), indicating a small but persistent interest. We attempted to contact all present and past collectors to survey their present interests and holdings. Unfortunately, we could not reach everyone, and responses were such that we saw little merit in including a summary here. We infer, however, that the state has had fewer than a hundred resident collectors in its entire history.

As recently as twenty years ago, very few individuals were active in lepidopteran research in the state. Because we could not visit every part of the state at weekly intervals and this aspect of the state's biodiversity was quite poorly documented, we have been encouraging individuals throughout the state to assist us in our collection efforts. Now perhaps as many as a dozen individuals are helping to document lepidopteran diversity. Because of these increased numbers of collectors, information on the distribution and abundance of Iowa's lepidopteran species has grown remarkably. Through these combined efforts, we were able to have input into the drafting of threatened or endangered lepidopteran lists by the Iowa Department of Natural Resources. Without the donation of many thousands of free hours and travel-miles by private individuals, such a list would have been difficult or impossible to compile.

All the data on individual collections by county gathered by these individuals in the state have been put in a single database by Jeff Nekola. From this source, we have been able to compile county occurrence maps and flight dates for this book and to make lists of species found on publicly and privately owned sites. These data are freely available to any person or organization (from Dennis Schlicht at the Iowa Lepidoptera Project in Center Point). Simply by asking, any owner or manager can obtain data collected and organized by a number of individuals over many thousands of hours. Such information would be very expensive for managers to gather on a contract basis.

In recent years interest in butterfly watching has increased. The North American Butterfly Association has been the umbrella organization for many of these activities. Jeffrey Glassberg's book *Butterflies through Binoculars: The East* (Glassberg 1999) is very useful for identifying butterflies with or without a net. An on-line list-serve for Iowa butterflies is a great communication tool for all butterfly enthusiasts (www.NABA .org).

Perhaps the added stimulus of the present work, which will aid in identifying local specimens and comparing county records, will attract more people to the discipline.

Attracting Butterflies

One of the great pleasures in studying butterflies is attracting them to your own site. Butterfly gardens have become very popular in recent years. In fact most of the inquiries we receive are about attracting butterflies. Having butterflies at hand especially captivates children. Many teachers routinely rear Painted Lady butterflies in the classroom. For adults the challenge is to design and maintain a garden that not only attracts the more cosmopolitan butterflies but also provides their life-cycle needs. Viewing butterflies with the naked eye, binoculars, or a camera is often the impetus for creating a garden.

Butterfly gardening can provide opportunities to do science. Behavior such as territoriality, mating, and reactions to daily cycles (for example, roosting or sheltering during rain) and seasonal cycles (such as overwintering strategies) can be studied. Relationships of caterpillars with various small wasp parasites and predation on caterpillars and butterflies can easily be studied in the butterfly garden.

Remember that by definition agriculture and horticulture (gardening) are human systems interjected into natural systems. Butterfly gardening mixes wild and cultivated species of plants and insects. Weeds and pests are part of the interaction that must take place. Learn to work with them and even use them to increase the diversity in your plot.

Considering Life Cycles

The egg came first, so we must have the proper plants for the females to lay eggs (oviposition). The caterpillars of each species eat one or more plant species. Some butterflies did not originate in your plot, and you may not be able to rear them there because you cannot meet the requirements for that species. A count of forty or so species may be seen in a diverse garden. Consult a good larval food plant list in *Butterfly Gardening* (1990) or one of the other references or start with the suggestions provided below.

The larva or caterpillar hatches from the egg in a few days to many months, depending on the species. The long incubators probably will be species that overwinter as eggs. Many species have more than one brood each summer, providing several opportunities to view hatching (see the species accounts). As they develop, the caterpillars outgrow their skins (exoskeletons) and must shed them by molting four or five times. Pupation is the beginning of the next stage.

Pupation may also be a short or long process, depending on the species and the season. The butterfly is recreated from the substance that was the caterpillar, to emerge as an adult with a completely different life role. The pupa body is called a chrysalis (as opposed to a cocoon for a moth). Each group of butterflies has a characteristic method of hanging the chrysalis and a specific place in the plant matter to position it.

The adult butterfly has one primary function: reproduction. To accomplish that, butterflies must find mates, accomplish mating, and locate the proper larval food plant for oviposition. Parental responsibilities are then complete. While this sounds simple, it takes all of their senses and most of their energy. Butterfly gardens are primarily for just this small part of the whole life cycle. The best gardens, however, have portions that provide for each of the life-cycle stages.

Creating and Maintaining Your Garden

Few of us have the luxury of choosing from multiple sites, but the following factors are important in site selection and design. Wind usually has a negative effect on the activities of butterflies. If your site is in the open, a windbreak will moderate conditions enough to help the insects go about their business. A site surrounded, but not shaded, by trees or houses will not need wind protection. A sunny, east-facing slope may be ideal.

Sunlight, of course, is critical to butterfly activities. Sites with excessive shading by trees or other structures should be avoided. Morning sun is necessary for the butterflies to dry away dew and become active.

Woodland sites with open areas may be used to good effect by naturalizing butterfly plants with woodland affinities. Be careful not to disturb native woodland flora. In fact, if high-quality native plants are present, disturbance and introduction of new plant species may well cause the *loss* of native butterflies. Tree and shrub species used by butterflies include prickly ash (although it is aggressive), hoptree, paw paw, sumac, wild cherry, wild plum, privet, hawthorn (including crabapple), alder, viburnum, oak, hickory, ash, walnut, hackberry, buckeye, willow, and elm. Woodland edges may be transitioned to butterfly garden by planting clumps of viburnum, sumac, willow, or alder. These shrubs may also be used for hedges in other settings.

Grassland-theme butterfly gardens offer the opportunity to use our beautiful prairie forbs such as purple and gray-headed coneflower, verbena (vervain), several species of milkweed (especially butterfly milkweed), blazing star, goldenrod, New England aster, silky aster, Joe-pye-weed, lead plant, black-eyed Susan, ox-eye daisy, meadowsweet, pearly everlasting, bee-balm, and New Jersey tea. Clumps of big bluestem, little bluestem, and Indian grass may be integrated for balance. Skippers use legumes, sedges, or grasses as larval food plants and are best habituated to the prairie garden.

Marshes have their own butterfly fauna, most of which are hard to entice to a garden. Fresh water is important in your garden, but open water is of little use to butterflies. Provide rocks or logs and sticks for perches at the water line. A marsh effect can be accomplished with a wet depression planted with cattails and sedges.

Many species of butterflies are territorial: that is, they defend space for the purpose of acquiring mates and food. This behavior is manifested by perching in prominent positions so that they can chase trespassers away or encounter potential mates and initiate mating behaviors. Patrolling back and forth along paths, tree lines, or watercourses is another way to encounter other individuals. Watch for these behaviors. They can help you to understand how the butterflies use your garden as well as how you can plan it to attract butterflies.

Chain-link fences are unintended barriers for butterflies. Some species will fly over, but many fly down the length of the fence to get around. Avoid locating your garden near them.

What should you plant? The answer to this question depends first on where you live. Check out local gardens and wild areas for the plant species that are attracting butterflies in each season. Several butterfly gardening books list plants by region. Two groups of plants should be needed in your garden. First and most glamorous are the nectar plants. These flowers should be chosen for their attractiveness to adult butterflies and for their blooming season. Look for species which flower in each 20- to 30-day period of the growing season.

You have the option of sowing seeds or using started plants for your garden. Seeds are inexpensive but more difficult to handle. Although many plants are easy to grow, some varieties are difficult to germinate. Some seedlings are so tiny that they are lost in just a few weeks; larger seedlings must be transplanted to the proper spacing. Started bedding plants are more expensive but are much easier to handle in the garden. Most varieties need to be planted one per square foot in patches of twenty to forty square feet to have the desired effect on butterflies as well as humans. Bedding annuals produce flowers quickly, offering nectar and the opportunity to change plants easily. Perennials often do not bloom the first year but are available as larval food plants. The second-year bloom is worth the wait.

Most of the seeds you will need are available from mail-order companies. Many bedding plants for a butterfly garden can be bought from your local garden center. A whole butterfly garden of bedding plants can be purchased in a single stop. At many full-service garden centers the employees are knowledgeable about butterfly plants. Some small greenhouse/garden center operations will even custom start specific plants if you provide the seeds. In recent years a number of prairie plant and seed businesses have emerged in Iowa and the Midwest. They will usually have the native species that you need.

When it comes to food plants, butterflies are either generalists or specialists. Generalists use a variety of plant species (probably from the same family), whereas specialists use a very narrow menu of plants (often only one species). Obviously your efforts are best spent on providing plants for the generalists like the Mourning Cloak, Eastern Comma, Buckeye, Gray Hairstreak, Clouded Sulphur, and Painted Lady. Generalists' palates change during the season, according to what is currently growing. Specialists include Monarchs, which eat milkweeds; fritillaries, which eat violets; and the Baltimore Checkerspots, which eat turtlehead. The nettle patch near the woods will provide larval food for at least four species of butterflies in Iowa.

One easy way to provide larval food plants is to share the human vegetable garden. Common garden plants like carrots, dill, cabbage, and parsley are food plants for swallowtails and whites. Other larval food plants include dock, lupine, sorrel, pearly everlasting, plantain, cress, aster, wild mustard, thistles, clover, and mallows (including hollyhock).

Adult butterflies feed on nectar from various species of flowers. In the absence of the introduced plants, each species uses a particular group of flowers during its adult life. When a butterfly senses a flower, it gets a different impression than we do. It sees a flower more in the ultraviolet portion of the spectrum. In ultraviolet light the flowers often have a "nectar guide" pattern to mark the center of the flower where the nectar is found. Large flowers provide landing areas for large butterfly species, and flowers in clusters offer more nectar in an arrangement that is easier to find.

Fragrance also is important for many insects to find flowers. The period of attraction to the blossom is often shorter than the time that a flower blooms (referred to as its phenology). The common milkweed in full bloom may not be attractive to butterflies and bees; but a few days later, with no apparent change to the human eye, the butterflies are all over it. Choose some of your flowers for fragrance. Good species include alyssum, herbs, lilac, milkweed, buddleia, summer phlox, moss-pink, mock orange, heliotrope, sedum, and bee-balm.

Other plants that should be included in the nectar garden are lupine, zinnia (*Zinnia elegans*, which is probably the single best butterfly plant), aster, daisy, yarrow, coreopsis, scabiosa, flowering tobacco, verbena, gaillardia, African marigold, gem marigold, Mexican sunflower, sweet William, phlox, blue salvia, chive, chrysanthemum, silver lace vine, Shasta daisy, cardinal flower, violet, spearmint, lavender, red clover, white clover, and cosmos (var. Klondyke, seashells, and others).

Care of the butterfly garden is like care of other flower gardens, with a few exceptions. Use patches rather than rows and mulch the space in between with grass clippings or wood chips. Weed the patches; however, leaving a patch with lamb's quarters, thistles, and nettles is beneficial to several species. No herbicides or insecticides should be used. Fertilize as needed, but remember that excess nitrogen causes vegetative growth and inhibits flowering, so a 5-20-20 mix is usually desirable. Apply at a rate of 1 pound per 100 square feet, but hold off on the nitrogen from August on (a 0-10-10 mix). Runoff with excess fertilizer will cause algae growth in your pond or puddle.

Weeds are best prevented with mulch and hand pulling; pesticides, of course, will kill butterflies. Keep in mind that some of the plants you may wish to use can become weeds in the surrounding areas. The dandelion, introduced from Europe for its vegetable properties, is now a weed from sea to sea. Plants that should *not* be used in gardens and yards include purple loosestrife, Jerusalem artichoke, obedient plant, tansy, crown vetch, bird's-foot trefoil, yellow coneflower, multiflora rose, leafy spurge, reed canary grass, common day lily, and pampas grass.

Constructing Shelter

Butterflies have two primary needs for shelter: roosting and hibernation. Adult butterflies survive the winter in a dormant state (hibernation). In the Midwest anglewings

(*Polygonia comma, P. progne, P. interrogationis*) and Mourning Cloaks hibernate as adults in tree hollows, in cracks, or under bark. Some species get through the winter in other life-cycle stages; for example, hairstreaks as eggs, Red-spotted Purples as early-stage larvae, and swallowtails as chrysalides. These will all overwinter at the place where the stage is found in the late fall.

Roosting is the behavior for night or bad-weather shelter. It is amazing how butterflies all disappear as rain threatens. Where do they go? What are the stimuli that cause this response? Where do they roost as night falls? Are all members of the same species in the same place (such as a tree), or are they mixed around the garden? These are interesting questions that may be answered in your butterfly garden.

Butterfly boxes have appeared in gardens in recent years. They are usually rectangular boxes with slits in the sides that are open at the bottom. Their use is probably limited to the few species listed above that hibernate. Bats may use them as well. Your garden should contain at least one woodpile with four- to five-foot limbs piled tepee style or crisscrossed to make a pyramid. Random piles of boulders or slab rock also provide some protection as well as perching space for territorial species such as skippers and swallowtails.

Encouraging Puddling

Puddling is a butterfly behavior often observed along moist roadways and paths. It involves sipping moisture from the soil or rocks, apparently for the water itself and for the minerals dissolved in it. The amazing thing about puddling is the speed at which the water moves through the butterfly's body. Close observation of the end of the abdomen will reveal a droplet being emitted every few seconds. This phenomenon is of interest to people researching human kidney function.

Several years ago we found a waterlogged blue butterfly in a swimming pool. When lifted from the water and placed on a dry deck board, it arranged its wings, legs, and antenna and then used its proboscis to siphon the water from its body and wings. It moved the proboscis around its thorax and abdomen and then between its wings; all the while, droplets were being expelled from the abdomen. After about five minutes it flew away.

Puddling can be encouraged by making wet patches in the soil or by making small open pools with sticks and stones for perches. Open water without perches is not useful. Spice your puddle with a pinch of salt or wood ash. It has been observed that butterflies may be solitary sippers or gather at a favorite watering hole in groups called puddle clubs.

Human perspiration is often attractive to butterflies. We have seen Hackberry Emperors, blues, and American Snouts on skin or clothing.

Using Feeders

Butterfly feeders have received much attention of late. Our experience with using them for midwestern butterflies is less than inspiring. Commercial feeders usually are plastic flower-shaped surfaces, with several feeding tubes for a sugar-water solution. A feeder can be made simply by placing a few small dishes around the garden. Put small sponges in the middle of several dishes to serve as a perch and a medium to hold the solution. Choices for solutions include salt, sugar, honey, or syrup (separately). Mix weak solutions and change them every day or two.

Even more effective than solutions are fermented, rotting, and cut fruits, placed either on a commercial feeder with prepared solutions or by themselves. Experiment with different fruits. Bananas, peaches, and melons are a sure bet. Butterflies are sometimes observed sipping fermented sap and often are unable to escape when touched, apparently inebriated.

Baits traditionally have been used to attract moths at night, but they can also be useful for butterflies. In *The Audubon Society Field Guide to North American Butterflies* Robert Pyle (1981) recommends a bait mix containing "a couple of pounds of sugar, a bottle or two of stale beer, mashed overripe bananas, some molasses or syrup, fruit juice, and a shot of rum." Paint the mixture on trees, rocks, or logs or put it in the dishes mentioned above. Scents from perfumes, wines, and commercial pheromones (chemicals that insects use to communicate) can be used to attract butterflies as well. Butterflies use natural scents to communicate, so they already have the olfactory equipment. Over the years there have been many anecdotal accounts of butterflies coming to someone's perfume or wine glass in an outdoor setting. Experiment with what you have at hand: you may well find the key to making feeders really successful.

We are sorry to report that these beautiful creatures have a fancy for animal dung, urine, and carrion. Use your imagination as to how it should best be served. Occasionally dog droppings and road apples are actually covered with butterflies. Such observations can be helpful in learning which species are currently out. These materials certainly contain some nutrients that are useful to butterflies.

School and Community Gardens

Probably the most common inquiry we get is from people interested in starting a butterfly garden, most often a school garden. School gardens provide a marvelous opportunity to incorporate environmental awareness, landscaping, and horticulture with butterflies. The first consideration is placing the garden away from high-traffic areas. Playgrounds and sites near athletic fields are too active for a butterfly garden. Look for a site that is visible from the school complex but along the edge of the property, such as near a waterway, woods, park, cemetery, or even residential area. Keep it simple, because you cannot expect maintenance help from the custodial staff or from the students during the summer months. Individual plots might be assigned to a student and his or her family or by grade level. Plots should be 25 to 50 square feet. Each plot should contain only one type of plant: masses of color attract both butterflies and humans.

Use the garden as an outdoor laboratory where students' ideas about the world can be studied and tested. Many of the questions posed at the end of each species account in this book can be investigated in a school butterfly garden.

Another great way to develop a large butterfly garden is to organize a community garden. Judy Pooler enlisted about 140 local volunteers who adopted plots in the butterfly garden at Bellevue State Park at Bellevue, Iowa. It was up to each community member to plant and maintain the plot according to the master plan. The plants (150 varieties) were provided by the state park. The adopters' names were placed on placards on their plots, along with placards with the names of the plants. Of course, friends and relatives were usually escorted to the butterfly garden to see this bit of competitive horticulture. An appreciation party was held at the end of the season to thank the plot-holders. A large number of the visits to the park surely can be attributed to this organizational design.

The Bellevue State Park garden is shaped like a large rectangle in a bowl, with a pond in the center. The beds are along terraces, with a mulched path between them. Each terrace is defined at the lower edge with a wooden board. The beds are laid out along the terraces, each five to six feet long. This design provides easy access, with a shelter at one edge.

Be sure to consider the needs of people in your garden. Use paths wide enough for wheelchairs, at least in several parts of the garden. Provide places for people to sit and observe the comings and goings of the butterflies. Photographers need space for tripods, and shelter may be appreciated by everyone.

Studying Butterflies

In addition to watching butterflies with the naked eye, many people use binoculars and cameras to aid observations. Binoculars are most useful if they are close focusing: to six or eight feet. Butterfly watching is very different from bird watching. Distances of five to ten feet are usually attainable. Due to their small size, however, identification of some species (especially skippers) is still difficult. When you test binoculars in the store, focus on a near object with print. Try every pair of the type you want. Each one focuses differently (despite what the salespeople say). More power usually means a longer minimum focus.

Photographic equipment for butterflies should include a macro lens (around 100 mm.) with flashes for primary light and a tripod. Butterfly photographer Jim Messina uses a "butterfly bracket" which holds two flashes. The primary flash is directed from about 30 degrees above the lens; a secondary flash may be used from the side to fill in shadows. Exposures are harder to calculate with this method, but the results can be stunning. Shoot quickly, and hope for a second chance. Messina says, "Once your system has been calibrated to render the proper exposure based on the relationship between aperture and flash distance, the beginner can expect one quality image in five." Careful editing of the images will yield a more pleasing result.

One way to control the conditions under which you can observe and study butterflies is to use enclosures. These can be as small as a mesh bag on a food plant so that you can associate a particular butterfly with its larva or pupa or as large as permanent structures like greenhouses, which can be used in conjunction with a butterfly garden to study a broader range of species and to extend the season. A net house (screen tent) such as those used to shelter a picnic table may also be helpful. Net houses are probably too shady for plant growth, however. Add screens to the roof for more light or use the net house as a short-term enclosure. A butterfly house made totally of screen over a light frame will also work to hold specimens on growing plants.

Taking notes is one of the most important activities in your garden. Journals come in many forms. Beautiful commercially published garden journals are available with both art and verse. A plain tablet with your own sketches, poetry, and prose may be even more precious. Record weather, seasonal factors, garden plan, plant performance, and butterfly associations and behavior. You will need to remember which cultivars (cultivated varieties) of the plants you planted and how well they germinated, grew, and attracted butterflies. Record the bloom times and the life-span of the bloom. Most importantly, keep records of which butterflies use which plants.

Many bird and butterfly watchers keep lifetime lists of all the species they have seen. Butterfly gardeners could keep a garden list. An Iowa butterfly garden might attract thirty to forty species in a season and accumulate fifty or more over time. We have even seen impressive data from individual patches of flowers, where each patch has a different combination.

One product of good data can be good science. Many experiments can be conducted in a butterfly garden if care is taken. Mark-recapture experiments, for example, can tell us how long a butterfly lives and how far it roams. The butterfly garden is also a great place for children's activities in natural history, such as drawing, writing, reading, or observing. Imagination is the only limiting factor.

Problems for Future Research

M uch work remains to be done on all aspects of the butterflies of Iowa. Reading through the species accounts will give you an excellent idea of appropriate problems in need of solution. Not a single species is completely known in terms of its total biology and natural history.

In this chapter, we have listed some questions under general headings that could result in significant contributions not only within the state but also to the science of lepidopterology. These issues are generally restricted to questions that may be answered by field and natural history observations. Laboratory and sophisticated problems which require expensive scientific apparatus are not included (though they are very important), simply because the general collector and naturalist may not have such specialized equipment.

Taxonomic Problems

Even in an area as well known as Iowa, some taxonomic problems remain which must be solved before we can truly say that we understand the systematic positions of our butterflies. Most of these concern the less-studied groups, the Lycaenidae and Hesperiidae, simply because few have taken the time and effort to study the relationships between closely related taxa.

Perhaps the most puzzling taxonomic problem is in the "*persius* group" of the Duskywings. Many species show superficial resemblances in wing characters, and it is often difficult to identify a specimen correctly by matching it with photographs of determined species. Specimens from Iowa include both the Wild Indigo Duskywing (*Erynnis baptisiae*) and the Columbine Duskywing (*E. lucilius*). The larval food plants of both — false indigo, a prairie plant, and columbine, a forest plant — occur commonly in Iowa, especially in the northeastern part of the state. The problem is that the two Duskywings often occur together. Some specimens from that area can easily be assigned to each type, but as many as a third show characteristics of both. Could each be reared on the other's food plant? What would the adults look like? Genetic studies will probably solve this issue or create more questions.

The Persius Duskywing (*Erynnis persius*) has been taken both east and (more commonly) west of Iowa. Several specimens from within our borders have been recorded as this species; however, most also have proven to be *E. baptisiae* upon examination of the genitalia. Still, there is no reason to exclude *persius*, because its lupine food plant occurs in Iowa. Series of bred specimens carefully documented in regard to food plants and other habitat data would go far toward determining which "*persius* group" members occur in Iowa. As with all taxonomic problems, definitive studies must include specimens from throughout the range of the species; they cannot be solved on the basis of Iowa populations alone.

Study of the Satyridae involves some pressing problems. What is the taxonomic and biological relationship between diverse populations of *Satyrodes eurydice eurydice* and *S. eurydice fumosa*? Are the differences that we see in Iowa and Minnesota due to genetics or to environment? The relationship between *S. eurydice* and *S. appalachia leeuwi* also needs study. Secondarily, does the last-named butterfly occur in Iowa? Similarly, the extreme variation of Common Wood-nymphs (*Cercyonis pegala*) requires much study at the population level to ascertain whether proper taxonomic discrimination has been made.

Life-history Problems

It is safe to say that we need to know much more about the life cycles and life history of all our butterflies. Not only do we need detailed morphological studies on each stage, but ecological and biological data are also lacking for most species. In particular, do we need intensive studies of single populations? Single populations exhibit many features not shown by the individuals in them. For instance, they have birth rates and death rates, sex ratios, and a host of statistical parameters that involve the population as a whole. The patterns of variability of these traits, both within and between populations, document evolutionary pathways and help explain why complex life cycles have developed. Also, comparative data might help explain why there is diversity not only among individuals within the same population but among the different species in the same area. At the base of these variables is the factor of adaptability. After the purely descriptive phase of recording life-cycle data, including morphological, physiological, behavioral, and genetic features, we should study how they might better adapt the individual, or the population, for its present ecological niche.

An urgent problem in Iowa concerns Reakirt's Blue (*Echinargus isola*). It is generally not believed to survive Iowa's winters and must immigrate each spring from the south. Nonetheless, we find good populations near its food plant on isolated prairies by early June. But we do not find it in other places. We hypothesize that it is overwintering on our prairies, possibly with the help of ants.

Genetic Problems

The genetics of various butterflies can be used to solve many of these taxonomic problems. The solutions must be applied intelligently, however, because species may (and probably do) react differently in nature than in the laboratory. Nevertheless, gene-flow problems do exist in gene pools, and their solutions may be very revealing. To assess gene flow adequately we must know a great deal more about the organism than just what happens when one morphotype is mated to another. For example, with our isolated habitat remnants, we must have an idea of how far individuals may stray from their birthplace: if individuals are incapable of moving more than a mile, important gene interchange with populations in areas ten miles away could not take place. If the species is more or less continuously distributed within a study area, however, it is quite possible to spread genes from one area to another over a succession of generations.

With this in mind, at least two good problems arise in Iowa butterflies. Most representatives of *Limenitis arthemis* are the Red-spotted Purple (*L. a. astyanax*), but in the northeastern part of the state the White Admiral (*L. a. arthemis*) or possible hybrids are occasionally encountered. Farther north the *arthemis* color pattern forms the entire population, with a broad to narrow (depending on the locality) blending zone where the two morphs come into contact. The situation is further complicated because it is not the influence of a single gene that determines "*arthemis*-ness." Many genes are involved. Perhaps the geographical distributions of these various component genes also differ, adding to the complexity of the situation. It is a significant problem to discover how we happen to have any *arthemis* genes in Iowa populations and, secondarily, what the distribution of this color pattern is in the Iowa populations. Is it spreading? In which direction? How? The list of questions is almost endless — but all need solutions.

In a similar manner, the Common Wood-nymph (*Cercyonis pegala*), which we often see as a dark and relatively small prairie species, seems to embody characteristics of three named subspecies in Iowa populations. Two of these, *C. p. nephele* and *C. p. olympus*, are uniformly dark brown above, without a trace of a yellow medial band on the fore wing. The other, *C. p. alope*, has this yellow band surrounding the fore-wing ocelli (eyespots). Larval differences between *nephele* and *olympus* were noted many years ago by W. H. Edwards. These need to be reevaluated in light of adult variability. Occasional Iowa females (and perhaps males) show the paler band characteristic of *alope*. All of these characters are genetically controlled and possibly environmentally modified. We need information about their expression in Iowa populations as well as changes in these populations through gene flow in time.

Ecological Problems

We are presently in a situation where the survival of up to half our butterflies depends on the intentional activities of humans. Butterflies live in rare habitats that are often managed under some plan. They are also frequently found in areas currently being managed for some entity other than insects (for example, plants). The ecological needs of the invertebrates are poorly known, let alone the effect of "prescribed" management or lack of it (neglect is also a management action). For rare species, we have little time to learn enough ecology to make wise decisions, although we lepidopterists do have strategies that may be part of the answer to this problem. For several species, including the Dakota Skipper and the Common (Prairie) Ringlet, it is probably already too late in Iowa.

The effects of bioengineered crops and the influences of invasive species of plants and animals on our isolated prairie species are poorly known.

Behavior Problems

Over a hundred behaviors have been logged in observations of larvae. Recording all these activities for each Iowa butterfly species would produce a compendium of descriptive and comparative behaviors. For example, studying the entire gamut of larval defensive postures (protective reactions against all the physical and biological hazards of their environment) might reveal significant categories of common responses and unique reactions. It would involve a considerable investment of time and energy in both field and laboratory but add many new data.

Similarly, the adult behavioral repertory for even a few of our most common species would require several lifetimes of study. We do not know some of the most elemental stimuli-response associations for our most common species. What makes adults groom or clean their antennae? What causes them to drum the surface on which they rest or drum prior to oviposition or feeding? What stimulates a given species to fly? Does it fly only at certain times during the day, or at certain temperatures or light intensities? What causes perching, courtship, pugnacity or territoriality, interpopulation movement, and migration? Several behavioral differences between the sexes are known—or at least we know that males and females may respond to different visual and chemical clues during courtship. But what stimulus provokes the mate rejection posture in a previously mated female? We should attempt to know not only the type and sequence of stimuli that bring the sexes together but what might keep them apart or discourage the advances of an aggressive partner at an unacceptable time.

It is our opinion that behavioral research will address some of the most fascinating biological problems in the next ten years. We have made significant advances with taxonomic problems in the last several decades. Even though not all problems in this area have been solved, the life history and biology of species have been exciting areas for research. We are just beginning to understand behavior, however, and how various species react to the environment. As the potential for understanding biological systems grows, so will our enthusiasm and insights into the behavior of the butterflies in the backyard.

Part Two. The Butterflies of Iowa

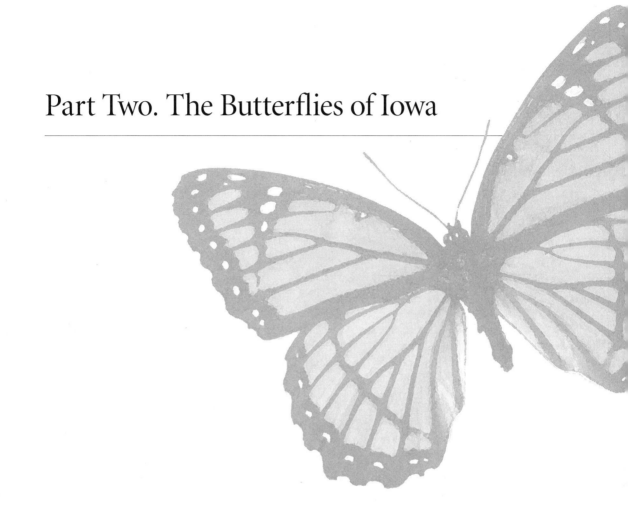

Introduction to the Species Accounts

In all, 131 butterfly species have been reported from Iowa. It is likely that 13 of these were errors due to misidentification or mislabeling of specimens. These dubious species (and their reasons for exclusion) are enumerated at the end of the species accounts. The remaining 118 have been documented in Iowa from at least one verifiable specimen. Of these, 6 stray only occasionally into the state from other regions and may not be observed every season. The Dakota Skipper has not been sighted since 1992 and is believed to have been extirpated, while the Cabbage White and the European Skipper represent our only introduced species.

The following accounts include all verified species, grouped by taxonomic family. Once you identify a specimen by photograph, you can determine its taxonomic associations and its family. We provide an introduction for each family, giving its characteristics and information about the number of species in Iowa and their habitats.

For each species, we include the common name, scientific name, Opler and Warren (2003) number, status, adult flight times and number of broods per season, distinguishing features, distribution and habitat, and natural history information such as behavior and food preferences.

Most common names are from Glassberg (1999). Scientific names are organized and therefore numbered based on the phylogenetic arrangement of Opler and Warren (2003). The Opler and Warren number indicates the sequential position of each butterfly in the classification list of the 780 butterflies in North America north of Mexico.

The status information for each butterfly includes comments on its commonness or rareness, whether it is a year-round resident of Iowa, and whether it breeds in the state.

We attempted to survey all the literature for published accounts on Iowa butterflies. In many cases we were not able to locate the specimens on which the published records were based and hence had to rely on the presumed accuracy of the determinations. In most cases, this method is reliable because of the commonness of the species or the usage of the name; presumed errors in distributional accounts are clearly indicated in appropriate places in the text. We have also relied heavily on our own fieldwork and on that of colleagues and collaborators over the last five decades.

The flight time of the adults is determined by date records obtained from all specimens observed or recorded in the literature. Refer to the introduction to the range maps and flight diagrams for more information about how to use and interpret these records.

To help you understand the section on distinguishing features, we have included diagrams (see figs. 1–4) that provide the terminology for general butterfly anatomy, wing regions, wing areas, and wing veins.

The distribution and habitat section refers to the species range maps (combined with the flight diagrams, for easier comparison of data). This section also includes information about the habitat and geographical preferences of each species.

Note that the section on the natural history of each species is not intended to include all the information available about its life history and host-plant preferences. As indicated earlier, you should use this book along with more comprehensive texts. For most plant names, we have relied upon Eilers and Roosa (1994) and Swink and Wilhelm (1994).

Because our knowledge of these species is far from complete, each account ends with some of the most important unanswered questions. It is our hope that the readers of this book will help answer these questions (and ask new ones), thereby advancing the understanding of these fascinating animals.

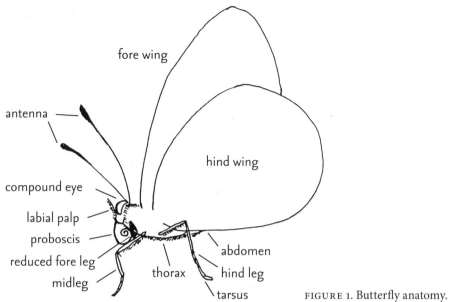

fore wing

antenna

hind wing

compound eye

labial palp

proboscis

reduced fore leg

midleg

abdomen

thorax

hind leg

tarsus

FIGURE 1. Butterfly anatomy.

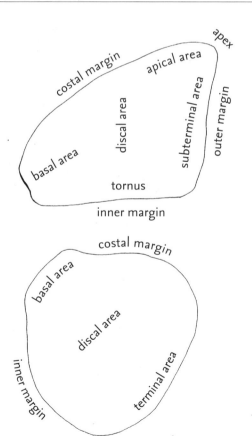

FIGURE 2. Butterfly wing regions.

apex

costal margin

apical area

discal area

subterminal area

outer margin

basal area

tornus

inner margin

costal margin

basal area

discal area

inner margin

terminal area

tornus

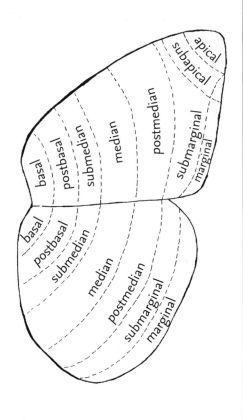

FIGURE 3. Butterfly wing areas.

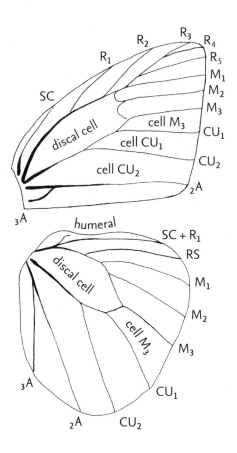

FIGURE 4. Butterfly wing veins.

Skippers: Family Hesperiidae

M any characteristics separate the skippers from the "true" butterflies. All skippers have twelve unbranched fore-wing veins arising from either the cell or the wing base. The head of the skipper is wider than the body, and the antennae clubs are usually hooked or bent. The early stages are also diagnostic: the larva is subcylindrical but has a reduced first body segment, making it appear to have a "neck" and a large, detached "head." Skipper larvae also make and live in nests of leaves fastened together by silken threads that help protect the pupae from predation.

Forty-two skippers are Iowa residents, while four migrate into the state each summer from the south. Two subfamilies, the Hesperiinae and Pyrginae, are represented. Pyrginae have an androconial fold on the fore-wing costa, while Hesperiinae have variously placed androconial bands, never contained within folds. Hesperiinae juveniles feed exclusively on monocotyledonous plants while Pyrginae larvae primarily feed on dicotyledonous plants. A very rough rule-of-thumb states that the Hesperiinae are more common in grassland habitats, while the Pyrginae are more characteristic of wooded areas. As monocots and dicots are found in all Iowa habitats, however, members of both subfamilies may be encountered in wooded and open habitats alike. Thus some Hesperiinae (e.g., Hobomok Skipper) are most common in woodlands, while some Pyrginae (e.g., Mottled Duskywing) are more common in grasslands.

An additional subfamily, the Megathyminae, is found as close as central Nebraska and may eventually be located in Iowa. This subfamily bores into leaves and stems of yuccas, agaves, and their relatives and includes the largest skippers known in North America.

Epargyreus clarus (Cramer [1775])

Status: Common breeding resident.

Flight: Multiple brooded, flying throughout the growing season. It is most often encountered from late May to mid July.

Distinguishing features: The Silver-spotted Skipper's large size, dark brown color, medial gold band on the upper and lower fore wing, and large silver band on the lower hind wing make it easy to identify. Wingspan: 4.5 – 5.5 cm.

Distribution and habitat: Map 5. Found throughout the state in a wide variety of wooded habitats. It was first reported in Iowa from Denison in Crawford County in 1869.

Natural history: The Silver-spotted Skipper is an extremely strong flyer. It is very pugnacious and will even dart at small birds. While Paul Opler and George Krizek (1984) report that its larvae consume a wide variety of legumes, no favored host plants have been recorded in Iowa. It is likely that it eats a wide variety of common woodland legumes, such as black locust, honey locust, hog peanut, and tick-trefoil.

Questions: Is the pugnacious behavior of perching adults toward flying intruders part of a courtship pattern or a form of territoriality? What is the selective advantage of the large silvery-white spot on the vertical hind wing?

Achalarus lyciades (Geyer 1832)

Status: Very rare breeding resident.

Flight: Single brooded in Iowa, with records ranging from middle May to early June. It has been reported to fly until August in other states along the northern margin of its range.

Distinguishing features: The upper wing surface of the Hoary Edge is very reminiscent of the wing of the Silver-spotted Skipper, being brown with a gold band along the upper fore wing. The lower hind wing of the Hoary Edge lacks the central silver patch, however, instead having a hoary-white suffusion along the outer wing margin. Wingspan: 3.8 – 4.5 cm.

Distribution and habitat: Map 41. The Hoary Edge has only been collected four times in Iowa during the past forty years: three times from Waubonsie State Park in extreme southwestern Iowa and once from Des Moines in Polk County. The most recent reported collection date is 1969. No habitat information is available from these collections. Based on its behavior in nearby states, however, it was probably found in open woods and woodland edges. Judging by its distribution in surrounding states, it may eventually be found to occur rarely across the southern tier of Iowa counties.

Natural history: No information is available on the activities of this species in Iowa. Based on reports from nearby states, it is likely that its larvae eat various tick-trefoils.

Questions: What are the Hoary Edge's favored habitats and host plants? Is it able to survive the coldest Iowa winters, or does it have to recolonize from the south following such years? If global warming occurs, will this species become more common across southern Iowa?

Southern Cloudywing 47

Thorybes bathyllus (Smith 1797)

Status: Infrequent breeding resident.

Flight: Most likely three broods, with adults flying from early May to mid August. It appears to be most often encountered in early May, from mid June to early July, and in mid August.

Distinguishing features: This species and *T. pylades* are quite similar. Both are brown with white spots on the upper fore wing and have a series of dark brown markings on the lower hind wing. In *T. bathyllus*, the dorsal white spots are larger and shaped like an hourglass, the wing fringes tend to be paler, and the dark brown hind-wing bands appear solid rather than hollow. Additionally, males lack the costal fold. Wingspan: 3.5 – 4 cm.

Distribution and habitat: Map 47. The Southern Cloudywing has been observed sporadically across the southern two-thirds of Iowa, with outlying populations also occurring in the Paleozoic Plateau. It is most frequently encountered in xeric grasslands, including Loess Hills prairies, sand prairies, limestone and sandstone glades, and occasionally in old fields.

Natural history: The larvae of this species favor wild beans and goat's-rue, which are most often found in dry, open, and sandy places. One of the most impressive Southern Cloudywing populations occurs on the state's largest goat's-rue population at the Big Sand Mound Preserve in Louisa County. Goat's-rue is quite uncommon in the state and essentially limited to the southeast, so it is likely that wild bean constitutes the more frequent larval host.

Questions: How often do *T. bathyllus* and *T. pylades* coexist? When both wild bean and goat's-rue are present, which is the preferred larval host?

Northern Cloudywing 48

Thorybes pylades (Scudder 1870)

Status: Common breeding resident.

Flight: Essentially single brooded, with adults flying from early May to mid August. Most individuals have been collected from the last few days of May through the first week of July.

Distinguishing features: Like *T. bathyllus*, this species is dark brown, with white spots on the fore wing above and darker brown bands on the hind wing below. It differs by having narrow, oblong fore-wing white spots, darker wing fringes, and hollow (rather than solid) dark brown hind-wing bands. Males possess a costal fold. Wingspan: 3.4–4 cm.

Distribution and habitat: Map 48. This species is relatively frequent in the southern two-thirds of the state. It occurs in a variety of dry, open habitats, including prairies and old fields.

Natural history: The larvae of the Northern Cloudywing have been reported to feed on a variety of legumes, including clover, bush clover, and tick-trefoil. These plants are more common in Iowa than those used by *T. bathyllus*, so it is not surprising that *T. pylades* is more common.

Questions: Is the apparent higher frequency of *T. pylades* populations, compared to *T. bathyllus*, due to the higher frequency of its larval host plants? How variable are the hyaline fore-wing spot patterns within and between populations?

Hayhurst's Scallopwing 70

Staphylus hayhurstii (Edwards 1870)

Status: Infrequent to rare breeding resident.

Flight: Double brooded, with adults flying from late May to mid June and from mid July to early August. Rarely a partial third brood will occur in early September.

Distinguishing features: This small dark brown skipper has scalloped wing edges in fresh specimens. The fore wing below appears to have a checkered fringe. Unlike its close look-alike the Common Sootywing, *Pholisora catullus*, *S. hayhurstii* rests with wings outspread against the surface of the substrate, which is reminiscent of some moths and metalmarks. It is also a lighter brown than *P. catullus*. Wingspan: 2.3–2.5 cm.

Distribution and habitat: Map 70. The Hayhurst's Scallopwing appears limited to the southern half of the state. It is most often encountered in sandy floodplain forests of river birch. It has also been sighted in Loess Hills forests and wooded groves adjacent to sand prairies.

Natural history: Most recent sightings of this species are of single individuals. Although its larvae have been reported to eat various members of the goosefoot family, including lamb's quarters, the actual host plants in Iowa remain undocumented. The Scallopwing's scattered occurrence and relatively high level of habitat fidelity suggest that it consumes a related species, which is less ubiquitous in the modern landscape.

Questions: What adaptive benefits are provided by resting with wings open and flat? What host plants are actually utilized by this species in the state? Do populations reside in floodplain forests or simply use these habitats as migrational corridors?

Dreamy Duskywing

Erynnis icelus (Scudder and Burgess 1870)

Status: Very rare breeding resident.

Flight: A single flight from late April to mid May.

Distinguishing features: Unlike most Duskywings in Iowa, the Dreamy Duskywing lacks clear spots on the fore wing. In this respect it is similar to the Sleepy Duskywing, but it is smaller and has less distinct and more jagged dark bars on the upper fore wing. Wingspan: 3 – 3.6 cm.

Distribution and habitat: Map 85. Very uncommon in Iowa, with only one authenticated record from black oak sand savanna in the far northeastern corner of the state. The specimen reported from Ledges State Park in Boone County likely represents a misidentified *E. brizo*.

Natural history: Very little is known about the behavior and activities of this species in the state. In northern Wisconsin it favors scrubby lowlands with willows and can become rather frequent. Its larvae are reported to eat willows and poplars.

Questions: Are populations of this species stable within the state, or do they undergo frequent colonizations and extirpations? What are the preferred larval hosts?

Sleepy Duskywing

Erynnis brizo (Boisduval and LeConte [1834])

Status: Rare breeding resident.

Flight: Single brooded, with adults flying from late April to mid May.

Distinguishing features: The fore wings of the Sleepy Duskywing, like those of the Dreamy Duskywing, lack clear spots. It is larger, however, and has two continuous and distinct black bands on the fore wing above. Wingspan: 3.5 – 4.5 cm.

Distribution and habitat: Map 86. This species is scattered and rare throughout the southeastern half of the state. It appears limited to dry oak woods, often in close proximity to dry prairie openings.

Natural history: This species is a harbinger of spring for butterfly enthusiasts. It is most often seen on prairie openings, where it nectars on early spring prairie flowers. Even though adults frequent dry prairie, the larvae almost certainly feed on oak.

Questions: How do larvae avoid being killed by tannins in oak leaves? Do *E. icelus* and *E. brizo* live in the same habitats? Do these species have different courtship behaviors or distinct pheromones? Why are most adults seen in prairie openings?

Juvenal's Duskywing

Erynnis juvenalis (Fabricius 1793)

Status: Uncommon breeding resident.

Flight: A single flight from mid April to mid June.

Distinguishing features: Juvenal's Duskywing is the only species of its genus in the state that has prominent hyaline spots on the fore wings, with two subapical pale spots on the ventral hind wing. Wingspan: 3.5 – 4 cm.

Distribution and habitat: Map 87. Essentially found across the entire state, although it appears to be more common in the eastern third. It occurs in a variety of oak-dominated forests and may be more common in undisturbed forest habitats.

Natural history: The larvae of Juvenal's Duskywing feed on oaks and make leaf-nests. The adults are fast flyers and may often be seen resting on vegetation or puddling along roadsides and trails.

Questions: Do the leaf-nests of different *Erynnis* larvae all look the same? Do all *Erynnis* larvae eat the same parts of oak leaves? Which oak species are favored by this species in Iowa? How do larvae avoid predation?

Horace's Duskywing 92

Erynnis horatius (Scudder and Burgess 1870)

Status: Uncommon breeding resident.

Flight: Apparently triple brooded in Iowa, with the first brood flying from late April to early May, the second from early June to late July, and the third from mid August to early September.

Distinguishing features: *Erynnis horatius* is close to *E. juvenalis* in appearance but is more uniformly brown and lacks the two subapical pale spots on the lower hind wing. Most of its flight occurs during the summer months, long after *E. juvenalis* has passed. Both of these species are larger than *E. baptisiae* and *E. lucilius*. Wingspan: 3.5 – 3.8 cm.

Distribution and habitat: Map 92. Scattered and rare throughout the state. No clear habitat preferences have been noted; it has been encountered from a wide variety of natural and altered habitats. In western Iowa it may be more common along oak-lined stream corridors.

Natural history: Although *E. horatius* has a wide distribution in the United States, Don C. MacNeil (in Howe 1975: 525) notes that it is "almost absent from the Great Plains." Its larvae have been reported to eat various oak species.

Questions: Why is *E. horatius* so much more uncommon in the state than *E. juvenalis*? What are its preferred habitats, if any? Is it more mobile than *E. juvenalis*?

Mottled Duskywing 94

Erynnis martialis (Scudder 1870)

Status: Rare breeding resident.

Flight: Up to four: from mid April to early May, late May to mid June, and early to late July. A partial fourth brood may occur in mid August.

Distinguishing features: The Mottled Duskywing is one of the most easily identified species in its genus. Particularly in the spring brood, the upper wing surface has a distinct mottling of light and dark brown patches. Wingspan: 3–3.4 cm.

Distribution and habitat: Map 94. Although collections are scattered across the state, it is absent from the northeastern quarter except in the vicinity of the Mississippi River. Most of the collections from south-central Iowa are over 100 years old, and it is probably now absent from this region. Only two collections have been made in eastern Iowa in the last twenty years, so it may soon be extirpated there as well. Its last stronghold is in the western third of the state, where it is limited to xeric prairie in the Loess Hills and on gravel ridges associated with the terminal moraines and outwash channels of the Des Moines Lobe.

Natural history: This species appears limited in Iowa to dry grasslands supporting an abundance of New Jersey tea.

Questions: Why have populations of this species apparently been more stable in western than in eastern Iowa? The presumed host plant (New Jersey tea) is found commonly throughout the state: what other factors limit it to so few sites? How much mortality do populations face when colonies of New Jersey tea are burned?

Wild Indigo Duskywing 98

Erynnis baptisiae (Forbes 1936)

Status: Once a very rare breeding resident. Populations have recently expanded. Now uncommon, but occurs regularly across the state.

Flight: Up to four broods over the growing season. The first occurs in May, the second from late June to early July, and the third from late July to mid August, with a possible fourth brood emerging from early September to early October. Native populations in Loess Hills prairies appear double brooded, with early May and July flights.

Distinguishing features: This species is very similar to the Columbine Duskywing, being on average larger and darker. It often possesses a lighter brown patch just proximal to the row of upper fore-wing clear spots. The only consistent distinguishing characteristics for these species, however, are their larval host plant choices. Wingspan: 2.8–4.4 cm.

Distribution and habitat: Map 98. Until the mid 1980s very rare and limited in Iowa to dry prairies supporting large colonies of wild indigo. Most verified colonies were restricted in the west to the Loess Hills and in the northeast to limestone and sandstone glades. Since that time, however, a race originating in Pennsylvania that eats crown vetch has moved rapidly through Iowa along roadside ditches where this plant has been established. It is now known from scattered sites across the entire state.

Natural history: Depending upon the population, wild indigo (especially cream wild Indigo) or crown vetch is used as the larval host.

Questions: Are there genetic, morphological, or behavioral traits that separate the races that feed on wild indigo and crown vetch? Do the populations that feed on wild indigo have two broods, while the populations that feed on crown vetch have three to four broods? Do these two populations interbreed? If so, does the crown vetch population pose the risk of genetically swamping the wild indigo population?

Columbine Duskywing 99

Erynnis lucilius (Scudder and Burgess 1870)

Status: Infrequent breeding resident.

Flight: Double brooded, with a spring brood from late April to mid May and a summer brood from late June to late July. A partial third brood may occasionally occur in mid to late August.

Distinguishing features: This species and the Wild Indigo Duskywing differ from other Iowa *Erynnis* by having very small clear spots on the fore wing and lacking dark brown mottling over both upper wing surfaces. Distinguishing these two species is quite problematic, however. Columbine Duskywings are often smaller and lighter brown than Wild Indigo Duskywings, but intermediate individuals are frequently encountered. Apparently no differences in genitalia exist (Burns 1964). The only consistent feature which can be used to separate them is their choice of larval hosts. Columbine Duskywings eat only columbine, and Wild Indigo Duskywings eat only wild indigo or crown vetch. Wingspan: 2.3 – 3.1 cm.

Distribution and habitat: Map 99. Generally limited to the northeastern tier of counties. Individuals were also noted from the Des Moines River valley in the 1960s. This species is limited to dry prairies that support columbine, often limestone or sandstone glades on south- or west-facing slopes. Interestingly, this species has never been observed in the more typical woodland habitat for columbine.

Natural history: As noted above, larvae for this species only consume columbine. Populations may be limited to glades, which are sunnier and may provide more nectar than woodlands. Individuals from the spring brood are darker than individuals from the summer brood.

Questions: Are the behaviors of Columbine Duskywing and Wild Indigo Duskywing different enough to allow for reproductive isolation, or do they interbreed? Why does the Columbine Duskywing occur only with grassland populations of columbine?

Common Checkered-skipper 106

Pyrgus communis (Grote 1872)

Status: Common nonoverwintering resident.

Flight: First emigrations from the south in early April through May. The bulk of flight occurs from late June to the first of October, although individuals have been encountered as late as early November.

Distinguishing features: As its name implies, this skipper is heavily white-checkered on a gray background. Specimens vary from quite dark to light in overall appearance. The hind wing below has three jagged transverse bands. Wingspan: 2.7 – 3.2 cm.

Distribution and habitat: Map 106. Found throughout the state in a wide variety of native and altered habitats. It is frequently encountered in sunny areas with low vegetation such as farm lots, heavily grazed pastures, and roadsides.

Natural history: Larvae have been reported to feed on a number of weedy species in the mallow family (Malvaceae). The Checkered-skipper can be common in some years and infrequent in others. Little is known about its courtship behavior, but this collection indicates that male flight activity does not play a critical role in female mate choice and that females may play an important role in moving genes.

Questions: What features of the environment affect the periodic fluctuations in abundance of *P. communis*? How often can this species overwinter in Iowa? How important is female movement in the distribution of genes across the landscape? How far can adults fly over a lifetime?

Common Sootywing   117

Pholisora catullus (Fabricius 1793)

Status: Abundant breeding resident.

Flight: Multiple brooded, with adult flight extending almost continually from early May to early September. Adults appear to be less frequently encountered in mid June.

Distinguishing features: Small with glossy black upper wing surfaces (in fresh specimens), with many small white spots on the fore wing. The somewhat similar Hayhurst's Scallopwing is dark brown and lacks the white spots on the fore wing. Wingspan: 2.6 – 3.2 cm.

Distribution and habitat: Map 117. Found throughout the state in a variety of natural and disturbed open habitats.

Natural history: Larvae of this species have been reported to eat a wide number of plants in the goosefoot, amaranth, and mint families. It is commonly observed making quick and erratic flights within a foot or so of the ground. The white spots on the dorsal fore wing, particularly in the discal area, seem to vary markedly within some populations.

Questions: Do both sexes fly erratically? How far do individuals fly? Are there preferred larval food plants in the state?

Least Skipper   146

Ancyloxypha numitor (Fabricius 1793)

Status: Common breeding resident.

Flight: Multiple brooded, ranging from the end of May to early October.

Distinguishing features: This distinctive little skipper has dark brown upper fore wings and orange upper hind wings with a dark border. This pattern is reversed below, with orange-bordered dark fore wings and orange hind wings. Only the orange can be seen at rest when the wings are folded up. Some individuals have uniformly dark dorsal fore wings; these may be termed *A. n. longleyi*. Wingspan: 2 – 2.3 cm.

Distribution and habitat: Map 146. Found throughout the state in a variety of open, moist, grassy habitats, including wet prairies and fens. It also tolerates disturbance and can be found in many degraded sites.

Natural history: Least Skipper larvae have been reported to eat a wide variety of grasses, including bluegrass and rice cut-grass. It differs from most skippers by having a relatively weak flight: it moves among the vegetation in a rather continuous motion. Individuals who are missed by a swung net often drop to the ground and feign death.

Questions: What natural history traits have allowed this species to tolerate human disturbance more than other native prairie skippers? Is the form *longleyi* more or less common in certain habitats and regions? Is this coloration produced by environment or by genetics?

Poweshiek Skipperling 149

Oarisma poweshiek (Parker 1870b)

Status: Rare breeding resident.

Flight: Single brooded, with adults flying from late June to late July. Rarely individuals have been observed emerging as early as mid June and as late as mid August.

Distinguishing features: This squarish skipper is dark brown above, with a golden fore-wing edge. The hind wing below is overscaled in white and has distinctive white veins contrasting with a dark anal margin. Females are slightly smaller and less distinctively marked. Wingspan: 2.5 – 2.8 cm.

Distribution and habitat: Map 149. Extant populations limited to the northern two tiers of counties, although collections made prior to 1920 document this species as far south as Woodbury and Poweshiek counties. This species is limited to high-quality, wet-mesic to xeric native prairie sites. Populations have proven susceptible to fire management and may no longer be present on sites where they were seen as recently as a decade ago. The 2004 flight was absent in many of the known preserve sites, making its future in Iowa precarious.

Natural history: Larvae were observed feeding on Indian grass at Cayler Prairie but also feed on big bluestem in the lab. The type location for this species was designated in 1870 as a prairie slope at Grinnell in Poweshiek County. It has not been observed there since. Populations have decreased at Cayler Prairie and other managed prairies in the state in the late 1980s and may be on the verge of disappearing from two Howard County sites (Crossman Prairie and Hayden Prairie). These population reductions began after the reintroduction of fire to these sites. Fire has been shown to cause high levels of mortality in Wisconsin populations (Borkin 1995).

Questions: Are there significant genetic or morphologic differences between populations? What factors determine on which prairies *O. poweshiek* has been able to persist? Why does it apparently not occur in the Loess Hills or prairie remnants in the central part of the state? Is a minimum habitat and population size required for the long-term maintenance of populations? Do populations living in wet-mesic and xeric prairies exhibit physiological or behavioral differences?

European Skipper 154

Thymelicus lineola (Ochsenheimer 1808)

Status: Infrequent (for now) breeding resident.

Flight: Single brooded, with adults flying during June.

Distinguishing features: This small, weak-flying skipper differs from the somewhat similar Least Skipper by its bright yellow-orange top and bottom wing surfaces. Wingspan: 2.5 – 3 cm.

Distribution and habitat: Map 154. Found with increasing frequency in a variety of old fields and roadside habitats in the southeastern quarter of the state.

Natural history: The larvae eat timothy, an introduced European pasture grass. This is the only nonnative skipper that has become naturalized in the state. It was introduced to North America near London, Ontario, in 1910, and was first collected in Iowa in Johnson County in 1975 (Gatrelle 1975). It has subsequently has been found with increasing frequency throughout eastern Iowa. Its range is likely still expanding and may eventually reach western Iowa. It is exceedingly abundant throughout northern Wisconsin.

Questions: At what rate is this species expanding its range? Is the drier climate of western Iowa conducive to establishment of populations? Can this species displace native skippers through depletion of nectar sources?

Fiery Skipper 155

Hylephila phyleus (Drury 1773)

Status: Frequent nonoverwintering resident.

Flight: First strays from the south in June. The offspring of these migrants constitute the bulk of the Iowa flight, which occurs from early August through late October.

Distinguishing features: Adults are tan-orange. Males have a prominent stigma with a gray shadow toward the rear. Dark fingerlike projections form a ragged border above. Females are larger and darker, with a nearly solid border above; the lower hind wing has a dark stripe in the area of the anal veins, with small dark patches throughout. Wingspan: 2.7 – 2.9 cm. (males) to 3.3 cm. (females).

Distribution and habitat: Map 155. Observed across the entire state, but most encounters have taken place in the western half. Adults are encountered in a wide variety of native and created habitats and often frequent flower gardens.

Natural history: The Fiery Skipper is not tolerant of Iowa winters, and populations are probably killed off each year. Caterpillars feed on weedy grasses such as crabgrass and Bermuda grass.

Questions: Do larval or adult Fiery Skippers ever overwinter in Iowa? Is this species more frequent in western Iowa, or is this simply an artifact of the activities of butterfly observers? What environmental factors might account for the higher frequency of this migratory animal in the west?

Ottoe Skipper

Hesperia ottoe (Edwards 1866 [1867])

Status: Rare breeding resident.

Flight: A single flight, with adults emerging from early June to mid August. The great majority of adults have been observed from late June to mid July.

Distinguishing features: The Ottoe Skipper can be differentiated from the similar (and more common) Delaware Skipper by its larger size, lemon-yellow (rather than orange) underwing color, and darker upper wing surface. Males of this species and the Leonard's Pawnee Skipper are essentially indistinguishable. These species are best separated based upon flight times, with the Leonard's Pawnee Skipper's flight ranging from the end of August through early October. Wingspan: 3.5–4.3 cm.

Distribution and habitat: Map 164. Limited to xeric prairie habitats dominated by midgrasses and short grasses in far western and eastern Iowa. Western Iowa populations are limited to the Loess Hills, gravel ridges along the Big Sioux River, and moraines along the western margin of the Des Moines Lobe. Eastern Iowa sites are restricted to limestone and sandstone glades, mostly along the Upper Iowa River. Although similar xeric habitats are found throughout northeastern and north-central Iowa, only two populations have been documented in these locations in spite of extensive searching.

Natural history: Larvae have not been observed feeding in Iowa but probably consume little bluestem, which is often abundant on xeric prairie sites. Oviposition has been noted on this plant, as well as on the flowers of pale purple coneflower, even though larvae do not eat this plant. Presumably, after hatching the larvae must crawl down the coneflower plants to reach appropriate food sources. The population at Freda Haffner Kettlehole State Preserve has not been observed in over a decade, and it was probably exterminated by management practices there.

Questions: Do genetic differences exist between eastern and western Iowa populations? How long have these populations been isolated? What advantages (if any) are afforded to larvae whose eggs are laid on coneflowers? What type, frequency, and coverage of prairie management will favor Ottoe Skipper populations?

Hesperia leonardus leonardus and *Hesperia leonardus pawnee* (Harris 1862b)

Status: Rare breeding resident.

Flight: Main flight from mid August to early October, although one adult was collected in early August.

Distinguishing features: No other *Hesperia* flies so late in the season in Iowa. It can easily be distinguished from the Sachem (which is in flight at this time) by its rusty-brown underwing and pale spots (for subspecies *H. l. leonardus*) or its pale yellow underwing (for subspecies *H. l. pawnee*). The two subspecies of *Hesperia leonardus* appear so different that they were long considered separate species. *H. l. leonardus* is generally darker above, with a light band in the center of the hind wing above and with light areas around the stigma on the fore wing. The hind wing below is rusty-red, with a row of pale patches in the center. Specimens of Iowa *H. l. pawnee* are typical of populations to the west (Howe 1975; Tilden and Smith 1986). The underwing color for both sexes is light yellow. While male underwings are usually unmarked (some have a faint row of white postmedial spots), females exhibit pronounced lighter patches in the center. Males are tawny above and are essentially indistinguishable from the earlier-flying Ottoe Skipper. These two subspecies completely intergrade in a genetic cline within a 60-km. band extending over Monona, Harrison, and Pottawattamie counties in the Loess Hills (Spomer et al. 1993). The Jackson County population is quite similar to individuals observed from the Paleozoic Plateau in southwestern Wisconsin, having a somewhat lighter underwing color with smaller light spots. Some have suggested that these populations represent *H. l. leonardus – H. l. pawnee* intergrades. These populations differ greatly from the true intergrades observed in the Loess Hills, however, and may represent a unique geographically isolated race. Wingspan: 2.9 – 3.2 cm. (males), 3.2 – 3.6 cm. (females).

Distribution and habitat: Maps 165a and b. While scattered locations across the southeastern half of the state have been recorded, the only extant *H. l. leonardus* populations known are from Mills and Fremont counties in the Loess Hills and from a single Jackson County site. *H. l. pawnee* occurs along the western border from northern Monona County to Lyon County. Both subspecies are limited to Loess Hills xeric prairies, gravel ridges, and limestone glades.

Natural history: Although larval host plants have not been recorded in Iowa, all populations occur in areas supporting a dense growth of little bluestem. *H. l. leonardus* adults appear to only use rough blazing star for nectar, although a few stray individuals may be seen in Wisconsin on other blazing star species, knapweed, and western sunflowers. A number of sites in northeastern Iowa support luxuriant little bluestem growth but little or no blazing star. Leonard's Skipper has not been located at any of these sites. *H. l. pawnee* has been observed nectaring on both rough and dotted blazing star.

Questions: What is the location of the *H. l. leonardus* and *H. l. pawnee* transition zone outside of the Loess Hills? Do the nectar sources for the two subspecies differ? Are the Paleozoic Plateau populations genetically and morphologically distinct? Why do adults use so few nectar sources? Is population size and occurrence limited by the size and distribution of blazing star populations? At what larval stage does overwintering occur? How sensitive is this species to prairie management?

Dakota Skipper 172

Hesperia dacotae (Skinner 1911)

Status: Probably extirpated breeding resident.

Flight: Last week of June and first week of July.

Distinguishing features: The male is tan with shaded wing edges above. The stigma is crisp and well defined, with gray, opalescent scales in the center (microandroconia). The fringe scales are lighter than the margins in both sexes. The wings are light tan below, with a short longitudinal black mark on the fore-wing base. The hind wing is sparsely overscaled in black, with a faint submarginal row of spots (macular band). The female is dark brown above. The fore wing is spotted above and below. The hind wing has a pale macular band above, and the hind wing below is overscaled with tannish-gray to greenish scales, which extend onto the body. This species is smaller and darker than the Ottoe Skipper, which flies at the same time in similar habitats in Minnesota. Wingspan: 2.9 cm. (males), 3.4 cm. (females).

Distribution and habitat: Only observed at a single Iowa location in the last eighty years: the xeric gravel prairie on top of an esker at Cayler Prairie State Preserve. Multiple individuals have not been seen there since 1980, and it is fairly certain that this population is no longer extant. In the late 1800s and early 1900s it was also located in Woodbury and Poweshiek counties.

Natural history: This species appears to be limited to xeric calcareous prairies at its few remaining sites in Minnesota and North Dakota. The entirety of this habitat type at Cayler Prairie lies within a single fire management unit. This population crashed after initiation of prescribed burning. Although a single male was seen in 1992, no additional individuals have been observed since then, in spite of extensive sampling efforts. This may be the clearest example of the loss of an endangered species population through management practices.

Questions: Do other populations exist in Iowa, particularly on xeric gravel prairies along the Big Sioux and Little Sioux rivers? Why are populations seemingly limited to calcareous prairies? What is the minimum habitat size required for long-term maintenance of populations?

Sachem 177

Atalopedes campestris (Boisduval 1852)

Status: Common immigrant, resident.

Flight: First migration north into Iowa from late April to early June. Offspring fly from mid June to late July, with a second brood emerging from mid August through mid September. Adults continue to fly until frost, as late as late October in some years.

Distinguishing features: Males have a very broad stigma that resembles a black patch with a grayish center. Females are larger and darker, having several clear spots on the fore wing and a green-gray under hind wing with a chevron of lighter spots. Females can be frustratingly similar to female Ottoe Skippers and Leonard's (Pawnee) Skippers at first glance, although they are easily distinguished upon more careful observation due to their unique fore-wing markings.

Distribution and habitat: Map 177. Found throughout the state, particularly in late summer, although it appears to be more common in the southwestern half. It is often seen with Peck's Skipper in a wide variety of open habitats, including gardens, open fields, roadsides, and pastures. It also can be frequent in prairies.

Natural history: This skipper is known to use crabgrass as a larval host, which helps to explain its frequent occurrence in human-modified habitats. It is not tolerant of cold winter temperatures and is exterminated from the state in most years.

Questions: Can adults occasionally overwinter in Iowa during mild years? Why does this species appear to be more frequent in the western half of the state? Which garden flowers are most favored?

Peck's Skipper 180

Polites peckius (Kirby 1837)

Status: Common breeding resident.

Flight: Two distinct broods in Iowa. Adults are most commonly seen from late April to October. A single early October collection suggests that a partial third brood may fly in some years.

Distinguishing features: This small skipper has a distinctive patchwork of light yellow on the underside of the hind wing, unlike any other skipper in the state. Wingspan: 2.5 cm. (males), 2.7 cm. (females).

Distribution and habitat: Map 180. One of Iowa's most abundant skippers, found in a wide variety of human-altered and natural open habitats across the state. It is often seen along creeks and in permanent pastures.

Natural history: Peck's Skipper exhibits some degree of phenotypic variability in its markings. For instance, the hind-wing undersurfaces on some specimens do not have clear-cut spots but instead form a large yellow patch reminiscent of the Whirlabout (*Polites vibex* [Geyer 1832]). In fact, the few records of the Whirlabout from the state likely represent this form. While Peck's Skipper has been reared on a number of different grasses in the laboratory, it apparently commonly feeds on rice cut-grass and panic grass in nature.

Questions: What food plants are utilized by the larvae in Iowa? Is the variability in wing appearance (spot pattern, size, etc.) more controlled by genetic or by environmental factors? Are adults preferentially attracted to particular flower colors or shapes?

Tawny-edged Skipper · 184

Polites themistocles (Latreille [1824])

Status: Common breeding resident.

Flight: Essentially flies continuously from mid May through September. Probably three overlapping broods: adults are more frequently encountered from late May to early June, from late June to mid July, and from early August to early September.

Distinguishing features: This small brown skipper is very similar to the Crossline Skipper (*Polites origenes*). It differs by having a small, sharp, sinuous stigma on the upper fore wing in males and an orange patch along the upper fore-wing costa in females. Females also lack faint light spots on the upper hind wing. Adults of both sexes tend to be smaller than Crossline Skipper adults. Wingspan: About 2.8 cm.

Distribution and habitat: Map 184. Abundant throughout the state in a wide variety of native and human-modified open habitats. Although commonly found in native prairies, it is also often seen in old fields and city parks.

Natural history: Larvae probably use panic grasses as their Iowa food plants, although other hosts have been reported from other states.

Questions: How far do adults travel from their site of emergence? Does this species avoid competition with other panic grass – eating skippers by feeding at different locations on the plant or at different times of the year?

Crossline Skipper · 186

Polites origenes (Fabricius 1793)

Status: Infrequent breeding resident.

Flight: Single brooded, with flight from mid June to the end of July.

Distinguishing features: The Crossline Skipper is superficially similar to the Tawny-edged Skipper (*P. themistocles*) but larger. The stigma in the male is less well defined than on *P. themistocles,* with the lower edge fading to brown. The female is dark brown, with a row of spots on the fore wing above, similar to *P. themistocles,* which often has blurred distal edges. The largest spot is often tan. Individuals of *P. origenes* and *P. themistocles* can be difficult to tell apart, but differences are clearer when comparing a series of specimens. Wingspan: 2.6 – 3.3 cm.

Distribution and habitat: Map 186. Essentially limited to dry native prairie tracts. It thrives in the Loess Hills in the west and limestone glades and sand prairies in the east. It has also been found on dry prairies in southern and central Iowa and xeric gravel prairies in the northwest.

Natural history: The only reported larval host, purple top, is uncommon in Iowa and limited to disturbed sand prairies in the southeast. It is clear that other native dry prairie grasses must be consumed.

Questions: What are the actual larval host plants used by this species in the state? What aspects of its ecology and behavior limit it to native prairies, compared to the more ubiquitous Tawny-edged Skipper? What is the dispersal ability of adults? Do individuals migrate between habitats?

Long Dash   187

Polites mystic (Edwards 1863)

Status: Infrequent breeding resident.

Flight: A single flight from late May through late July.

Distinguishing features: As its common name implies, the stigma on males extends over two-thirds of the fore wing. The hind wing below is brown, with a series of equal-sized tan spots that parallel the wing margin. The female has a broad, dark band winding through the center of the upper fore wing. Wingspan: 2.7 cm. (males), 3.0 cm. (females).

Distribution and habitat: Map 187. Confined to isolated populations in the northern half of the state. In the northwest it is most commonly observed on dry prairies, where it may be found flying with Poweshiek Skipperlings and Crossline Skippers. In northeastern Iowa it is limited to fens and occasionally wet prairies. A few scattered populations have also been located in southwestern Iowa.

Natural history: Larval host plants are unrecorded from any Iowa habitat. Specimens collected from dry prairies in the northwest appear somewhat lighter in color as compared to the wetland forms in the northeast. It is possible that the dry prairie populations represent the subspecies *P. m. dacotah*, which is known from Northern Plains prairies. The northeastern Iowa populations appear identical to those from northern Wisconsin wetlands, which are typical *P. m. mystic*.

Questions: What differences in larval hosts and adult behavior separate northwestern and northeastern Iowa *P. mystic* populations? How great are the genetic differences between these populations? Should individuals from northwestern Iowa be considered *P. m. dacotah*?

Northern Broken-dash   191

Wallengrenia egeremet (Scudder 1864)

Status: Infrequent breeding resident.

Flight: Generally from late June to early August.

Distinguishing features: Males may easily be distinguished by their double stigma on the upper fore wing. Females are very similar to female Dun Skippers and female Little Glassywings but have orange spots on both the upper and the lower wing surfaces.

Distribution and habitat: Map 191. Scattered records throughout most of the state, although it has yet to be seen in the north-central counties. It occurs in a wide variety of habitats, ranging from fens and xeric prairies to forests. It is perhaps most often encountered in open areas adjacent to woodlands.

Natural history: While various grasses, including panic grass, have been listed as larval hosts in other states, the favored food plants have not been identified in Iowa. Given the wide range of habitats in which it has been found, it likely consumes a number of species.

Questions: Why is this species only infrequently encountered, given its apparent wide habitat tolerance? Does it often compete with other generalist grass feeders such as the Tawny-edged Skipper?

Little Glassywing   192

Pompeius verna (Edwards 1862b)

Status: Infrequent breeding resident.

Flight: Single brooded, flying generally from mid June to mid July.

Distinguishing features: This uniformly dark brown skipper has one large and several small clear spots in the center of the upper fore wing. The large spot is shaped like a parallelogram in males and is rectangular in females. Wingspan: 3 cm.

Distribution and habitat: Map 192. Scattered locations across the state. It seems to favor woodland margins.

Natural history: The only listed larval host plant (purple top) is absent from the bulk of Iowa sites, indicating that some other grass must be used for food. It avidly visits flowers such as milkweed and is docile enough to be easily observed and photographed.

Questions: What are the larval hosts used by this species in the state? Why is it found in so few woodland edge habitats? What other factors limit its range? Why are nectaring adults so docile?

Arogos Skipper   193

Atrytone arogos (Boisduval and LeConte [1834])

Status: Rare breeding resident.

Flight: Single brooded, flying from mid June to early August. Rarely a partial second brood emerges in mid September.

Distinguishing features: The Arogos Skipper is rather small, with an unmarked yellow-tan color below. The upper wing surfaces are orange-tan with dark margins, with a pale diffused appearance. Wingspan: 2.7 cm.

Distribution and habitat: Map 193. Restricted to high-quality prairie remnants in the northwestern half of Iowa, favoring mesic to xeric sites. It can persist on small, unmanaged railroad prairies, although some populations have apparently crashed on larger fire-managed sites.

Natural history: On Cayler Prairie it occurs in the same areas as the Poweshiek Skipperling, although it flies immediately after the Poweshiek populations have waned. Competitive phenological displacement could be involved, as has been shown with other skippers in the Loess Hills (Schlicht and Orwig 1992). Big bluestem has been reported as a larval host in Kansas, although other grasses may also be eaten. The type for this genus is based upon 1869 Crawford County and Greene County collections.

Questions: Why are populations absent from seemingly appropriate dry prairie sites in the northeastern corner of the state? How far can adults fly during their lifetime? How often is the Arogos Skipper double-brooded in Iowa, and what climatic conditions favor this second brood? Why do populations shrink following the introduction of fire management?

Delaware Skipper   194

Anatrytone logan (Edwards 1863)

Status: Common breeding resident.

Flight: Main flight period from mid June to early August, with scattered individuals encountered until early September.

Distinguishing features: Females are darker above than males. Males are exceedingly similar to female Byssus Skippers and can be most easily distinguished by the orange vein which extends to the margin at the base of the upper hind wing. It can be distinguished from the rare Ottoe Skipper and Arogos Skipper (which share pale yellow, unmarked lower wing surfaces) by having an inverted, narrow black V at the tip of the upper fore wing. Wingspan: 3 – 3.3 cm.

Distribution and habitat: Map 194. Collected from many localities throughout the state. While it inhabits a large number of open habitats (including marshes, pastures, meadows, and roadsides), it is also one of the more commonly encountered skippers of native prairies.

Natural history: Delaware Skipper larvae apparently eat a wide range of grasses, including big bluestem and switchgrass.

Questions: How long do adults live? How far can they fly? How do larvae overwinter? Does this species compete with the rarer prairie skippers with which it sometimes occurs?

Byssus Skipper   196

Problema byssus (Edwards 1880)

Status: Rare breeding resident.

Flight: Most adults observed during a brief flight in the first half of July.

Distinguishing features: Males are unmarked orange beneath and orange with a dark brown, unbroken border on the upper wing surfaces. Females are larger and darker above, with a distinctive band of orange spots on both the upper fore-wing and hind-wing surfaces and rusty-brown lower hind wings with lighter central patches. Iowa material appears to be paler than individuals from farther south. Wingspan: 3.3 cm. (males); 3.6 cm. (females).

Distribution and habitat: Map 196. Restricted to native prairies in the southeastern part of the state. It occurs on mesic to xeric sites, including sand prairies and limestone glades.

Natural history: Although the only reported larval host is gama grass, this species does not occur at any of the Iowa stations. Rather, the Byssus Skipper consistently is found in prairies that support dense swards of Indian grass. This grass is very successful on restored prairies, so it should not be surprising that the Byssus Skipper has been able to colonize at least one restored prairie in Iowa.

Questions: Is Indian grass the preferred larval host for this species in the state? How far can adults disperse within their lifetimes? How close must restored prairies be to native populations to allow for recolonization? What are the minimum habitat requirements to maintain populations over long periods?

Hobomok Skipper 201

Poanes hobomok (Harris 1862b)

Status: Common breeding resident.

Flight: Essentially restricted to a single brood which flies from mid May to early July. Rarely a partial brood flies in August.

Distinguishing features: This skipper has an orange upper wing surface with black borders, lacks a stigma, and has a rectangular black patch in the center of the upper wing tip. Elsewhere in its range, dark females with scattered rectangular orange patches on both upper wing surfaces occur (form *pocahontas*); these may rarely be found in Iowa. This form differs from the similar Zabulon Skipper by having a solid yellow patch on the lower hind wing. Wingspan: 2.8 – 3.1 cm.

Distribution and habitat: Map 201. Found in woodlands and woodland edges throughout the state.

Natural history: Although this species is reported to eat panic grass and bluegrass, larval hosts in Iowa have not been observed.

Questions: How often does the dark form of the female occur in the state? What larval host plants are used by this species? How variable are wing color patterns within populations?

Zabulon Skipper

Poanes zabulon (Boisduval and LeConte [1834])

Status: Rare breeding resident.

Flight: Possibly triple brooded, with the first flight in June, the second in early July, and the third in August.

Distinguishing features: Males are similar in appearance to the Hobomok Skipper, but their light yellow under-hind-wing patches are flecked with small brown spots, creating an almost checkered appearance. Females are dark above, with white angular spots on the fore wings. The hind wing below is dark tan to brown, with a violet over-scaling toward the outer edge. Wingspan: 3.2 cm.

Distribution and habitat: Map 202. Scattered and rare in the southern part of the state, where it appears to favor woodland edges, prairies, and remnant savannas. The Clinton County collection was made in a xeric prairie.

Natural history: This skipper's life history and ecology are essentially unknown in Iowa. It has only been recorded a dozen times since 1961. It is reported elsewhere to use various grasses as larval hosts.

Questions: What are the larval hosts used by this species in Iowa? How do its ecological requirements compare to those of the much commoner Hobomok Skipper? Do populations require both forest and grassland for survival?

Mulberry Wing

Poanes massasoit (Scudder 1864)

Status: Rare breeding resident.

Flight: Single brooded, with a short flight from late June to mid July.

Distinguishing features: Males are uniformly dark brown above. Females are dark brown with a chevron of orange spots on the upper hind wing and scattered orange spots on the upper fore wing. Both sexes have an arrangement of arrow- or X-shaped orange patches on the lower hind wing. Wingspan: 2.8 cm.

Distribution and habitat: Map 205. Restricted to fens, marshes, and wet prairies in the northwestern quarter of the state. This is one of our rarest wetland skippers. Contrary to the maps published in Opler and Krizek (1984), this species has never been found in eastern Iowa (or southwestern Wisconsin), meaning that the northwestern Iowa and southern Minnesota populations are disjunct form population centers farther east.

Natural history: This skipper is not easily observed, as it often flies among the sedge and grass tops. Tussock sedge has been reported elsewhere to serve as its larval host, but no observations of larval activity have been made in Iowa.

Questions: What are the larval hosts for the Mulberry Wing? Why is it absent from seemingly appropriate fen and wet prairie sites in northeastern Iowa? Can the Iowa and Minnesota populations be genetically or morphologically differentiated from the Great Lakes and northern Atlantic Coast populations? If so, how long have these populations been isolated?

Broad-winged Skipper 206

Poanes viator (Edwards 1865)

Status: Rare breeding resident.

Flight: Single brooded, flying from the last of June through mid August.

Distinguishing features: The Broad-winged Skipper is most easily identified by a large bright orange patch (bordered by dark brown) on the upper hind wing and by its mostly dark upper fore wing, with only a small amount of orange. The lower hind wing is rusty-colored, with faint light orange spots surrounding a central orange ray between two central veins. Wingspan: 3.2 – 3.5 cm.

Distribution and habitat: Map 206. Restricted to prairie marshes, lake margins, and fens from the Lake Okoboji region in the northwest to eastern Jones County in the east-central part of the state. It was first located in Iowa at the poor fen at Dead Man's Lake in Pilot Knob State Park (Miller 1961). It ranks among Iowa's rarest wetland skippers.

Natural history: The Broad-winged Skipper seems to prefer undisturbed wetland sites with an abundance of large-leaved sedges, such as lake sedge. Its larvae have been reported to feed on this species in other states.

Questions: Do Broad-winged Skippers avoid competition with other skippers whose larvae eat broad-leaved wetland sedges (such as the Dion Skipper) by consuming different parts of the plant? Why are Broad-winged Skippers absent from disturbed wetland sites? How resilient are populations in regard to changing water levels?

Black Dash 212

Euphyes conspicua (Edwards 1863)

Status: Infrequent breeding resident.

Flight: Single brooded, flying from mid June through mid August.

Distinguishing features: Males are orange above, with broad dark borders and a large and prominent jet-black stigma. Females are darker above, with orange coloration restricted to small areas in the center of both upper wing surfaces. Females look much like female Byssus Skippers above but are uniformly brown toward the body, lack an isolated orange-yellow cell near the fore-wing tip, and live in very different habitats. Both sexes are dark orange-brown below, with four prominent orange cells, one twice as long as the others. Wingspan: 3.3 – 3.5 cm.

Distribution and habitat: Map 212. Perhaps the most common wetland skipper in Iowa, found in all but the southwestern quarter of the state. It occurs in fens, wet prairies, and marshes.

Natural history: This is our most tolerant wetland skipper and can be found even in degraded sites. The Black Dash has been reared in the laboratory on tussock sedge, a very common wetland sedge in Iowa. Some believe that Iowa populations represent the subspecies *E. c. buchholzi*, which tends to be darker and larger than typical specimens. Much of the Iowa material, however, seems identical to the typical subspecies.

Questions: Is there significant variation in adult wing coloration across Iowa? Why is this species more able to withstand habitat disturbance than other Iowa wetland skippers? How wide an array of sedge species will larvae feed on? What is the typical oviposition behavior of this species?

Dion Skipper   214

Euphyes dion (Edwards 1879)

Status: Infrequent breeding resident.

Flight: Single brooded, flying from late June through mid August.

Distinguishing features: The Dion Skipper is one of the largest Hesperiinae skippers in Iowa. In both sexes, the hind wing is dark brown above, with a single orange streak that ends before the edge of the wing. The hind wing below is orange with two yellowish streaks. The upper one is more pronounced in Iowa material. Wingspan: about 3.5 cm. (males) to 4 cm. (females).

Distribution and habitat: Map 214. Principally found in the northern half of the state, where it is restricted to wetlands supporting dense stands of lake sedge.

Natural history: The first report for this species in Iowa was made at the poor fen at Dead Man's Lake in Pilot Knob State Park (Miller 1961). This species rarely strays far from lake sedge patches, even within wetland sites. Its larvae have been reported elsewhere to feed on lake sedge and other wide-leaved sedges.

Questions: How many lake sedge stands support Dion Skipper colonies? Does this percentage change across the state? What is the minimum amount of lake sedge required to support stable populations of the Dion Skipper? How is it able to differentiate its host plant from the many other sedge species in Iowa?

Two-spotted Skipper   217

Euphyes bimacula (Grote and Robinson 1867)

Status: Rare breeding resident.

Flight: Single brooded, flying from mid June to late July.

Distinguishing features: This dark skipper is quite similar to the Dun Skipper, except that both sexes have a white fringe of scales on the outer wing margin, an orange-tan suffusion on the lower hind wing, and two prominent white spots on the lower fore wing. Wingspan: 3 cm. (males); 3.5 cm. (females).

Distribution and habitat: Map 217. Found in very few widely scattered sites across the state, being mainly restricted to fens, low prairies, and wet meadows. Lindsey (1917 [as Lindsay], 1921, 1922) indicated that this species was quite rare in the state, and little has changed in eight decades.

Natural history: The only reported host plant for this species (hairy-fruit sedge) is quite uncommon in the state and is not present at any of the known sites. Its larvae likely feed on some other sedge, perhaps tussock sedge or woolly sedge. Hibernation occurs when the larvae are half grown.

Questions: What are the habitat requirements for this species? What is its larval food plant? What makes it so much more unpredictable in its occurrence than the other wetland *Euphyes* species? Does its basking behavior differ from the behavior of other related species due to its darker color?

Dun Skipper 219

Euphyes vestris (Boisduval 1852)

Status: Common breeding resident.

Flight: Adults observed in flight from late May through late September, with most encounters occurring in the first half of July. While this species likely has multiple broods, collection records do not clearly indicate when these might occur. Perhaps there is only a single adult brood, which emerges over an extended period in the summer.

Distinguishing features: This is a uniformly dark brown skipper. Males have a black stigma, and females have a few white spots on the upper fore wing. Females often have a faint crescent of light brown spots on the mid hind wing below. It differs from the Little Glassywing and Northern Broken-dash by having reduced light markings (if any) on the upper fore wing. Wingspan: 3 cm.

Distribution and habitat: Map 219. Common throughout the state in a wide variety of open habitats.

Natural history: The larval hosts are unreported but are believed to be various members of the sedge family.

Questions: What are the larval hosts for this species in Iowa? How does it overwinter? What factors have allowed it to become the most abundant member of its genus in the state?

Dusted Skipper 221

Atrytonopsis hianna (Scudder 1868a)

Status: Rare breeding resident.

Flight: Primarily mid May through early June, with stray adults being encountered until mid July.

Distinguishing features: This distinctive dark brownish gray skipper has pointed fore wings with small white spots and white overscaling on the hind wing below. Some females in the Loess Hills are more highly marked and do not resemble the illustrated specimens. Wingspan: 3 cm.

Distribution and habitat: Map 221. Only known from far western and eastern Iowa, except for a century-old collection from Poweshiek County and an apocryphal Marion County sighting in 1962. Populations are restricted to xeric prairie habitats and occur in the Loess Hills, on dry gravel ridges along the terminal moraine of the Des Moines Lobe, and in limestone and sandstone glades near the Mississippi River. Although seemingly appropriate habitats exist on xeric limestone glades throughout the Iowan Surface, no populations have yet been observed in spite of extensive survey efforts.

Natural history: This is the earliest-flying prairie-restricted skipper in Iowa. It is seen on sunny south-facing hillsides perching on the ground or on low vegetation. Its flight is rapid, and it is very wary of approach. While both big and little bluestem have been listed as larval hosts, the limitation of this species to xeric prairie sites suggests that it probably prefers little bluestem in Iowa.

Questions: Do significant morphologic or genetic differences exist between eastern and western Iowa populations? Do environmental or historical factors account for its apparent absence from the Iowan Surface? How far can adults fly from their site of emergence? How sensitive are populations to fire management?

Pepper and Salt Skipper   236

Amblyscirtes hegon (Scudder 1864)

Status: Very rare breeding resident.

Flight: A single yearly flight from mid to late May.

Distinguishing features: The Pepper and Salt Skipper is very small and dark. It has a series of small white dots on the upper wing surfaces, with unworn individuals exhibiting a brown and white checkered margin. The brown lower surface is overscaled with gray, with an arc of white patches on both the fore wings and hind wings. Wingspan: 2.3 cm.

Distribution and habitat: Map 236. Known only from Allamakee County, except for a collection from Crawford County more than a century old. The first twentieth-century sighting of this species in Iowa occurred on May 20, 1978, at Yellow River State Forest. Only one other station has been discovered. In both sites it frequents moist, grassy trails or roadsides passing through mesic upland forest.

Natural history: Little is known of the ecology of this species in Iowa. Its larvae are reported to eat various grasses (including Kentucky bluegrass), but it likely feeds on other species.

Questions: Do colonies exist in other northeastern Iowa counties? What larval food plants are used in the state? What environmental factors are required for the persistence of populations? How susceptible is this species to logging activities?

Amblyscirtes vialis (Edwards 1862a)

Status: Infrequent breeding resident.

Flight: Apparently double brooded, with the first flight from late April to early June and the second from early July through early August. Double brooded populations previously have been reported only from Illinois and the Delaware River south (Opler and Krizek 1984).

Distinguishing features: This species is small and dark, with checkered edges and a violet overscaling on the hind wing below. Wingspan: 2.5 cm.

Distribution and habitat: Map 244. Limited to the southern third of Iowa, with populations extending north along the Loess Hills and the Mississippi River. It is restricted to xeric prairie habitats, including Loess Hills prairies, sand prairies, and limestone and sandstone glades.

Natural history: The Roadside-skipper overwinters in the pupal stage. While its larvae have been reported elsewhere to consume a wide variety of weedy grasses, its limitation to high-quality prairies suggests that this is not the case in Iowa.

Questions: Which grass species do larvae eat? Do larval host plants remain the same between the two broods? Why is this species limited to prairie sites in Iowa, even though it is common in weedy and disturbed habitats elsewhere?

Swallowtails: Family Papilionidae

All Iowa Papilionidae are members of the subfamily Papilioninae, large butter-flies with tails at the end of hind-wing vein M_3. The fore legs are completely developed in both sexes, and the tarsal claws are simple. The larvae are large, smooth, and often brightly colored. Some species have false eyes on the thorax to frighten predators. The larvae also bear an osmeterium (a fleshy, forked organ on the dorsal part of the thorax that emits an unpleasant odor). The pupae of all our species suspend themselves from branches and leaves by a girdle of silk around the middle and a silk pad at the caudal end, into which the cremaster is thrust.

The swallowtails in Iowa fall into several not too closely related genera. The Pipe-vine Swallowtail is a member of the *Aristolochia* swallowtails (genus *Battus*), which are characterized by scent scales on the hind wing of the male and by larvae bearing prominent tubercles. Substances gathered by the larvae from their food plants, in the pipevine family, protect these species. The Zebra Swallowtail is our representative of the kite swallowtails (*Eurytides*), which are characterized by long swordlike tails on the hind wing, fat larvae, and stubby pupae. The remaining species are more closely related to each other and are characterized by lack of androconial hairs on the hind wing and by their smooth and more elongate larvae.

Battus philenor (Linnaeus 1771)

Status: Breeding resident in the southeastern quarter, rare stray elsewhere.

Flight: Probably multiple brooded, because adults have been observed from early May through August. The few documented reports of this species make determination of flight times difficult.

Distinguishing features: The Pipevine Swallowtail is easily distinguished from other Iowa swallowtails by its black upper wing surface, with greenish-blue iridescence in the outer half of the hind wing. The rear hind wing below has bright orange submarginal spots surrounded by iridescence. Wingspan: 6.5 – 13 cm.

Distribution and habitat: Map 285. Strays reported from the southeastern half of the state, but breeding colonies are very rare and limited to old-growth, rocky woodlands in the southeastern quarter.

Parker first reported this butterfly from the Shimek State Forest area in Lee County in 1870. For years Iowa collectors believed that it was a stray from Missouri, where it is more common. Apparently the next specimen of the Pipevine Swallowtail collected in Lee County was on May 2, 1987. The resident status of this colony was verified by the location of the host plant, Virginia snakeroot, at this site in 1989 by Jeff Nekola. This plant had last been collected in Iowa in 1894, from Muscatine County. Many individuals were flying in 1987, so it was apparent that a population of the host plant must be present. With that hint from the butterflies, the plant was relocated.

Natural history: The larval host for this species is the Iowa-endangered Virginia snakeroot. This butterfly is the model for several mimics in Iowa, including the Spicebush Swallowtail, the female Black Swallowtail, the dark female Eastern Tiger Swallowtail, and the Red-spotted Purple. These apparently palatable species are afforded some protection from predation by resembling the Pipevine Swallowtail. Predatory birds may have had unpleasant previous experiences with it in their wintering grounds.

Questions: How frequently do Virginia snakeroot populations in Iowa support Pipevine Swallowtail colonies? How are these butterflies able to find such rare plants in our fragmented landscape? Are existing populations stable, and how may they best be protected?

Zebra Swallowtail   289

Eurytides marcellus (Cramer 1777)

Status: Breeding resident in the extreme south, stray elsewhere.

Flight: Double brooded: one from mid April into July, with a partial second brood in August.

Distinguishing features: This striking butterfly is the only Iowa swallowtail that is black-and-white striped, with tails to 2.5 cm. Wingspan: 6.4 – 10.4 cm.

Distribution and habitat: Map 289. Very rare in Iowa and restricted to mesic lowland forests. The only known breeding colony occurs in Waubonsie State Park (adults are seen in flight there during most years), but others should be sought in the southern tier of counties.

Natural history: The larval host in Iowa is paw paw, which is itself quite uncommon in the state. While this species is double brooded in Iowa, only a single specimen of the larger, darker, long-tailed summer brood has been reported.

Questions: How common are second-brood individuals in Iowa? Do breeding colonies occur in Iowa outside of Waubonsie State Park? Why are breeding colonies more limited in Iowa than its host plant, which occurs along the Mississippi River as far north as Clayton County?

Black Swallowtail 294

Papilio polyxenes (Fabricius 1775)

Status: Breeding resident.

Flight: Multiple brooded, with flights from April through early June, mid June through mid July, late July through August, and September through early October.

Distinguishing features: This easily recognized swallowtail is black, with two rows of submarginal yellow spots. The hind wing has a blue band between the yellow rows of spots, which are more extensive in females. The hind wing has a red spot at the anal angle and always has a black center. Wingspan: 6.7 – 11 cm.

Distribution and habitat: Map 294. Found commonly throughout the state in a variety of open habitats.

Natural history: Larvae of this species are particularly fond of cultivated and naturalized members of the carrot family, including parsley, dill, and carrots (including Queen Anne's lace), often decimating garden plantings of these vegetables. Because of the abundance of its host plants, it is often the most commonly observed swallowtail. Larval appearance changes across each of its four instar stages: the first two are bird-dropping mimics, the third is mostly black, and the fourth is green.

Questions: How often does this species use native members of the carrot family as a larval host? What are the selective advantages of having each larval stage appear different? What factors account for the marked size differences between populations often observed?

Eastern Tiger Swallowtail 297

Papilio glaucus (Linnaeus 1758)

Status: Breeding resident.

Flight: Generally double brooded, with flights from April through June and early July through August. A partial third brood may be present in some years from mid September to first frost.

Distinguishing features: This familiar butterfly is yellow with black margins and black tigerlike stripes on the front edge of the fore wing. Females are dimorphic. One form resembles the male, with yellow wings and black markings. The other form is melanic: the yellow may be completely obscured by black scaling, but under close examination the tiger stripes may be seen. Some individuals appear intermediate, with the yellow scaling only partially blacked out. Wingspan: 9–16 cm.

Distribution and habitat: Map 297. Common throughout the state in a wide variety of habitats. It is particularly frequent along forest edges, where adequate nectaring sites occur.

Natural history: The larvae feed on a number of common trees, such as ash and wild cherry. They derive protection from predators in at least two ways. First, the dorsal part of the thorax has two large eyespots. When larvae are disturbed, they shake the front part of their body, calling attention to these spots, intimidating predators, and discouraging further attack. Second, the brightly colored two-pronged osmeterium (normally kept tucked under the mid dorsal region of the thorax) can be made to release a bright, unpleasant-smelling liquid. Adult males frequently congregate at mud puddles or along streambanks.

Questions: Does the percentage of melanic to yellow females vary from population to population, and what environmental factors influence any such changes? Is the dark form mimetic and related to the protection derived from other swallowtails (e.g., Pipevine or Spicebush Swallowtails)? How protective are the eyespots against predation by native birds? What is the chemical nature of the odor-producing osmeterium?

Spicebush Swallowtail 303

Papilio troilus (Linnaeus 1758)

Status: Southern stray.

Flight: July. Two flights, with a partial third, are reported elsewhere in its range.

Distinguishing features: This large black swallowtail is best distinguished by its upper hind wing with a blue-green patch on top and pale green marginal spots. Wingspan: 8.5–12 cm.

Distribution and habitat: Map 303. Rare records, generally dating from 1876 to 1917. More recent observations have been made in Monona, Winneshiek, and Keokuk counties.

Natural history: The preferred larval host, spicebush, is not known to occur in Iowa, although populations are recorded from adjacent counties in Missouri and Illinois. If this shrub could be located in the state, it is possible that a resident colony of this butterfly might also be identified. Its larvae may also rarely utilize other shrubs that are native to Iowa, such as prickly ash and sassafras.

Questions: Why has this species apparently become much less common over the last century? Do breeding colonies occur in Iowa? If present, do they use spicebush as their larval hosts? What environmental factors favor long-distance movement of this species beyond its normal range (such as far northern Iowa)?

Giant Swallowtail 308

Papilio cresphontes (Cramer 1777)

Status: Breeding resident.

Flight: Multiple brooded: the first from mid May to early June, the second from mid July through August, and a partial third from mid September through frost.

Distinguishing features: The Giant Swallowtail is black-brown, with a band of yellow spots running from the upper fore-wing tip through the base of the upper hind wing. The ground color below is mostly yellow. Wingspan: 9 – 15.5 cm.

Distribution and habitat: Map 308. Widely scattered throughout the state in a variety of brushy habitats.

Natural history: This species is particularly fond of brushy open woods and margins, where its larval hosts (prickly ash and wafer ash or hoptree, Iowa's only members of the citrus family) occur.

Questions: Do spring brood adults represent resident individuals or migrants from farther south? What are the minimum winter temperatures that its pupae can withstand? How far can adults fly in a lifetime?

Whites, Sulphurs, and Marbles: Family Pieridae

Pierid butterflies in Iowa are generally small to medium species with white, yellow, or orange wings, making them some of the most visible members of our fauna. The Iowa Pierids belong to two subfamilies, the whites and marbles (Pierinae) and the sulphurs (Coliadinae). One of the species (Cabbage White) is a garden pest, while another (Orange Sulphur) can be an important alfalfa pest.

Pierids are distinguished from other groups by their split tarsal claws. In both sexes, the fore legs are fully developed. The larvae are smooth to slightly hairy, green with yellow or white stripes. In our area, most feed on mustards or legumes. A silk girdle around the middle and a silk pad at the caudal end into which the cremaster is thrust suspend the pupae from the substrate.

Pontia protodice (Boisduval and LeConte [1830])

Status: Breeding resident.

Flight: Multiple broods from mid April to mid October. This species is common in Minnesota during April and May, so the rarity of early spring Iowa records is probably due to incomplete field observations.

Distinguishing features: Females have a distinctive dark brown checkered pattern above on both the upper and lower wings; males often lack this pattern, having only a few black patches on the fore wing. The hind wing below is yellowish. Wingspan: 4.2 – 6 cm.

Distribution and habitat: Map 323. Found statewide, but most common in western and east-central Iowa, where it flies along railroad tracks and in old fields, disturbed areas, and pastures.

Natural history: The larvae consume a wide variety of weedy mustards. Olsen (1990) observed a tenfold decrease in the population size of this species at Rock Island Preserve in Linn County from sequential dry (1989) and wet (1990) years. This population has not been seen since then.

Questions: What factors affect the population density of *P. protodice*? What effect does the Cabbage White (*P. rapae*) have on *P. protodice*? Is the early spring brood uncommon in Iowa or simply overlooked?

Cabbage White 326

Pieris rapae (Linnaeus 1758)

Status: Naturalized breeding resident.

Flight: Multiple overlapping broods, with flights extending from early April through mid October.

Distinguishing features: The Cabbage White is white with a black fore-wing tip. Males have a single spot on the fore wing, while females have two. Spring males tend to be small and have more basal black, with darker undersurfaces; summer forms are larger and lighter in color. Wingspan: 4 – 5.5 cm.

Distribution and habitat: Map 326. Abundant statewide and found across a wide variety of habitats. It is particularly common in farmyards and gardens.

Natural history: Larvae consume a wide variety of mustards and are especially fond of domesticated cabbages and their relatives, making the Cabbage White one of Iowa's few pest butterflies. While this species has been in the state since 1878 (Scudder 1889), later records of movement across the state (Osborn 1890) do not seem well documented and should be treated with caution.

Questions: What advantages are afforded by having different wing colors in spring and summer broods? How often does this species consume native mustards? Has it had a negative impact on the size and distribution of Checkered White populations? What is the ecology of the braconid wasp parasitoids that feed on the Cabbage White larvae?

Olympia Marble 337

Euchloe olympia (Edwards "1871")

Status: Breeding resident.

Flight: Early April to late May.

Distinguishing features: This gorgeous butterfly is named for the striking green marbling on the hind wing below, which barely shows through. The fore wing above is flecked with short bands of gray. These wing colors help it blend into the early spring landscape of dead grass with the first hint of new green growth. Some fresh specimens exhibit a rosy blush over the apical third of the fore wings, which fades following pinning and storage. Wingspan: 3.5 – 5 cm.

Distribution and habitat: Map 337. Found throughout the Loess Hills; rare in northwestern Iowa on dry gravel prairies and in the northeast on sandy bedrock glades.

Natural history: Larvae consume various rock cress species, likely hairy rock cress in western Iowa and rock cress in the northeast. Adults are weak flyers, often barely rising above the dead grass of the previous summer. Populations are often small; only single individuals are observed at a given time. This, in combination with the emergence of this species before most other species, has led Loess Hills lepidopterist Tim Orwig to call it our "loneliest butterfly." These factors suggest that it may be overlooked and may be more common than current records indicate.

Questions: Do preferred host plants differ between eastern and western Iowa Olympia Marble populations? Do these preferences have a genetic basis? Why are population sizes often so small, given that host plants are usually quite common? Why does it appear not to colonize algific talus slopes, which support large rock cress populations?

Clouded Sulphur 348

Colias philodice (Godart 1819)

Status: Breeding resident.

Flight: Multiple overlapping broods from late April through October.

Distinguishing features: This species has predominantly bright yellow wings with black borders above. On females these borders are interrupted by several yellowish spots. Females are often white, making them difficult to distinguish from white females of the Orange Sulphur. It is smaller, with narrower black bands. Wingspan: 4 – 5 cm.

Distribution and habitat: Map 348. Abundant statewide in a variety of native and disturbed open habitats.

Natural history: Larvae feed on a variety of native and naturalized legumes but are particularly fond of clovers. Population sizes can vary by as much as a factor of ten on the same sites in consecutive years (Olsen 1990). Currently the Clouded Sulphur is less abundant than the Orange Sulphur; but this pattern was reversed when clover was the major hay source several decades ago. Natural hybridization occurs in Iowa between *C. philodice* and *C. eurytheme*, often complicating the identification of a given individual. While courtship differences ordinarily keep these two species genetically isolated, such mechanisms begin to break down when host plants are cultivated side by side.

Questions: What behavioral factors tend to keep *C. philodice* and *C. eurytheme* from commonly interbreeding? Have rates of hybridization changed over time? Do these two species compete for similar limiting resources?

Orange Sulphur   349

Colias eurytheme (Boisduval 1852)

Status: Breeding resident.

Flight: Multiple overlapping broods from early May through mid November.

Distinguishing features: This butterfly has orange wings with black borders that are generally wider than those of the Clouded Sulphur. Early spring adults are less orange and have considerably narrower black margins than adults from later broods. Significant portions of females in all broods are albinic and are difficult to distinguish from white Clouded Sulphur females. The relative widths of the black wing margins are often the only features that help distinguish these individuals. Wingspan: 4–5 cm. (males), 4.5–6 cm. (females).

Distribution and habitat: Map 349. One of the most abundant butterflies throughout the state, found in a wide variety of open habitats, including alfalfa fields and old pastures.

Natural history: Temperature is thought to be the factor that affects the proportion of albinic individuals in the population. Larvae consume alfalfa, vetch, and a variety of other legumes.

Questions: Does the proportion of white to orange females vary between populations? Is this proportion consistent from year to year and season to season? What factors maintain this dimorphism?

Southern Dogface   366

Colias cesonia (Stoll [1790])

Status: Spring and early summer southern stray, summer resident.

Flight: First migrants by early to mid June in most years. Two broods later in the season, the first flying July to mid August and the second from September to October.

Distinguishing features: The Dogface is named for the yellow dog's face (including an eye) framed in the black border of the upper fore-wing surface. The wings are yellow below. Late autumn specimens may have a rosy cast on the underside and have been referred to as the form *rosa*. Wingspan: 6 – 7.5 cm.

Distribution and habitat: Map 366. Frequently found in the Loess Hills; incidental throughout the rest of the state. Individuals demonstrate a strong preference for dry meadows and prairies.

Natural history: Larvae feed on a large number of legumes, including the native lead plant, prairie bush clover, and false indigo. Adults, larvae, and eggs are unable to withstand harsh Iowa winters, and this species must repopulate the state each year by migration from the south. Because of this, population sizes may fluctuate greatly on a yearly basis.

Questions: What minimum winter temperatures can this species survive? Do the Loess Hills represent a migration route for this species? What is the selective advantage to the rose coloration of late-season adults?

Cloudless Sulphur 370

Phoebis sennae (Linnaeus 1758)

Status: Midsummer stray, late summer and early fall resident.

Flight: First rare migrants from the south in late June and early July; more in late July through mid August. These individuals found resident populations that fly from September through frost.

Distinguishing features: The large lemon-yellow, unmarked wings of the Cloudless Sulphur make it easy to identify in the field. Wingspan: 6 – 8 cm.

Distribution and habitat: Map 370. Scattered throughout the southern half of Iowa, where it favors a variety of open habitats, including old fields, roadsides, and prairies.

Natural history: The most frequent Iowa larval host is probably partridge pea. This butterfly is a fast flyer, making it very difficult to net. Population sizes vary greatly, from almost absent in some seasons to relatively abundant in others.

Questions: What environmental factors best predict good seasons for the Cloudless Sulphur in Iowa? What cues do migratory adults use to locate the relatively uncommon host plant?

Little Yellow 385

Eurema lisa (Boisduval and LeConte, [1830])

Status: Early to midsummer southern stray, late season resident.

Flight: First arrival of adults from mid June to mid July. Overlapping broods fly from late July to frost.

Distinguishing features: Wings are yellow above; the apical one-third of the fore wing is black. The hind wing has a black margin above. The maculation of the lower wing surface shows marked variability. Orange and white forms of females are also known. Wingspan: 3.1–4 cm.

Distribution and habitat: Map 385. Frequently scattered throughout the state, with populations favoring dry, open habitats such as meadows, old fields, roadsides, and prairies.

Natural history: Like many other Iowa late summer resident Pierids, Little Yellow larvae consume partridge pea. It is much commoner in the state than other members of this genus.

Questions: Why is this species so much commoner in Iowa than the other small sulphurs? Do the larvae of these species compete for access to partridge pea? How much yearly variability occurs in late summer population size? What advantage (if any) exists for the nonyellow females?

Dainty Sulphur   389

Nathalis iole (Boisduval 1836)

Status: Spring to early summer southern stray, midsummer to fall resident.

Flight: First migrants from late May through June, founding a series of overlapping later broods that fly from late July to frost.

Distinguishing features: This is the smallest Pierid in the state. It is typically yellow above, with black apices and a black bar on both wings where they meet. The color varies, with some females being white or orange. Males have a very apparent sex-patch on the dorsal hind wing, which may vary from red to yellow (Clench 1976). This color may fade in preserved specimens. Wingspan: 2.2–2.6 cm.

Distribution and habitat: Map 389. Scattered throughout the southwestern two-thirds of Iowa in various open, mesic, disturbed habitats.

Natural history: Unlike the larvae of other small sulphurs, larvae of this species consume members of the aster family, especially tickseed. Its range of host plants may be wider, however; Lulu Berry (1934) reared larvae on chickweed in Benton County. The species flies rather close to the ground, with sporadic stops at low-growing flowers.

Questions: How far must initial migrants travel to reach the state? What range of host plants do larvae consume? How much yearly variability occurs in population size and location?

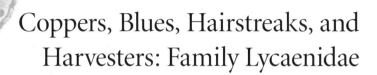

Coppers, Blues, Hairstreaks, and Harvesters: Family Lycaenidae

While the Lycaenids represent the world's largest family of butterflies, they are only the third largest Iowa family. Lycaenids are characterized by a reduced male tarsus bearing a single claw, absence of the humeral vein on the hind wing, and reduced fore-wing veins (ten to eleven). The genitalia of both sexes are often distinctive and useful for taxonomic identification.

Our species belong to three main subfamilies, the Miletinae (harvesters), Lycaeninae (coppers and hairstreaks), and Polyomnatinae (blues). The taxonomic distinction between these groups is based on groups of complex morphological characters, but in Iowa assignments can usually be made by general appearance: harvesters have noniridescent orange and brown wings; coppers have orange, brown, or purple upper wings and lack tails and eyespots; blues have upper wings with iridescent blue areas; and hairstreaks have noniridescent brown-gray wings that are interrupted on the undersurface by bands of a different color. Unfortunately, such rules do not apply for Lycaenids from the tropical regions.

The eggs of Lycaenids are frequently turban-shaped, with a variety of pits, prominences, and sculptures. They may be laid directly on the food plant or may be broadcast nearby. The larvae are sluglike, tapered toward both the head and the anal region; most have some short hairs (often in bizarre patterns), and they usually possess honeydew glands on the seventh abdominal segment. The solution from this gland is avidly sought by ants, which occasionally tend the larvae and protect them from enemies. The pupae tend to be stout and relatively immotile and are suspended by a silken median girdle and the cremaster. The pupae are capable of making tiny chirping or creaking noises, which are thought to serve some protective function against predators or parasites.

Harvester

Feniseca tarquinius (Fabricius 1793)

Status: Breeding resident.

Flight: Apparently multiple overlapping broods, with adults flying almost any time between late May and late September. Adult populations may reach peak abundance in August.

Distinguishing features: The upper surface is orange and has a highly sculptured brown border with a row of dark spots in the marginal area of the hind wing. The colors are more diffuse below; the hind wing is covered with gray circular patterns. Wingspan: 2.9–3.2 cm.

Distribution and habitat: Map 390. Scattered throughout the southeastern three-quarters of the state, where it is most often found in woods along trails, gravel roads, and streams.

Natural history: The Harvester is our only carnivorous caterpillar. It is generally reported to live on woolly aphid colonies associated with alder. This shrub is rare in Iowa, however, with a much more restricted range than the range for this butterfly. Perhaps woolly aphid colonies on dogwood are more often used, although harvester caterpillars have yet to be observed in such situations. To find larvae, look for large woolly aphid congregations near plant branch tips. The larvae are usually found near the margin of these colonies and camouflage themselves with aphid detritus and cast skins. Probing such colonies with a twig is usually sufficient to dislodge this camouflage and reveal the larva. The larval stage only lasts about ten days, so they are easily reared by keeping cut branches with aphid colonies in a jar of water.

The flight pattern is darting and fast, and netting adults on the wing is very difficult. Capture is made easier by waiting for adults to alight on a leaf (often dogwood) then rapidly swinging the net up from below.

Questions: What aphids are most often eaten by this butterfly in Iowa? What are the most common host-plant associations for these aphid species? Do Harvesters frequent Iowa's only large alder wetlands at the headwaters of the Cedar and Wapsipinicon rivers? What factors contribute to their scattered distribution and low population numbers in Iowa? Larvae (presumably) have lost the ancestral "honey glands" to establish a relationship with ants (even though the pupae still stridulate), so how do the larvae "prevent" attacks by ants which tend the aphids?

American Copper 392

Lycaena phlaeas (Linneaus 1761)

Status: Naturalized breeding resident.

Flight: Three broods: the first flying from late April to early June, the second from late June to early August, and the third from late August through September.

Distinguishing features: Adult top fore wings are copper-colored, with a dark brown margin and spots. The hind wing above is the opposite: dark brown with a copper margin. The hind wing below is grayish, with a wavy copper line in the margin. Wingspan: 2.5 – 3.5 cm.

Distribution and habitat: Map 392. Scattered in the southeastern half of the state in a variety of dry, open, sandy habitats. It is particularly common in the sandy ground adjacent to the Iowa, Cedar, and Wapsipinicon rivers.

Natural history: Larvae feed on red sorrel, a naturalized Eurasian pasture weed. This species also occurs in Europe. While native North American populations are known from the high arctic and western alpine tundra, our populations originated in Europe and were brought to eastern North America in hay during colonial times. Distinctive color-pattern forms are known.

Questions: How rapidly did the American Copper colonize the state following European settlement? Why are populations so uncommon in northwestern Iowa? How frequent are *fasciata* phenotypes in local populations?

Gray Copper 395

Lycaena dione (Scudder 1869)

Status: Breeding resident.

Flight: Early June through July.

Distinguishing features: The male is gray above, with several orange-bordered black spots on the hind-wing margin. Below it is light gray to whitish with black spots and has an orange hind-wing margin. The female is similar but has black spots above.

Distribution and habitat: Map 395. Common in the western half of Iowa but more scattered in the east; restricted to a variety of open, upland habitats such as native prairie, old fields, roadsides, and open woods. In the east it appears more frequently in sandy sites.

Natural history: Larvae consume dock species. In 1892 Willard sent Skinner some larvae that had been collected in Grinnell from what was claimed to be yard dock, an introduced species not known from the state. The actual host plant was probably curly dock, which is an abundant Iowa weed.

Questions: What environmental factors allow this species to become more common in western Iowa? What variety of dock species do larvae consume? What are the oviposition behaviors in relation to its host plant?

Lycaena hyllus (Cramer [1775])

Status: Breeding resident.

Flight: Double brooded, with the first flying from late May to early July and the second from late July to early September. A partial third brood rarely emerges some years from late September through frost.

Distinguishing features: The male is coppery brown above, with a copper hind-wing margin. The female hind wing is similar, but the fore wing is copper with black spots and a brown margin. Below the fore wings of both sexes are orange with a light margin, and the hind wings are white with an orange margin. Wingspan: 3.2 – 4.5 cm.

Distribution and habitat: Map 398. Abundant statewide in open, moist meadows and wetlands.

Natural history: Larvae consume a number of dock species. They may be easily found by looking on the underside of the largest leaves of the host plant. As with many members of the genus, the Bronze Copper displays marked sexual dimorphism.

Questions: What advantages are gained by being sexually dimorphic? Do larvae of this species and the Gray Copper use the same host plants? If so, do they compete?

Lycaena helloides (Boisduval 1852)

Status: Breeding resident.

Flight: Double brooded, with the first largely flying from late May to early June and the second in early July. Scattered individuals have been observed from early May to early September, suggesting other partial broods in some seasons.

Distinguishing features: The sexes are strongly dimorphic. Males are copper-brown above, with a purplish iridescence, scattered black spots, and a band of orange spots on the hind-wing margin. Females are orange, with triangular black spots and gray margin on both upper fore-wing and hind-wing surfaces. Males of this species and the Bronze Copper may be almost indistinguishable based on the upper wing surface. Both sexes of the Purplish Copper have gray-orange under-hind-wing surfaces, however, with a margin of orange crescent-shaped spots on the outer margin. Wingspan: 2.4 – 3.2 cm.

Distribution and habitat: Map 403. Scattered and rare throughout the northeastern half of Iowa in wet-mesic prairies, marshes, and wet meadows.

Natural history: Larvae consume a variety of dock and knotweed species. This is the most uncommon copper species in Iowa.

Questions: What factors limit the Purplish Copper's population range and abundance in Iowa? Given that they share the same host plants, what makes it so much rarer in the state than the Bronze Copper? What is the response of Purplish Copper populations to fire management?

Callophrys gryneus (Hubner [1819])

Status: Breeding resident.

Flight: Double brooded: the first flying from late April through May, the second from late June through early August.

Distinguishing features: The wing underside is a striking green, with a jagged white postmedial line bordered medially in brown. The wing appearance above changes between the two broods. In the spring form both the fore wings and hind wings have orange-brown centers with brown margins. In the summer form the upper wing surface is unmarked and dark brown. Wingspan: 2.2–3.2 cm.

Distribution and habitat: Map 422. Uncommon, with populations concentrated in the eastern and western thirds of the state. It occurs most frequently on limestone and sand prairies in the east and the Loess Hills and xeric gravel prairies in the west.

Natural history: Larvae consume red cedar, living on the margins of or within native xeric prairies. Adults rest in cedar branches with wings closed, allowing the green cast of the hind-wing underside to afford a good degree of camouflage. Sweeping (or beating) cedar branches is often an effective sampling method when adults are not active. Active individuals may commonly be seen in spiral encounter flights above cedar trees. Although cedar is common throughout Iowa in a variety of disturbed habitats (like old fields), populations of the Juniper Hairstreak have yet to be found in such situations. It has not been found in the central third of the state, in spite of repeated location attempts.

Questions: What factors limit the Juniper Hairstreak in Iowa to cedars growing in native prairie habitats? How many cedars are needed to support stable Juniper Hairstreak populations on prairies? Is this species absent from central Iowa? If so, what ecological factors are responsible? What advantages are afforded by having light-colored spring and dark-colored summer adults?

Henry's Elfin

432

Callophrys henrici (Grote and Robinson 1867a)

Status: Breeding resident.

Flight: Mid to late April.

Distinguishing features: Henry's Elfin is brown above, with a golden cast in the limbal area of the hind wing. The wing is dark brown below on the medial area basal to the body. A jagged line separates this region from the discal and limbal areas, which are greenish tan with gray overscaling at the margin. It has a row of small brown spots between the center and the margin. The hind-wing margin is scalloped. Wingspan: 2.4–3 cm.

Distribution and habitat: Map 432. Apparently scattered and rare in the southern third of the state, where it occurs in woodlands.

Natural history: Larvae consume redbud. Pupae stages diapause through summer and winter and are capable of sound production (as are most hairstreaks). Adults fly only in the immediate vicinity of redbud trees. This species may be overlooked in Iowa, owing to its very early and short flight and strict restriction to native redbud stands.

Questions: How common are Henry's Elfins in southern Iowa? How many native redbud stands support this species? What is the minimum amount of redbud necessary to support stable colonies? What nectar sources do adults most often use? Do adults demonstrate territoriality?

Coral Hairstreak   445

Satyrium titus (Fabricius 1793)

Status: Breeding resident.

Flight: Mid June through July.

Distinguishing features: This is one of the few resident hairstreaks without hind-wing tails. Both sexes are dark brown above and slightly lighter brown below. Males have triangular wings, while females' wings are rounded. Females have two orange and black spots on the trailing edge. The fore wing has one to two rows of submarginal and marginal black spots below, and the hind wing has one row of black spots and a marginal row of coral-colored spots. Males have a gray sex spot in the middle of the front margin of the fore wing. Wingspan: 2.8 – 3.4 cm.

Distribution and habitat: Map 445. Common statewide along wood edges and in brushland, old fields, prairie, and savanna.

Natural history: Larvae consume shrubby wild cherries and plums. Adults are particularly fond of milkweed flower nectar. While they may swarm around some milkweed plants, nearby plants of the same species may be ignored.

Questions: What triggers attraction of Coral Hairstreaks to certain milkweed plants? What is the biology of the larval stages? Where does pupation most frequently occur?

Acadian Hairstreak   446

Satyrium acadica (Edwards 1862a)

Status: Breeding resident.

Flight: Late June to mid July.

Distinguishing features: The underwing surface is grayish; each of the median round black spots is surrounded by a thin white line. A distinct orange spot occurs on the dorsal surface of the hind wing above. Wingspan: 2.9 – 3.3 cm.

Distribution and habitat: Map 446. Uncommon to rare, largely limited to native wet prairies, fens, sedge meadows, and marshes in the northwestern three-fourths of Iowa.

Natural history: Larvae feed on willows. Adults may be found perching on shrubs, from which they dart at intruders. Adults are fond of dogbane flowers.

Questions: Do larvae favor some willow species over others? Given the abundance of its host genus, why are Acadian Hairstreak populations almost completely limited to native prairie and wetland habitats? How readily can new populations be founded? Can prairies on railroad right-of-ways serve as migration corridors?

Hickory Hairstreak 449

Satyrium caryaevorum (McDunnough 1942)

Status: Breeding resident.

Flight: Mid June through July; a single early September observation has also been recorded.

Distinguishing features: This species is very similar to the Banded Hairstreak except that the underside is lighter brown in contrast to the macular band, which is broken into offset segments rather than being straight. The blue eyespot on the hind wing below usually is tall enough to reach the macular band. The amount of variation found within both species, however, often makes distinguishing individuals difficult. Certain identification requires dissection and comparison of the genitalia. Wingspan: 2.6 – 2.9 cm.

Distribution and habitat: Map 449. Scattered and rare, with the bulk of colonies known from the northeast and Loess Hills, where it is found in mature upland forest. Because of confusion with the Banded Hairstreak, it seems likely that the Hickory Hairstreak may be more common in Iowa than these few records suggest.

Natural history: Larvae consume shagbark hickory, a common upland forest tree throughout Iowa. While the Hickory Hairstreak flies with the Banded Hairstreak and Striped Hairstreak, it is possible that slight differences in flight times exist.

Questions: Is the Hickory Hairstreak rare in Iowa or simply overlooked due to confusion with the Banded Hairstreak? Do Hickory Hairstreak larvae eat other hickory species? Do small but significant differences in the emergence times of Hickory, Banded, and Striped Hairstreaks exist? Do these species compete for nectar resources?

Edwards' Hairstreak 450

Satyrium edwardsii (Grote and Robinson 1867a)

Status: Breeding resident.

Flight: Mid June through July.

Distinguishing features: The underwing surface is warm brown; the postmedian macules are separated and oblong or rectangular, with a white margin that is more prominent on the outer surface. The hind wing has tails and a blue eyespot, with a weak orange spot on the top dorsal surface. Wingspan: 2.9 – 3.5 cm.

Distribution and habitat: Map 450. Rare and scattered throughout the state (perhaps absent in the southeast), where it occurs in savanna, prairie-forest margins, and dry, open woods.

Natural history: Larvae consume oak species. It may be easily confused with *S. calanus* and *S. acadica*.

Questions: In what stage does the Edwards' Hairstreak overwinter? Do adults patrol certain areas and show territorial restriction during perching? Why does this species avoid typical mesic oak forests in the state?

Banded Hairstreak 451

Satyrium calanus (Hubner [1809])

Status: Breeding resident.

Flight: Early June through late July.

Distinguishing features: The lower wing surface is dark brown, with a submarginal row of nearly connected darker brown spots bordered on the outer margin with white. The close placement of these spots gives the impression of a dark brown and white band. The lower hind wings have tails and a blue eyespot that does not reach the macular band. Wingspan: 2.4–3.6 cm.

Distribution and habitat: Map 451. Frequent statewide in dry, upland forests.

Natural history: Larvae consume various upland forest trees, such as oaks and hickories. Most adults in a given population typically fly at almost the same time, seemingly flooding the location with individuals for a week or so.

Questions: How do populations synchronize the flights of individual adults? Are genetic or environmental factors more important in creating high levels of variability between individuals? How much genetic interchange occurs between adjacent populations?

Striped Hairstreak 453

Satyrium liparops (LeConte 1833)

Status: Breeding resident.

Flight: Late June to mid July.

Distinguishing features: Similar to the Banded Hairstreak, but with highly offset dark macular bands, two to three times wider, with prominent white lines on both sides. Wingspan: 2.8–3.6 mm.

Distribution and habitat: Map 453. Scattered and uncommon throughout the state, occurring on the margins of dry upland forests, such as woodland edges of bedrock glades or Loess Hills prairies.

Natural history: Larvae consume a variety of dry woodland trees, such as hawthorn, wild cherry, wild plum, ironwood, and oak. Adults often rest on woodland edge shrubs, dart out to encounter passing individuals, and then return to the same perch.

Questions: Do significant behavioral differences exist between adult Striped Hairstreaks and Banded Hairstreaks? What plants serve as the favored larval hosts in

Iowa? Why is it less common than the Banded Hairstreak? How do mating adult Striped, Banded, and Hickory Hairstreaks distinguish each other?

Gray Hairstreak   470

Strymon melinus (Hubner [1813])

Status: Spring and early summer southern stray, midsummer to fall resident.

Flight: Initial southern migrants from late April through early June. At least three resident broods: one flying from late June to mid July, a second from early August through early September, and a third from late September through frost.

Distinguishing features: The blue-gray underwing color and the prominent orange spot at the anal angle on both sides of the hind wing make this species easy to identify. Wingspan: 2.5 – 3.2 cm.

Distribution and habitat: Map 470. Scattered but frequent throughout the state (especially in the southern two-thirds) in a variety of open, weedy habitats.

Natural history: Larvae consume a wide variety of host plants, including many commercial crops and garden plants. Adults are particularly fond of clover nectar. Although most butterfly guides (e.g., Opler and Malikul 1998) suggest that this species is resident throughout the northern states, its frequency over the growing season appears identical to the frequency of many small sulphurs that are early summer strays, which found breeding populations by the end of the season. Given the dearth of collections before mid June, it seems likely that this species simply cannot overwinter in Iowa.

Questions: Can individuals survive Iowa winters? How far can adults fly in a lifetime? Do they have any host-plant preferences in Iowa?

White M Hairstreak   490

Parrhasius m-album (Boisduval and LeConte, "1833")

Status: Southern stray or very rare breeding resident.

Flight: April through September.

Distinguishing features: This species is unlike any other Iowa butterfly. The under fore wing is brown-gray, with two medial bands of dark brown and white. The under hind wing is also brown-gray, with a distinct brown and white medial band in the shape of an upside-down M. Large orange, iridescent blue, and black spots occur on the lower margin. The upper wing surfaces are dark iridescent blue with a wide brown-black margin. Wingspan: 3.2 – 4.1 cm.

Distribution and habitat: Map 490. Extremely rare, with only seven sites reported in the southeastern half of the state. Little is known of the habitats, except that they are woodlands.

Natural history: Larvae consume oaks. While the May records suggest pupal diapause and resident populations, colonies do not appear to persist in the same locations from year to year. The apparent rarity of this species, however, could be due to the fact that adults principally fly above the forest canopy and only rarely stray to ground level. The Linn County record was nectaring on goldenrod.

Questions: Is this species a resident or stray in Iowa? Do adults spend most of their lives patrolling forest canopy tops? What are its favored woodland habitats? If it is not a resident, what are the origins of the adults found in May?

Eastern Tailed-blue 499

Everes comyntas (Godart [1824])

Status: Breeding resident.

Flight: Multiple overlapping broods, with flights from late April through fall frost.

Distinguishing features: Males are blue above and females slate-gray, with an orange eyespot on the hind wing. Both sexes are white below, with a postmedial row of small black spots on the fore wing. The hind wing below has two orange eyespots and a tiny tail. Wingspan: 2 – 3 cm.

Distribution and habitat: Map 499. Abundant throughout the state in a wide variety of open and forested, native and disturbed habitats. This is one of our most common butterflies.

Natural history: Larvae consume white clover, red clover, and assorted species of bush clover. Many other legumes may be used as a host. The white clover found in lawns often supports flourishing populations of this blue. Mowed road and railroad right-of-ways also support countless populations. Ants of at least three species have been found associating with larvae, though the incidence of attendance is very low. The pupae make noise (Downey 1966), though the amplitude is very slight; they must be placed in a vial in order to be heard.

Questions: Do host-plant preferences change over a growing season in one locality in any predictable manner? What is the impact of insecticide spraying on local populations?

Spring Azure 501

Celastrina ladon (Cramer [1780])

Status: Breeding resident.

Flight: Single brooded, flying from late April through May.

Distinguishing features: The males of this species are characterized by almost unmarked "matte" violet-blue upper wing surfaces. Under the microscope the rows of wing scales overlap more than on *C. neglecta*. The upper surfaces of the fore wings and hind wings have the same color and color density. Hind-wing veins are not distinctively marked. Females have a slate-colored margin above, which is about half as wide as in *neglecta*. Below, it is gray and heavily marked with black spots and chevrons. Both sexes often have checkered wing fringes. Wingspan: 2.2–2.6 cm.

Distribution and habitat: Map 501. Found throughout the state in a variety of woodland-associated habitats.

Natural history: In general Spring Azure larvae consume a large number of woody plant species, including dogwood, viburnum, wild cherry, and New Jersey tea. Ants often tend the larvae. In Iowa flight dates are earlier than those of *neglecta*.

Questions: Are ant associations more common on one host plant than on another? Can habitat, behavior, and food-plant differences between *ladon* and *neglecta* be documented in Iowa?

Summary Azure   503

Summer Azure   503

Celastrina neglecta (Edwards 1862a)

Status: Breeding resident.

Flight: Multiple overlapping broods with emergences from early June through mid September. They are most common during the third week of June, with a lack of records in early August.

Distinguishing features: This species is characterized by its sky-blue upper wing surfaces, with the fore wing darker than the hind wing. The hind-wing veins are distinctively darker above. It is larger and lighter than *C. ladon*, and the female has wider slate-colored margins, especially at the apex of the fore wing. The overlap of the fore wings and hind wings is usually dark. The wings below are white with rows of small marks. Wingspan: 2.5–3.3 cm.

Distribution and habitat: Map 503. Abundant throughout the state in a variety of open and woodland habitats.

Natural history: Summer Azure larvae consume a large number of woody plant species, including dogwood, viburnum, wild cherry, and New Jersey tea. Ants often tend the larvae. The pupae stridulate and probably represent the overwintering stage.

Comment: Alice B. Walton (1880) used the names *neglecta* and *pseudargiolus* (*ladon*) to describe these two species in her list for Muscatine County.

Questions: Do larval host plants change over a growing season? Are ant associations more common on one host plant than on another?

Silvery Blue   510

Glaucopsyche lygdamus (Doubleday 1841)

Status: Breeding resident.

Flight: Early May to early June.

Distinguishing features: The almost metallic, blue iridescence on the upper wing surface distinguishes this species. The females have a darker margin than the males. The underwing surface is dark gray below, with a row of white bordered black spots on the fore wing and a row of smaller dots on the hind wing. Wingspan: 2.2–3.2 cm.

Distribution and habitat: Map 510. Rare and local in the northwest and northern counties; also known from a single site in Shimek State Forest in the far southeastern part of the state. Populations are limited to native prairie and open, dry forest and are usually small.

Natural history: Larvae consume native vetches and perhaps other native legumes. Ants frequently tend them. Adults are often found nectaring on wild strawberry.

Questions: Do host-plant associations differ between the northern and southern Iowa populations? How dependent are they on their associated ant populations? What is the impact of prairie management techniques on population survival? Why are populations seemingly absent from most of central and southern Iowa?

Reakirt's Blue 526

Echinargus isola (Reakirt [1867])

Status: Breeding resident.

Flight: Multiple brooded: the first from late May to early June, the second from late June through July, the last from mid August to early September. A rare partial fourth brood may appear from late September to frost.

Distinguishing features: The sexes differ: the males are blue above and the females slate-gray above, with blue limited to a basal area on the dorsal surface. Two black spots are usually found at the anal angle of both sides of the hind wing. The fore wings below have a narrow submarginal band of small rectangles and a prominent post-medial row of white-circled black spots. The hind wings below also have three or four black spots in the basal area. Wingspan: 2.1–2.5 cm.

Distribution and habitat: Map 526. Scattered but frequent in the western half of the state; scattered and uncommon to rare in the east. Populations across Iowa appear essentially limited to native prairies.

Natural history: Larvae consume a wide assortment of legumes. Iowa populations often seem to occur in prairies with large amounts of lead plant; perhaps this species serves as a preferred host in the state. Even though most authorities (e.g., Opler and Malikul 1998) state that it does not overwinter in Iowa, our observations suggest that this is not always true. First, it is essentially limited to native prairies; if it was a migrant, it should be found across a wide variety of habitats. Second, at a given site, many fresh adults mark their initial emergence in spring; this also seems unlikely for an emigrating species, when a few worn adults should mark the initial occurrence. Finally, populations have proven to be persistent on given sites over multiple years.

Questions: Does lead plant serve as the primary larval food source for this species in Iowa? In what stage does it overwinter? Where does it overwinter? What is the effect of fire management on population size? How long do individual adults survive?

Melissa Blue 531

Lycaeides melissa (Edwards 1873)

Status: Breeding resident.

Flight: Multiple overlapping broods with emergences ranging from late May through fall frost. Adult population size apparently peaks during June.

Distinguishing features: The upper wing surfaces of the sexes are strikingly different. The wings of males are purplish-blue with a black margin and a contrasting white fringe above. The wings of females are dark gray, with an overcast of blue and a bold orange band near the margin. They are much more similar on the underwing surface, which is light gray with an orange band near the margin and a row of black spots on the inside. Wingspan: 2.1 – 2.6 cm.

Distribution and habitat: Map 531. Infrequent in the northwest, where it is limited to dry native prairies in the Loess Hills and on gravel ridges. It has recently been located at several sites in Lucas County in south central Iowa.

Natural history: Larvae consume various native prairie legumes. At Cayler Prairie, larvae were observed to be tended by ants. While individual populations are quite localized, these colonies can be sizable. Within the last decade, however, some of these larger populations (for example, at Cayler Prairie) have drastically declined.

Questions: What has caused the decline of some of the populations on managed preserves? What host plants are preferred by this species in Iowa? How capable is this species of recolonizing appropriate unoccupied sites? Do any populations of the Karner Blue occur on the few native lupine colonies in northeastern Iowa?

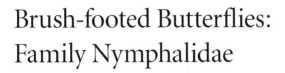

Brush-footed Butterflies: Family Nymphalidae

T he Nymphalids are a diverse group of small to large butterflies characterized by aborted fore legs covered with short hairs in both sexes. The pupae of all Nymphalids are suspended from the substrate by their cremasters. The family is quite diverse in Iowa, with eight subfamilies being represented: the Libytheinae (snouts), Danainae (milkweed butterflies), Heliconiinae (longwings and fritillaries), Nymphalinae (typical brushfoots), Limenitidinae (admirals and sisters), Charaxinae (leafwings), Apaturinae (emperors), and Satyrinae (nymphs).

The Libytheinae are a very small subfamily of primitive nymphaloid butterflies known from fossils 30 million years old (Pyle 1981). They are distributed throughout much of the world. Their elongated labial palpia project forward about four times the length of the head itself.

The Danainae or milkweed butterflies are a largely tropical group, venturing as far north as Iowa only as migrants or strays. Our species are characterized by their large size, bright orange and black wings, and the presence of scent patches on the male hind wing. The fore legs are reduced in both sexes. The caterpillars are naked, with fleshy tubercles on the anterior and posterior body segments. The cylindrical pupae are pendant from a silk button. All stages are emetic to birds because they concentrate poisons contained in host-plant leaves.

The Heliconiinae are longer winged than other Nymphalids, with open cells on both wings. The early stages of the longwings resemble those of fritillaries. The fritillaries are distinguished as adults by their orange wings with various black, white, or silver spots and as larvae by being densely spined.

The checkerspots and crescents belong to the subfamily Nymphalinae: smaller butterflies with less-spined larvae. The angelwings belong to the subfamily: they have the most heavily spined larvae and have pupae with dorsal prominences, giving them a serrated appearance. Brushfoots appear to have four legs rather than six because the front pair of legs is reduced to brushlike appendages.

The Limenitidinae are represented in our fauna by the genus *Limenitis*. The caterpillars in this group are adorned with spines and warts, and the pupae have a greatly humped wing case.

The Charaxinae (leafwings) are represented by one species in Iowa. The ventral wing surfaces are patterned like a dead leaf. They are often seen on rotted fruit.

The Apaturinae (emperors) are represented by the genus *Asterocampa* in Iowa. They share robust adult bodies and rapid flight. The larvae (like those of the Satyrinae) have twin horns at the caudal end.

The Satyrinae (nymphs) are small to medium butterflies recognized by their dull coloration and slow, jerky flight. Adults of all Iowa species are characterized by swollen fore-wing vein bases and closed cells of both wings. The body is exceptionally pubescent (fuzzy, with fine hairs), and eyespot patterns are usually prominent on the wings. This subfamily shares with other Nymphalids fore-leg reduction in both sexes. The larvae are cryptically colored, slightly pubescent, and cylindrical and have bare tails at the caudal end, a character shared only by the Apaturinae in our fauna. The pupa is slender and either is suspended by its cremaster or lies free in the grass.

American Snout 571

Libytheana carinenta (Cramer 1777)

Status: Early summer migrant, late summer and fall resident.

Flight: Strays from the south in June found a mid July through August brood, with a partial second brood emerging from mid September to frost.

Distinguishing features: No other Iowa butterfly has a long, beaklike snout. The upper wing surface is orange with brown on the margins and has subapical white patches and square tips on the fore wing. Wingspan: 4.2 – 4.8 cm.

Distribution and habitat: Map 571. Scattered throughout the state on the margins of mesic forests.

Natural history: Larvae consume hackberry. This butterfly is often seen puddling in small groups. Because its presence in Iowa is based on migration, population sizes vary greatly from year to year. Nocturnal copulation has been reported (Heitzman 1969).

Questions: Do Iowa populations occasionally overwinter? Are there favored nectar sources? What climatic conditions favor development of large midsummer populations?

Monarch 573

Danaus plexippus (Linnaeus 1758)

Status: Spring and early summer southern migrant, midsummer and late summer resident.

Flight: Some migrants in early April; most from mid May to mid June. These found a series of overlapping generations, with emergences from late June through August. Adults congregate in September and begin the southern migration to their wintering grounds in the mountains of central Mexico.

Distinguishing features: This is one of our most conspicuous butterflies; a description is hardly necessary. The Monarch has large, bright orange wings, with black lines and a black margin with white spots. Unlike the Viceroy, it lacks a black line crossing the hind wing. Wingspan: 9–10 cm.

Distribution and habitat: Map 573. Abundant throughout the state in a wide variety of open habitats, wherever its host plant is plentiful. It is frequent in disturbed sites.

Natural history: Larvae consume various species of milkweed, especially the common milkweed. Adult population sizes slowly climb until mid September, when the bulk of the migration passes through Iowa. Their annual routes have been studied for many years by Fred Urquhart (1960) and others, who are assisted each year by hundreds of co-workers (including Iowans) in applying wing-tags to help trace distances and directions traveled. Eventually the wintering site was located in the Sierra Madre of central Mexico. During migration Monarchs may gather in great numbers on trees, often on high points, or in wind-protected areas for a day or two before continuing their southward journey. The same roosting points may be used year after year. The continued existence of this species may be in more jeopardy than its current distribution suggests. Deforestation in the Mexican highlands has increased the frequency of killing frosts. Millions perished in a single night in late December 1995. Given that many of our common milkweed plants live in ditches and fencerows immediately adjacent to croplands, methods of controlling crop pests may well have serious negative impacts.

Questions: What climatic events can be associated with migratory behaviors such as communal roosting? How much exposure to transgenic BT (*Bacillus thuringiensis*) corn pollen is required to cause significant reductions in population size? What cues do females use to identify potential oviposition plants?

Variegated Fritillary   585

Euptoieta claudia (Cramer [1775])

Status: Southern stray in spring, summer resident.

Flight: Initial southern strays from late April through May; at least three resident broods: the first emerging from late June to mid July, the second from August through early September, and a partial third from late September to frost.

Distinguishing features: This butterfly is characterized by the variegated or mottled appearance of the under hind wing. On both sides, the dorsal surface is brown basally to tan distally, with a jagged black line between. Wingspread: 4.5-5.5 cm.

Distribution and habitat: Map 585. Scattered frequently throughout the state in various open habitats, including old fields, flower gardens, roadsides, parks, and prairies.

Natural history: Larvae consume a large variety of plants, including violets. Adult density often varies greatly from year to year, but they are only rarely seen in large numbers.

Questions: Can Iowa populations overwinter? What host plants are preferred? Are some nectar sources favored? What environmental factors correlate with large population sizes? How far can adults fly in a lifetime?

Great Spangled Fritillary 588

Speyeria cybele (Fabricius 1775)

Status: Breeding resident.

Flight: Either a single long brood or a series of multiple overlapping broods flying from late May through August, with few flying adults when the Monarchs migrate in the fall. Peak flight densities occur from mid June to Mid July.

Distinguishing features: The wing is orange above, diffused with brown basally, with rows of black crescents then spots and crescents in from the margin. The hind wing below has a rusty-brown discal area with white-silver spots, a tan limbal band, a submarginal row of triangles, and a brown margin. Wingspan 5.5 – 7.5 cm.

Distribution and habitat: Map 588. Abundant throughout the state in a wide variety of native and disturbed habitats, including woodlands, forest margins, old fields, and roadsides.

Natural history: The larvae consume violets; adults are attracted to many kinds of flowers. Fall populations seem to disappear just as the Monarch migration arrives. It may be single brooded in northern counties of the state.

Questions: Are certain violet species favored as larval hosts? Does the reduction in population size at the initiation of Monarch migration represent a form of competitive displacement? Do Great Spangled Fritillaries and Monarchs use the same nectar sources?

Aphrodite Fritillary 589

Speyeria aphrodite (Fabricius 1787)

Status: Breeding resident.

Flight: Double brooded: the first from mid June to mid July and a larger second one from early August through early September.

Distinguishing features: The dorsal wing surface is fulvous brown and slightly darker at the base. The fore wing below is light brown with a darker apex. The hind wing below is dark brown with a hint of a limbal band. This species can be most readily distinguished from the Great Spangled Fritillary by the dark spot on the dorsal fore wing above, between veins Cu_2 and $_2A$. Subspecies (or form) *alcestis* is very dark below without a limbal band. Wingspan: 6.6 – 8.4 cm.

Distribution and habitat: Map 589. Once found statewide; now infrequent and scattered only over the northern half of the state. These populations are restricted to high-quality native prairie, prairie marsh, and fen habitats.

Natural History: Larvae consume violets. This butterfly is more uncommon in Iowa than its distribution map suggests, with many counties being represented by only a single small colony. Populations seem to be small and isolated. Like many other insects they use only the portion of a preserved habitat with the required food plants and ecological parameters; the placement, timing, and type of management are crucial to their survival on a site.

Questions: What limits *aphrodite* populations to native grasslands? Why do populations seem to have disappeared from the southern half of Iowa? How easily can this species recolonize sites?

Regal Fritillary   590

Speyeria idalia (Drury 1773)

Status: Breeding resident.

Flight: Apparently multiple overlapping broods, with emergences from late May through mid September. Peak flight densities occur early to mid July.

Distinguishing features: The male fore wing above is orange-brown; the hind wing is blue-black with brown basally and has two rows of spots, the outer orange and the inner white. The female has two rows of creamy-white spots. The female's fore wing above is darker on the margin and apex. The hind wing below is brown-black with large silver-white spots. Wingspan: 8 – 10.5 cm.

Distribution and habitat: Map. 590. Found infrequently, but scattered throughout the western half of Iowa; rarer in the east. While populations are most commonly observed in native dry-mesic to xeric prairie, they are also consistently seen in very small numbers on fens.

Natural history: Larvae consume bird's-foot violet and perhaps other violet species. Adults are strong flyers and appear to be long-lived. It may be extremely numerous on small patches of native prairie and be virtually absent from intervening farm and grasslands. While populations are often found to dwindle after application of fire management to sites, large populations commonly persist on hayed prairies (Swengel 1998).

Questions: Are populations stable, or is this species declining throughout the state? How readily can it recolonize vacant sites? Why are populations much rarer and smaller in the eastern half of Iowa? Are the small populations observed on fens residents or strays from the surrounding landscape? What violets serve as larval hosts? Grazing is said to be a favorable management practice: why does it appear better than prescribed burning?

Silver-bordered Fritillary   605

Boloria selene (Denis and Schiffermuller 1775)

Status: Breeding resident.

Flight: Probably three broods: the first emerging from late May through mid June, the second from early to late July, and the third from late August through mid September.

Distinguishing features: The wings above are orange with black marks. The hind wing below is patchy orange and brown with three rows of silver spots and several more spots in the basal area. Wingspan: 3.5 – 4.5 cm.

Distribution and habitat: Map 605. Infrequently seen in the northeastern third of Iowa, where most populations are limited to fen areas. Some additional populations occur in wet prairies and meadows.

Natural History: Larvae consume violets, likely favoring the bog violet. Adults rarely stray beyond the margins of fen sites and may be restricted to patches less than a few thousand square meters in size.

Questions: Is a minimum habitat size required for maintenance of stable populations? How frequent is gene flow between populations? How much has this rate changed since the draining of over 90 percent of Iowa's fens in the last century?

Meadow Fritillary 606

Boloria bellona (Fabricius 1775)

Status: Breeding resident.

Flight: Multiple broods: the first emerging from late April to late May, the second from mid June through July, the third from early August though early September, and a partial fourth rarely flying in late September.

Distinguishing features: The wings are orange-brown above, with black marks and a clipped apex on the fore wing. The hind wing below is mottled with brown-purple and orange and lacks silver spots. Wingspan: 3.5 – 4.5 cm.

Distribution and habitat: Map 606. Scattered throughout the northeastern two-thirds of the state, with populations becoming increasingly frequent to the northeast. It occurs in various wet, open habitats such as wet meadows, pastures, open stream margins, wet prairies, fens, and marshes.

Natural history: Larvae consume violets. Even though adults are perhaps most commonly encountered within open streamside pastures in the Paleozoic Plateau, this habitat has only existed since European settlement.

Questions: Within what native habitats in the Paleozoic Plateau does this species occur? How long do adults live, and what are their dispersal abilities? In areas where the Meadow Fritillary and Silver-bordered Fritillary are sympatric, how are resources partitioned? What violet species do larvae favor?

Gorgone Checkerspot 631

Chlosyne gorgone (Hubner 1810)

Status: Breeding resident.

Flight: Apparently three broods: the first emerging in late April to early June, the second from late June to late July, and the third in August. A partial fourth brood emerges some years in late September.

Distinguishing features: The upper wing surface is dark, with a dark band, an orange band with spots, and a tan band moving from the margin to the body. The hind wing below is highly figured, with a central row of white arrowheads. Wingspan: 2.8 – 3.5 cm.

Distribution and habitat: Map 631. Occurs regularly throughout the southern three-fourths of the state. Its frequency appears higher toward the west, however, with populations becoming increasingly uncommon toward the east. They occur in a wide variety of open habitats, including old fields, roadsides, pastures, vacant lots, and native prairie.

Natural history: Larvae consume various members of the aster family, including sunflowers. It overwinters as half-grown larvae. Pupation lasts six days in the July brood. This very distinctive species may be expanding its range in Iowa as it did in Illinois (Irwin and Downey 1973).

Questions: Is the range of this species increasing in Iowa? How often does it use disturbed versus native habitats? What plant species are its favored larval hosts? What are the dispersal capabilities of adults? Why does it appear to be less common in northern and southeastern Iowa?

Silvery Checkerspot   632

Chlosyne nycteis (Doubleday and Hewitson [1847])

Status: Breeding resident.

Flight: Perhaps multiple overlapping broods, with adults emerging from early June through early September. Peak flight densities occur from mid to late June.

Distinguishing features: Both upper wing surfaces are orange, with a black margin and interior patches. The lower hind wings have two white crescents within the dark limbal area, a light central band, and weblike basal markings. Wingspan: 3.5 – 4.5 cm.

Distribution and habitat: Map 632. Frequent statewide, though perhaps less common in the north-central counties. It occurs in various native and disturbed open and forested habitats such as old fields, roadsides, parks, open woods, woodland margins, and prairies.

Natural history: Larvae consume various members of the aster family, including asters and black-eyed Susans. Eggs are laid in clusters; while the early instars appear semigregarious, mature larvae scatter to nearby shoots.

Questions: Do the Silvery Checkerspot and Gorgone Checkerspot compete for limiting resources? How long do adults live? What are adult dispersal abilities? How many broods are typically reared in Iowa?

Pearl Crescent

Phyciodes tharos (Drury 1773)

Status: Breeding resident.

Flight: Multiple overlapping broods from early April through late October.

Distinguishing features: The wings have an orange background above, with brown markings on the margins. Below the hind wing is largely clear, with a brown margin containing an ivory crescent. The cool-weather form *marcia* and females are darker below. Wingspread: 2.6–3.6 cm.

Distribution and habitat: Map 648. The most abundant Nymphalid in Iowa, found across the entire state in a wide variety of natural and disturbed habitats, including old fields, parks, woodland edges, pastures, roadsides, open forests, and prairies.

Natural history: Larvae consume asters. Populations are often large, and dozens of individuals are commonly found congregating around single puddles. Males are aggressive courters and have been observed attempting to mate with other species, even other families!

Questions: What aspects of the Pearl Crescent's life history traits have allowed it to become the most abundant crescent in Iowa? Do larvae prefer certain aster species? At what stage do individuals overwinter? Are courtship patterns ritualized and sequential or relatively simple (generalized) and random?

Baltimore Checkerspot

Euphydryas phaeton phaeton (Drury 1773)

Status: Breeding resident.

Flight: Mid June to mid July.

Distinguishing features: This striking butterfly has black wings with rows of white rectangles, spots, and crescents, bordered with red-orange half-moons on the margin. Brick-red spots occur near the costal margin of the upper fore wing. Females are approximately 25 percent larger than males. Wingspan: 4–6 cm.

Distribution and habitat: Map 659a. Scattered and rare across the northeastern quarter of the state, where it is limited to high-quality fens, open woodland seeps, and marshes.

Natural history: Larvae consume the relatively infrequent wildflower turtlehead. Although of limited distribution, this plant occurs on almost all 160 remaining fens in northeastern Iowa. Yet the Baltimore Checkerspot has only about eighteen documented populations in the state. Larvae are initially gregarious but disperse to individual plants by later instars. Adults disappear immediately after the sun becomes cloud-covered but resume flight as soon as the sun returns.

Questions: What factors limit Baltimore Checkerspots to so few of the appropriate fen sites in northeastern Iowa? What is the minimum number of turtlehead plants needed to establish a stable Baltimore Checkerspot colony? Is a minimum fen size required for establishment of colonies? What are the dispersal abilities of adults? How much genetic variability occurs between isolated colonies?

Ozark Baltimore Checkerspot 659b

Euphydryas phaeton ozarkae (Masters 1968)

Status: Breeding resident.

Flight: Early to late June. As in Illinois (Irwin and Downey 1973), this subspecies flies one to two weeks earlier than *E. phaeton phaeton.*

Distinguishing features: Very similar to the Baltimore Checkerspot, the Ozark Baltimore Checkerspot is larger and darker, with smaller marginal white and orange spots and orange spots near the costal margin of the upper fore wing. Wingspan: 5.4 – 6.5 cm.

Distribution and habitat: Map 659b. Very rare in the far southeast, where it occurs in open, dry upland forest.

Natural history: Because this butterfly lives in a completely different habitat, eats a different larval food plant, and flies at a different time than *E. phaeton phaeton,* we deal with it as a separate entity. Hoffmeister (1881) reported Lee County populations feeding on what is likely mullein foxglove. This plant is a hemiparasite on oak and is most frequent in margins and openings of dry oak forest.

Questions: How extensive is the range of the Ozark Baltimore Checkerspot in Iowa? Does it exclusively consume mullein foxglove or eat other woodland members of the figwort family? How large are individual colonies? How persistent are these colonies? What is the dispersal ability of this butterfly? What proportions of appropriate sites have been colonized by this subspecies?

Buckeye 664

Junonia coenia (Hubner 1806 – 1824 [1822])

Status: Southern stray.

Flight: Multiple overlapping broods or successive waves of migrants from late May through late October.

Distinguishing features: This spectacular brown butterfly has three large-pupiled eyespots on the upper wing surface. The anterior spot on the hind wing is reflective. The lower wing surface has one large and two small spots. The autumnal form has a gorgeous rosy color on the lower hind wing. Wingspan: 4 – 6.5 cm.

Distribution and habitat: Map 664. Scattered throughout the state, with encounters perhaps more common in the western half. It is found in a wide variety of dry open habitats, including old fields, pastures, roadsides, parks, prairies, and railroad rights-of-way.

Natural history: Larvae consume a number of open-ground low plants, including snapdragon, toadflax, plantain, and wild petunia. Occasionally minor population explosions have been noted.

Questions: Do populations ever overwinter and breed in Iowa? If so, what are the favored larval hosts? Do individuals use rivers as migration corridors? Why is the species less frequently encountered in eastern Iowa?

Question Mark 672

Polygonia interrogationis (Fabricius 1798)

Status: Breeding resident.

Flight: Multiple overlapping broods from early May through mid October.

Distinguishing features: The Question Mark is the largest and perhaps the most familiar anglewing in the state. It is easily identified by the pearly, question mark–shaped spot in the center of the hind wing below. It is seasonally dimorphic; the winter form is lighter and more uniformly colored on the undersurface; the summer form has blackish hind wings above and a much more mottled underside. No two individuals have quite the same color and pattern. Wingspan: 6–6.6 cm.

Distribution and habitat: Map 672. Abundant throughout the state in a variety of woodland habitats.

Natural history: Larvae consume a number of woodland trees and plants, including elms, hackberries, and nettles. Resting adults mimic dead leaves and when startled fly rapidly through sunlit glades. Adults eat fermented sap, fruit, and dung and can easily be baited at a butterfly feeder, using old fruit and a fermented brown sugar mix. Adults are the overwintering phase.

Questions: Is environment or genetics more important in determining wing variation among adults? How long do adults live? What are their dispersal abilities? What are the favored larval host plants? How much body weight do overwintering adults lose? What are their preferred hibernacula?

Eastern Comma 673

Polygonia comma (Harris 1842)

Status: Breeding resident.

Flight: Four major flight times for the three broods. Overwintering adults from last season's fall brood awaken in mid April and fly through mid May. These parent a brood that flies from mid June to mid July. A second brood emerges in August. The third brood emerges in mid September and flies through mid October then locates hibernacula.

Distinguishing features: The Eastern Comma's wings are orange-brown above, with a dark brown border, which has lighter crescents on the hind wing. The bottom surface is a collage of browns, rusts, and tans. Wing color tends to be darker toward the body. The comma-shaped mark is found in the middle of the lower hind wing; it is silver and barbed on one or both ends. Like other Iowa anglewing species, the Eastern Comma has a darker summer form and a lighter spring form. Individual variability in spot patterns is also more apparent in some populations than in others. Wingspan: 4.5 – 5 cm.

Distribution and habitat: Map 673. Common throughout the state in woodlands. The Eastern Comma is generally more common in Iowa than the Question Mark.

Natural history: Larvae consume nettles, hops, and elms. Like other anglewings, they prefer fermented juice, sap, and dung piles as adult food sources and are easily baited.

Questions: Is the general similarity of the three common Iowa anglewings of mimetic origin? Do adults demonstrate any preferences for some tree saps or rotting fruit over others? How far can adults travel in a lifetime? Do the hibernacula of this species differ from those of the Question Mark?

Gray Comma 677

Polygonia progne (Cramer [1775])

Status: Breeding resident.

Flight: Four flight times for the three broods. Overwintering adults from last season's fall brood awaken in early April and fly through early May, founding a brood that flies during June. A second brood flies from late July through August. The third brood emerges in mid September and flies through mid October then locates hibernacula.

Distinguishing features: The ventral wing surface of this species is dark gray, with a silver mark on the hind wing below that tapers at both ends. It is seasonally dimorphic, with a summer form that is very dark on the hind wing above and a lighter overwintering form. Wingspread: 5 – 5.5 cm.

Distribution and habitat: Map 677. Scattered throughout the state in woodland habitats. This is the most uncommon of Iowa's *Polygonia* species.

Natural history: Larvae consume gooseberry and currant species. Like other anglewings, Gray Commas prefer fermented juice, sap, and dung piles as adult food sources and can easily be baited.

Questions: Gooseberries tend to increase in density in grazed forests, so has this species become more common in Iowa since European settlement? What color patterns characterize the early summer brood? What is the adaptive significance (if any) of light-colored overwintering forms? How far do adults fly in a lifetime?

Roddia vaualbum (Denis and Schiffermuller 1775)

Status: Breeding resident in the far northeast, occasional stray elsewhere.

Flight: Scattered occurrences from mid June through mid October.

Distinguishing features: This large species has an orange upper fore wing marked with black patches, two white patches at the apex, and a brown-and-white banded margin. The upper hind wing is brown near the body, with a black and white patch on the costal margin and a yellow-orange outer margin with a single interior brown band. The lower wing surface mimics tree bark and is mottled in gray and white. Wingspan: 7.2 – 7.8 mm.

Distribution and habitat: Map 679. Extremely rare resident colonies, known only from a very few large tracts of mature forest in extreme northeastern Iowa. Additional records scattered over the remaining northeastern half of the state probably represent strays.

Natural history: Larvae consume birch and aspen. Adults prefer fermented sap, fruit, and dung piles and can be baited. They are extremely rapid flyers, quite wary and extraordinarily hard to net. Adults are reported to overwinter in other parts of its range.

Questions: What is the minimum forest size needed to support Compton tortoiseshell breeding colonies in Iowa? What other factors limit it to the northern part of the state? How far can it travel in a lifetime?

Milbert's Tortoiseshell 680

Aglais milberti (Godart 1819)

Status: Breeding resident.

Flight: At least two broods, with the first flying from early June through mid July and the second from August to frost. Stray adults can be active on warm days to late November.

Distinguishing features: This species has brown-black wings with overlying bands of red and yellow. The margin above is dark and finely lined and contains small blue chevrons on the hind wings. The leading edge of the fore wing has a pair of red bars, making the upper wing surface look like a cat's face from a distance. Wingspan: 4.8 – 6.2 cm.

Distribution and habitat: Map 680. Frequent in northeastern Iowa; scattered and rare through the rest of the state, where it occurs in and around rich, moist woods.

Natural history: Larvae consume nettles. Eggs are laid in batches, and larvae live within a communal web. Adults not only eat fermented sap, fruit, and feces but also avidly visit flowers. While adults overwinter elsewhere in its range, this does not appear to be the case in Iowa, owing to the lack of spring records. This species can occasionally undergo large population increases.

Questions: What environmental factors trigger rapid increases in population size? What is the most frequent overwintering stage? Nettles are found statewide, so why are most populations restricted to the northeast corner? How well does the "cat-face" appearance protect adults from native potential predators?

Mourning Cloak 682

Nymphalis antiopa (Linnaeus 1758)

Status: Breeding resident.

Flight: Multiple overlapping broods, with flights from early March through mid October.

Distinguishing features: The wing of this species has a brown-black interior with maroon iridescence above, a yellow margin, and a row of brilliant blue spots. The lower wing surface is a cryptic dark gray-black, with a pale yellow border and a small white chevron in the center of the hind wing. Wingspan: 7.3 – 8.5 cm.

Distribution and habitat: Map 682. Common statewide in a variety of forested situations.

Natural history: Larvae consume a number of common trees, such as willow, birch, cottonwood, elm, and hackberry. It hibernates as an adult and may activate on any warm winter day. Thus it is usually one of the first butterflies to be seen in the spring. Adults use fruit, sap, and animal feces as food sources. It has been reported to make a grating sound with its wings.

Questions: What environmental factors trigger activation of hibernating adults? What are the favored hibernacula? How are adults physiologically able to withstand typical Iowa winters? What are the lowest temperature and humidity that overwintering adults can withstand? How long do adults live?

Red Admiral 684

Vanessa atalanta (Linnaeus 1758)

Status: Breeding resident.

Flight: Multiple overlapping generations, with broods emerging from late March through late September. Occasionally adults have also been observed on warm, late fall days.

Distinguishing features: This distinctive species has a black upper fore wing with a bright, diagonal red band and a red marginal band on the hind wing. The lower hind wing is mottled, with a complex jumble of light tan to black areas. Wingspan: 4.5 – 5.5 cm.

Distribution and habitat: Map 684. Abundant statewide in forests.

Natural history: Larvae consume nettles and wood nettles. While some guides (e.g., Opler and Malikul 1998) contend that this species does not overwinter in Iowa, the data do not support this. The first individuals seen in early spring Iowa woodlands are fresh and clearly just emerged. The spring flight is also the largest during the year. Given that 5 to 10 percent of the individuals observed during the 1992 mass *Vanessa* migration were of this species, however, it seems clear that southern migrants are continually reinforcing local resident populations. During the day adults exhibit a certain wariness, which makes them difficult to net. At dusk, however, individuals gather in openings and make only short circular flights around a given perch, so they are easier to net.

Questions: What percentages of spring adults represent migratory individuals? Do some adults or pupae overwinter? How much gene flow is provided by the annual spring influx of southern adults? How long do adults live?

Painted Lady   685

Vanessa cardui (Linnaeus 1758)

Status: Spring southern stray, summer resident.

Flight: Multiple overlapping broods, with flights occurring from early April through mid November. Peak flight times occur in July and August.

Distinguishing features: Similar to the American Lady, but with four to five blue-centered eyespots on the lower hind wing. Wingspan: 5.1–5.5 cm.

Distribution and habitat: Map 685. Common throughout the state in a wide variety of open habitats, including old fields, pastures, parks, roadsides, and vacant lots.

Natural history: While larvae generally consume thistle species, over a hundred different host plants have been recorded worldwide. This species is one of the most widely distributed butterflies, being known from all continents except Australia and Antarctica. The early flight dates suggest that some populations overwinter. This species is migratory, however, and any such permanent colonies are continually reinforced with southern individuals. A striking example of this occurred during late April and May 1992. From April 21 to 25 only two to twelve individuals were seen at a given eastern Iowa site per day. By April 29 this number had increased to over a thousand. During this time northward-moving individuals were passing between two observers (spaced 50 m. apart) about once every thirty seconds at a height of 1–3 m. In early August 1992 an unprecedented population explosion of this species was noted.

Questions: What climatic factors stimulate rapid population growth and large northward spring migrations? How genetically similar are Iowa populations to populations from other areas in North America and from other continents?

American Lady   687

Vanessa virginiensis (Drury 1773)

Status: Breeding resident.

Flight: Multiple overlapping broods emerging from mid April through mid August. Occasional adults also have been seen in late September and early October. This species tends to fly earlier than the related Painted Lady, with peak flight times of late April to early May and late June to early July.

Distinguishing features: The wings are orange and black above, with several white spots in the fore-wing apex. The two large eyespots on the hind wing below distinguish this from the similar Painted Lady. Wingspan: 4.5 – 5.4 cm.

Distribution and habitat: Map 687. Frequent in the eastern half of Iowa, more scattered in the west. It occurs in a variety of dry, open, grassy habitats, including old fields, pastures, and prairies.

Natural history: In Iowa larvae consume pussytoes. This is the least common of our three *Vanessa* species.

Questions: Why are populations more frequent in eastern Iowa? What is the impact of grazing on larval survival? How much do populations fluctuate annually? What cues do adults use to locate the larval host plants?

White Admiral 692a

Limenitis arthemis arthemis (Drury 1773)

Status: Northern stray.

Flight: Late June through mid August.

Distinguishing features: This black butterfly has a bold white band running postmedially down both wings. Wingspan: 7.3 – 7.9 cm.

Distribution and habitat: Map 692a. Very rare northern stray found in the northern three tiers of counties in a variety of open or partially wooded sites.

Natural history: Within its breeding range, larvae consume a large variety of forest trees, including wild cherry, poplar, aspen, and oak. Most Iowa specimens are referable to the form *proserpina*, which demonstrates various degrees of expression of the white band and lacks submarginal red spots on the hind wing. Such individuals are intermediate with the Red-spotted Purple, and it is doubtful that pure individuals of this subspecies penetrate as far south as Iowa.

Questions: What factors prevent the establishment of breeding colonies in the state? What environmental conditions are conducive to the southern movement of individuals into the state? Is there gene flow in Iowa between this form and the Red-spotted Purple? How far can adults fly?

Red-spotted Purple 692b

Limenitis arthemis astyanax (Fabricius 1775)

Status: Breeding resident.

Flight: Multiple overlapping broods from mid May through August. Rare individuals have been observed from September through mid October.

Distinguishing features: The upper wing surface is black, with marginal banding; the outer half of the hind wing is iridescent blue. The undersurface has orange-red spots along the margin, with several spots near the body. Wingspan: 7.5 – 10 cm.

Distribution and habitat: Map 692b. Common throughout the state in a variety of open and wooded habitats.

Natural history: Larvae consume a large variety of forest trees, including wild cherry, poplar, aspen, and oak. Because of apparent limited genetic exchange with occasional White Admirals that stray into Iowa, many Red-spotted Purples demonstrate a slight development of the white banding, especially on the undersurface.

Questions: At what life stage do individuals overwinter? Does consumption of different larval host plants lead to morphological differences in adults? How mobile are adults?

Viceroy 693

Limenitis archippus (Cramer [1776])

Status: Breeding resident.

Flight: Multiple overlapping broods, with emergences from mid May through early October; peak flight times in August.

Distinguishing features: The Viceroy is familiar as the classic mimic of the Monarch: its wings are rusty-orange above with black veins, the fore wing has a cross-band near the apex which contains white spots, and the undersurface is similar but a lighter shade of orange. The main difference is that the hind wing above has a black line crossing the veins in a perpendicular fashion. Wingspan: 6.7 – 7.5 cm.

Distribution and habitat: Map 693. Common throughout the state in a variety of open and wooded habitats.

Natural history: Larvae consume willows and aspens. The adults reach peak abundance just before the start of the Monarch fall migration. Recent research has shown that this species and the Monarch represent Müllerian mimics; both have defensive compounds that make birds ill if consumed. Interspecific hybridization between the Viceroy and the Red-spotted Purple can occur, although such progeny are extremely rare (Platt and Greenfield 1971).

Questions: What mechanisms serve to prevent more active interspecific breeding between the Viceroy and Red-spotted Purple? What environmental cues are used to synchronize the reduction in adults with the start of Monarch migration? What are the preferred nectar sources?

Goatweed Leafwing

Anaea andria (Scudder 1875)

Status: Rare breeding resident or southern stray.

Flight: Adults observed from early April through late September.

Distinguishing features: The upper wing surface is dark red-orange, with a hooked fore-wing apex and a short tail on the outer hind-wing margin. The lower wing surface is a plant-brown to gray color and mimics the appearance of a dead leaf. Wingspan: 6–8 cm.

Distribution and habitat: Map 722. Limited to the southern half of the state, where it is very rare. Adults have generally been seen in sandy woods and fields adjacent to rivers.

Natural history: Larvae consume croton species, which are uncommon plants in southern Iowa sand prairies. Adults feed on fermented fruit, sap, and dung piles. This species has been observed on multiple occasions in Waubonsie State Park in Fremont County, making it likely that a resident colony exists there. The remaining sightings are once-only occurrences. The location of a slightly worn female in April in Linn County in 1991, however, suggests that other temporary breeding colonies may periodically exist in the state.

Questions: Do breeding colonies of this species occur in Iowa outside of Waubonsie State Park? What cues do females use to locate larval host plants, which are uncommon in the state? Do adults use river valleys as migration corridors?

Hackberry Emperor

Asterocampa celtis (Boisduval and LeConte 1835)

Status: Breeding resident.

Flight: Apparently double brooded, with the first emerging from early June to early July and the second during late July and August. Stray individuals may be found on wing from mid May to early October.

Distinguishing features: The upper wing surface is flat tan-brown, with two spots in the base of the fore-wing discal area and a small eyespot near the fore-wing apex. The hind wing has a white centered spot between each set of veins. Males have concave hind-wing margins, while females have rounded margins. Wingspan: 5.1–6.3 cm.

Distribution and habitat: Map 726. Common statewide in a variety of woodland habitats.

Natural history: Larvae consume hackberry. Adults tend to return to the same perch after darting out to encounter almost any moving object. They not infrequently land on a butterfly net or collector and occasionally fly into the car and go home with you. In some years local populations can become very large. They are often seen puddling on forest roads.

Questions: What environmental factors favor development of very large populations? What visual function does movement of the highly reflective antennae tips accomplish?

Tawny Emperor 728

Asterocampa clyton (Boisduval and LeConte 1835)

Status: Breeding resident.

Flight: Likely multiple overlapping broods, with adults emerging from mid June to early September.

Distinguishing features: Unlike the Hackberry Emperor, this species has a tawny orange-brown upper wing surface. The fore wing has three rows of cream spots on the outer margin and two black bars on the costal margin. The eyespots on the hind wing below often have blue pupils. The hind wing is concave in males and rounded in females. Wingspan: 5–7 cm.

Distribution and habitat: Map 728. Scattered statewide in a variety of wooded habitats.

Natural history: Larvae consume hackberry and are gregarious during the first two instars. Although it is usually sympatric with the Hackberry Emperor, it is much less common.

Questions: How do the Tawny Emperor and the Hackberry Emperor partition larval host-plant resources? Why is the Tawny Emperor rarer in Iowa? During what life stage does overwintering occur? What are the dispersal abilities of adults?

Northern Pearly-eye 734

Enodia anthedon (Clark 1936)

Status: Breeding resident.

Flight: Perhaps double brooded, with the first emerging from early June through late July and a second during August and September.

Distinguishing features: The wings are dull-brown above, with two full jagged lines across all four wings. The dorsal fore wing often has a creamy cast beyond the jagged postmedial line. The fore wing usually has four pupiled eyespots (ocelli) and the hind wing six. The wing margins below have a scalloped appearance. Wingspan: 4.6–5.3 cm.

Distribution and habitat: Map 734. Infrequent and scattered over the southeastern half of the state, with a few records from northwestern counties. Populations occur in moist woodlands, often near water, and tend to congregate on trails or in clearings.

Natural history: Larvae are known to consume a number of woodland grasses. In Iowa, the most likely host plants are rice cut-grass, bottlebrush grass, and bearded shorthusk. Adults are territorial and aggressive in defense of their realm. They escape to high trees when startled.

Questions: What cues do females use to locate cut-grass for oviposition? What is the size of the average adult territory? What environmental factors limit the abundance of this species in Iowa? Do the wing eyespots provide any selective advantage to individuals?

Eyed Brown 736

Satyrodes eurydice (Linnaeus 1763)

Status: Breeding resident.

Flight: Mid June through July.

Distinguishing features: The wings are dull brown above with small ocelli on both (the posterior ones haloed) and usually with pupils. The underwing surface is tan-brown near the body and a lighter brown beyond a jagged postmedial line. It has four or five ocelli on the fore wing and six or seven on the hind wing. These extra ocelli are paired within the same set of rings. Wingspan: 4.5 – 5.4 cm.

Distribution and habitat: Map 736. Scattered throughout the northeastern half of the state, with populations being limited to fens, wet prairies, and marshes.

Natural history: Larvae probably consume common wetland sedges, such as tussock sedge. Oviposition has only been noted on nearby broadleaf plants (Opler and Krizek 1984). Carde et al. (1970) suggest that our material should be segregated as its own species, *Satyrodes fumosa*, based on its larger size, darker wing color, and other subtle wing and genital differences. If *S. fumosa* represents a valid species, due to habitat destruction and range reduction, it may be considered endemic to Iowa. The distinction appears problematic, however, as a great amount of morphological overlap exists between Iowa and northern populations.

Questions: Does the dark *fumosa* represent a morphologically distinct form, genetically isolated from *eurydice*? If so, what percentage of the world population of the Eyed Brown resides in Iowa? Is a minimum wetland size required for development of stable populations? What is the dispersal ability of adults?

Little Wood-satyr 745

Megisto cymela (Cramer 1777)

Status: Breeding resident.

Flight: Principally late May through early July.

Distinguishing features: The wings are dull brown above, with two ringed ocelli on the fore wing and one or two on the hind wing. The undersurface is lighter, with two reddish lines across both wings and two ringed ocelli on either wing, sometimes with several smaller adjacent ones. Wingspan: 4.4 – 4.8 cm.

Distribution and habitat: Map 745. Common throughout the state in a variety of wooded situations.

Natural history: Larvae consume a variety of grasses, including the nonnative orchard grass. Adults have a slow, bobbing flight and rarely visit flowers, preferring rotting fruit and animal droppings for food. When populations peak, this can become the dominant woodland butterfly.

Questions: Does Iowa have more than one species within this complex? If so, what are their distinguishing characteristics, ranges, and preferred habitats? How do adults avoid predation? What native grass species do their larvae in Iowa use?

Common Ringlet 749

Coenonympha tullia (Muller 1764)

Status: Very rare breeding resident.

Flight: Early to mid June.

Distinguishing features: This butterfly is orange-tan to orange-brown above, without marks. The underside has orange-tan fore wings with one ocellus at the apex. The hind wing is olive-brown, with a diffuse light mark across the end of the discal cell that sometimes crosses the whole wing. Wingspan: 3.4 – 3.8 cm.

Distribution and habitat: Map 749. Extremely rare and limited to high-quality xeric gravel prairies in the far northwest.

Natural history: Larvae consume various grasses; the preferred host species in Iowa are unknown. Adults were once common in the Blood Run Valley in far northwestern Iowa as recently as a decade ago. Since the initiation of fire management in this area and at Cayler Prairie, however, these populations have vanished. The only remaining population may survive along a railroad/highway prairie in Osceola County, but the precarious nature of this site leaves even the fate of this population in serious doubt.

Questions: What are the dispersal abilities of the species? What is the likelihood of recolonization on sites that have been recently burned? What are its larval host plants? At what stage does it overwinter? What is the long-term impact of light grazing or haying on population size and persistence?

Common Wood-nymph 750

Cercyonis pegala (Fabricius 1775)

Status: Breeding resident.

Flight: Apparently two broods, the first emerging from early June through late July and a second from August through mid September.

Distinguishing features: The wings on both sides are dark brown with two large ocelli on the fore wings. On the hind wing above the anal margin is one small ocellus, with up to six ocelli below it. Wingspan: 4.4 – 5.6 cm.

Distribution and habitat: Map 750. Abundant throughout the state in a wide variety of open and wooded habitats, including old fields, pastures, parks, prairies, woodland margins, and roadsides.

Natural history: Larvae are known to consume various grasses; the specific Iowa host-plant species are unknown. Adults have sound-sensing organs on the ventral fore wing and can be startled by loud noises. Most Iowa material can be placed in *C. p. olympus*, a dark subspecies which has less well developed ocelli than the more northern *C. p. nephele*. It is especially frequent in native upland prairies. Some females have a hint of a pale band on the upper side of the fore wing around the ocelli, which suggests the eastern *C. p. alope*.

Questions: What are the preferred larval host plants in Iowa? At what stage does it overwinter? How many broods occur in Iowa? Is the basal swelling on vein SC of the fore wings used for sensing sound?

Occasional Strays and Old Records

Uncas Skipper 158

Hesperia uncas (Edwards, 1863)

Doubtful occurrence. Reported from Linn County, but we question several of George Berry's (1914) Linn County records, particularly the occurrence of this western species in eastern Iowa.

Comma Skipper 160

Hesperia comma (Linnaeus 1758)

Doubtful occurrence. Reported from Winneshiek County. *Hesperia comma colorado* is presently restricted to the southern Colorado Rocky Mountains, and we seriously doubt that it has ever occurred in Iowa. The specimens reported (Lindsay [for Lindsey] 1917) to have been taken by Porter at Decorah in Winneshiek County were very likely misidentified or mislabeled.

Cobweb Skipper 168

Hesperia metea (Scudder 1864)

Must be considered an uncertain resident. Reported from Story County. Hendrickson (1928) reported specimens of *H. metea* on June 23, 1925, and remarked that this species was common in Story County in June of 1925 and 1926. This record seems unlikely from our perspective today. Its presence in Wisconsin from mid May to early June (Ebner 1970) and in Minnesota as well as in Missouri and Illinois suggests that Iowa populations are possible. It would probably be found in the northeast Iowa hill prairies if present, but intensive searches have not located it.

Attalus Skipper 170

Hesperia attalus (Edwards, "1871")

Doubtful status, even though reported from Linn County. Berry's (1914) record of *H. attalus* is probably the female of *Atalopedes campestris*, which is not included in Berry's Linn County list. William J. Holland's (1940) figure of the female undersurface can nearly be matched by local specimens of *A. campestris*, a common species in Linn County and throughout Iowa.

Indian Skipper 174

Hesperia sassacus (Harris 1862b)

Must be considered an improbable occurrence. Reported from Crawford, Dickinson, and Linn counties. All primary records of this species in Iowa date from over fifty years ago. Recent secondary sources (Klots 1951; Howe 1975) indicate an Iowa distribution but probably represent an extension from unverified and early records. We doubt its resident status. An occasional summer brood populated from Wisconsin sources is not discounted, but these would be far from the records above. Two misidentified specimens labeled "Ioa" only were located in the Strecker collection, but these are unquestionably *H. dacotae*.

Whirlabout 189

Polites vibex (Geyer 1832)

Doubtful occurrence. Reported from Henry and Winneshiek counties. This skipper is very common in the southeastern states and the tropics. The latest Iowa record noted (in the collection at Iowa Wesleyan College, October 6, 1937) might have been a casual or windblown stray. We have sufficient experience with odd but authentic distributions that we do not discount the possibility of its occurrence in the state.

Eufala Skipper 252

Lerodea eufala (Edwards 1869)

Status: Very uncommon nonoverwintering stray.

Flight: Strays from the south in early summer. These give rise to the main brood, which flies from late August through early October.

Distinguishing features: This small, light brown skipper has small white spots on the upper fore wing. Wingspan: 2.8 cm.

Distribution and habitat: Widely scattered across the state, where it frequents alfalfa fields along with late flying Pierids and skippers such as the Sachem. Only three collections have been made since 1980.

Natural history: Although it has southern affinities, the Eufala Skipper colonizes each summer northward as far as Minnesota. Its offspring cannot survive winters north of the southern Gulf Coast, however. Its larvae are reported to eat a number of weedy grasses, including Johnson grass, although its northern host plants are unreported.

Questions: What grasses do the larvae of this species eat in Iowa? Why does it appear to have been more common in the state in the 1970s? Is it more common than records indicate, being unobserved due to its weedy habitat and late flight? Could this species become more frequent in the event of global warming?

Mexican Yellow 380

Eurema mexicana (Boisduval 1836)

Status: Southern stray.

Flight: Migrants seen from mid June to frost.

Distinguishing features: The wings are pale yellow to cream above, with a black forewing margin deeply indented with yellow in the center. The hind wing below is bright yellow, with a bit of a tail. Wingspread: 3.5–4.6 cm.

Distribution and habitat: Found across the state, but a very rare stray, with only a few observations since 1960. These few records seem to indicate this species favors dry, open habitats.

Natural history: Larvae consume various legumes; in Iowa the most likely host is partridge pea. Migratory flights have been reported in Illinois (Irwin and Downey 1973).

Questions: Why does this species so rarely stray into the state? Why has occurrence frequency apparently fallen over the last century? Do adults breed in Iowa?

Sleepy Orange 388

Eurema nicippe (Cramer [1779])

Status: Southern stray.

Flight: Migrant individuals from mid June through frost.

Distinguishing features: This butterfly has orange-yellow wings with an irregular black margin above and no margin below. Females are larger, with brighter yellow hind wings than the Little Yellow. Wingspan: 3.6–4.6 cm.

Distribution and habitat: Infrequently scattered throughout the southern half of the state in dry open meadows, old fields, roadsides, and prairies.

Natural history: If breeding occurs in Iowa, larvae will be limited to partridge peas. This species may be overlooked in the state due to its similarity to the Little Yellow.

Questions: Do migrant individuals breed in Iowa? How much do population sizes and locations vary on a yearly basis? Does this species occur more frequently along river courses?

Leptotes marina (Reakirt 1868)

Status: Southwestern stray.

Flight: Late May through late September.

Distinguishing features: This small, pale-blue butterfly has a bold brown-and-white striped pattern beneath and two dark eyespots at the hind-wing angle below. Females are darker above. Wingspread: 2.5-2.8 cm.

Distribution and habitat: Rare and scattered, with individuals reported from the far west and north in a variety of open habitats. The September record was made near a major highway on a planted prairie at the edge of Decorah.

Natural history: Larvae consume a number of legumes, including alfalfa, clover, and milk vetch. The nearest overwintering of this species is in coastal Texas; thus its appearance in late May is remarkable. Perhaps these individuals were transported to the state in truckloads of hay.

Questions: How can butterflies whose adult phase probably lasts only five days migrate to Iowa? Can individuals that arrive early in the growing season found ephemeral populations in alfalfa or clover fields?

Queen 574

Danaus gilippus (Cramer [1775])

Status: Very rare southern stray.

Flight: Late August.

Distinguishing features: Similar to the Monarch, but with a chestnut-brown wing, a double row of white spots on the hind-wing outer margin, and scattered white spots across both upper fore wings and hind wings. Wingspan: 8–10 cm.

Distribution and habitat: Collected only a few times in the state (the first a 1912 Cass County record, the last a 1999 collection from Plymouth County).

Gulf Fritillary 579

Agraulis vanillae (Linnaeus 1758)

Status: Southern stray.

Flight: Late summer to fall.

Distinguishing features: Dark orange above, with a black hind-wing margin consisting of six orange triangles. The hind wing below is dark brown, with reflective silver-white streaks. Wingspread: 6.5–7.2 cm.

Distribution and habitat: Very rare stray, with scattered occurrences throughout the state from a variety of open habitats.

Part Three. Plates, Range Maps, and Flight Diagrams

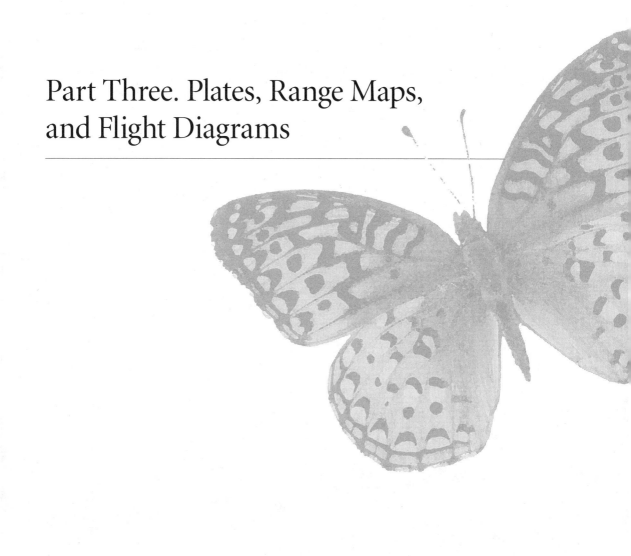

Introduction to the Plates

This section includes photographs of the adult forms of all butterflies known to occur in Iowa. Each was digitally recorded against a photographically neutral gray background. No attempt has been made to preserve the scale of different species; the reader should check the sizes in the species accounts for comparisons. Male and female as well as top and bottom views are shown for most species. The first pair of illustrations for each species shows the dorsal and ventral views of the male; the second pair shows the female. When both sexes are essentially identical, only one pair of photographs is included. Species with important polymorphisms are documented with more than four illustrations.

Browse through the photographs until you locate the one that matches, or nearly matches, the specimen you wish to identify. Further reading in the sections on distinguishing features and comparisons with related species will usually confirm your identification. Where additional information is warranted, you might use the scientific name of the butterfly you have identified for a further search of the literature. For example, other texts on butterflies may have additional photographs or information about the same species that will be helpful for identification.

Information about the location and date of collection of each specimen, along with the name of the collector, can be found following the checklist; all but a few are in the collections of the authors.

5 Silver-spotted Skipper, Epargyreus clarus

41 Hoary Edge, Achalarus lyciades

47 Southern Cloudywing, Thorybes bathyllus

48 Northern Cloudywing, Thorybes pylades

70 Hayhurst's Scallopwing, *Staphylus hayhurstii*

85 Dreamy Duskywing, *Erynnis icelus*

86 Sleepy Duskywing, *Erynnis brizo*

87 Juvenal's Duskywing, *Erynnis juvenalis*

92 Horace's Duskywing, *Erynnis horatius*

94 Mottled Duskywing, *Erynnis martialis*

98 Wild Indigo Duskywing, *Erynnis baptisiae*

99 Columbine Duskywing, Erynnis lucilius

106 Common Checkered-skipper, Pyrgus communis

117 Common Sootywing, *Pholisora catullus*

146 Least Skipper, *Ancyloxypha numitor*

149   Poweshiek Skipperling, *Oarisma poweshiek*

154   European Skipper, *Thymelicus lineola*

155 Fiery Skipper, Hylephila phyleus

164 Ottoe Skipper, Hesperia ottoe

165a   Leonard's Skipper, Hesperia leonardus leonardus

165b   Hesperia leonardus pawnee

172 Dakota Skipper, *Hesperia dacotae*

177 Sachem, *Atalopedes campestris*

180   Peck's Skipper, Polites peckius

184   Tawny-edged Skipper, Polites themistocles

186 Crossline Skipper, Polites origenes

187 Long Dash, Polites mystic

191 Northern Broken-dash, Wallengrenia egeremet

192 Little Glassywing, Pompeius verna

193 Arogos Skipper, *Atrytone arogos*

194 Delaware Skipper, *Anatrytone logan*

196 Byssus Skipper, *Problema byssus*

201 Hobomok Skipper, *Poanes hobomok*

202 Zabulon Skipper, Poanes zabulon

205 Mulberry Wing, Poanes massasoit

206 Broad-winged Skipper, *Poanes viator*

212 Black Dash, *Euphyes conspicua*

214 Dion Skipper, *Euphyes dion*

217 Two-spotted Skipper, *Euphyes bimacula*

219 Dun Skipper, Euphyes vestris

221 Dusted Skipper, Atrytonopsis hianna

236 Pepper and Salt Skipper, *Amblyscirtes hegon*

244 Common Roadside-skipper, *Amblyscirtes vialis*

285 Pipevine Swallowtail, Battus philenor

289 Zebra Swallowtail, Eurytides marcellus

294 Black Swallowtail, Papilio polyxenes

297 Eastern Tiger Swallowtail, Papilio glaucus

303 Spicebush Swallowtail, Papilio troilus

308 Giant Swallowtail, Papilio cresphontes

323 Checkered White, Pontia protodice

326 Cabbage White, Pieris rapae

337 Olympia Marble, *Euchloe olympia*

348 Clouded Sulphur, Colias philodice

349 Orange Sulphur, *Colias eurytheme*

366 Southern Dogface, Colias cesonia

370 Cloudless Sulphur, Phoebis sennae

385 Little Yellow, *Eurema lisa*

389 Dainty Sulphur, *Nathalis iole*

390 Harvester, *Feniseca tarquinius*

392 American Copper, *Lycaena phlaeas*

395 Gray Copper, Lycaena dione

398 Bronze Copper, Lycaena hyllus

403 Purplish Copper, Lycaena helloides

422 Juniper Hairstreak, Callophrys gryneus

432 Henry's Elfin, Callophrys henrici

445 Coral Hairstreak, Satyrium titus

446 Acadian Hairstreak, *Satyrium acadica*

449 Hickory Hairstreak, *Satyrium caryaevorum*

450　Edwards' Hairstreak, *Satyrium edwardsii*

451　Banded Hairstreak, *Satyrium calanus*

453 Striped Hairstreak, *Satyrium liparops*

470 Gray Hairstreak, *Strymon melinus*

490 White M Hairstreak, Parrhasius m-album

499 Eastern Tailed-blue, Everes comyntas

501 Spring Azure, Celastrina ladon

503 Summer Azure, Celastrina neglecta

510   Silvery Blue, Glaucopsyche lygdamus

526   Reakirt's Blue, Echinargus isola

531 Melissa Blue, *Lycaeides melissa*

571 American Snout, *Libytheana carinenta*

573 Monarch, *Danaus plexippus*

585 Variegated Fritillary, *Euptoieta claudia*

588 Great Spangled Fritillary, *Speyeria cybele*

589 Aphrodite Fritillary, *Speyeria aphrodite*

590 Regal Fritillary, Speyeria idalia

605 Silver-bordered Fritillary, Boloria selene

606 Meadow Fritillary, Boloria bellona

631 Gorgone Checkerspot, Chlosyne gorgone

632 Silvery Checkerspot, Chlosyne nycteis

648 Pearl Crescent, Phyciodes tharos

659a   Baltimore Checkerspot, Euphydryas phaeton phaeton

659b   Ozark Baltimore Checkerspot, Euphydryas phaeton ozarkae

664 Buckeye, *Junonia coenia*

672 Question Mark, *Polygonia interrogationis*

673 Eastern Comma, *Polygonia comma*

677 Gray Comma, *Polygonia progne*

679 Compton Tortoiseshell, *Roddia vaualbum*

680 Milbert's Tortoiseshell, *Aglais milberti*

682 Mourning Cloak, *Nymphalis antiopa*

684 Red Admiral, *Vanessa atalanta*

685 Painted Lady, *Vanessa cardui*

687 American Lady, *Vanessa virginiensis*

692a   White Admiral, Limenitis arthemis arthemis

692b   Red-spotted Purple, Limenitis arthemis astyanax

693   Viceroy, Limenitis archippus

722 Goatweed Leafwing, *Anaea andria*

726 Hackberry Emperor, *Asterocampa celtis*

728 Tawny Emperor, Asterocampa clyton

734 Northern Pearly-eye, Enodia anthedon

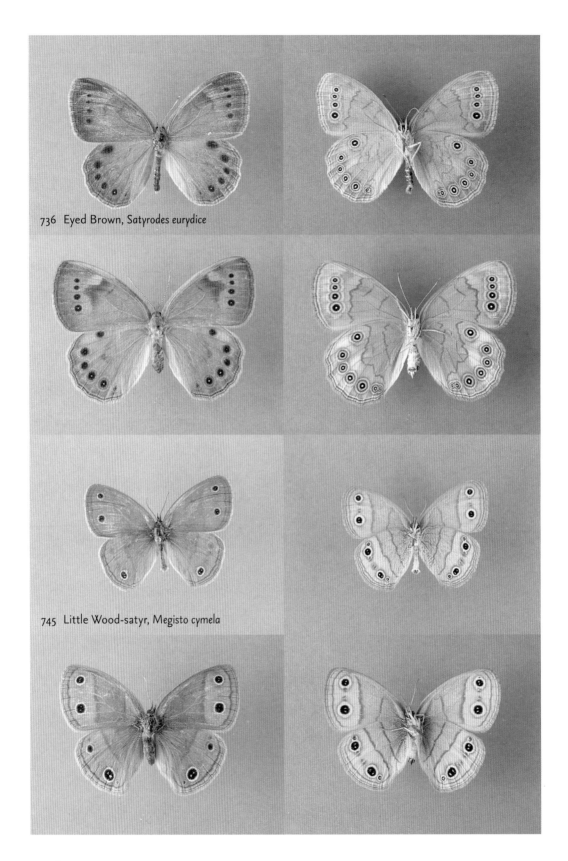

736 Eyed Brown, *Satyrodes eurydice*

745 Little Wood-satyr, *Megisto cymela*

749 Common Ringlet, Coenonympha tullia

750 Common Wood-nymph, Cercyonis pegala

Introduction to the Range Maps and Flight Diagrams

The distribution maps indicate in which of Iowa's ninety-nine counties specimens have been collected. Each county dot is shaded based on the year of most recent collection: black dots represent collections made from 1980 to 2005; double open circles represent collections made from 1960 through 1979; single open circles represent collections made before 1960.

The flight time for each species is shown by marking the date of collection for each verified specimen on a yearly calendar. You can use this information in a variety of ways. The accumulated records indicate when to look for adults — the probable flight times for butterflies to be on the wing. An absence of records for specific periods may indicate the lack of records or of actual specimens or of both. It might also indicate things such as a low adult density between broods during a season. We expect that each collector will add data to the flight times and to the county records for a given Iowa butterfly.

You might also use adult flight periods to determine when eggs and larvae might be expected to occur on the host plants. For those species that overwinter as eggs or young larvae, you might search for the immatures some days or weeks ahead of the time when adults of that generation begin to fly.

The range maps and flight diagrams are based on all Iowa butterfly specimens or photographs verified by the authors, amounting to more than 14,000 individual records. These are based on collections made by John Fleckenstein, Brian Scholtens, Ron Harms, Diane Debinski, Jessica Skibbe, Tim Orwig, Mike Christenson, David Cuthrell, Jerry Selby, John Downey, Jim Durban, Frank Olsen, Ed Freese, Michael Hafner, Judy Pooler, Jeff Nekola, Robert Howe, Steve Milne, John Nehnevaj, M. J. Hatfield, Mark Leoschke, Ray Hamilton, Dennis Schlicht, Scott Mahady, Bob Cecil, Brian Blevins, and others, who all contributed to the Iowa Lepidoptera Project of Center Point, Iowa.

We have not included records based solely upon sight observations (such as those available from the 4th of July Butterfly Counts), because these reports cannot be independently verified. Our experience with such information suggests that it can often be unreliable for groups like skippers and hairstreaks that are difficult to observe and identify due to their small size, rapid flight, and subtle markings. Furthermore, due to habitat destruction, populations at the sites of older records may no longer exist.

5 Silver-spotted Skipper, *Epargyreus clarus*

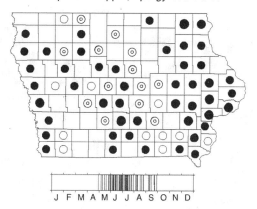

41 Hoary Edge, *Achalarus lyciades*

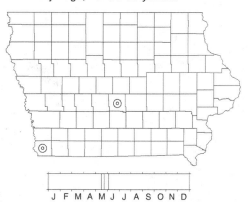

47 Southern Cloudywing, *Thorybes bathyllus*

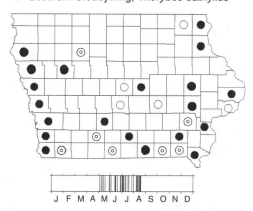

48 Northern Cloudywing, *Thorybes pylades*

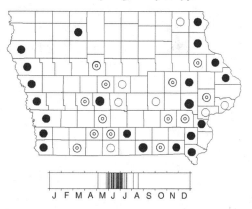

70 Hayhurst's Scallopwing, *Staphylus hayhurstii*

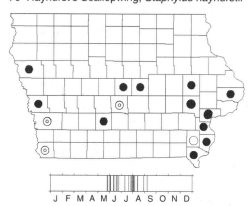

85 Dreamy Duskywing, *Erynnis icelus*

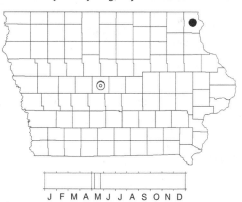

86 Sleepy Duskywing, *Erynnis brizo*

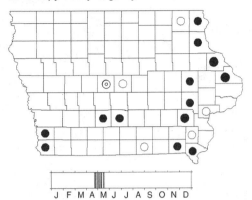

87 Juvenal's Duskywing, *Erynnis juvenalis*

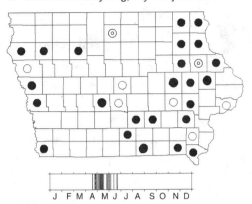

92 Horace's Duskywing, *Erynnis horatius*

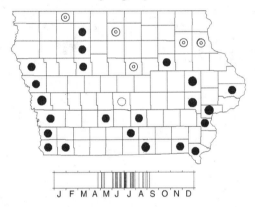

94 Mottled Duskywing, *Erynnis martialis*

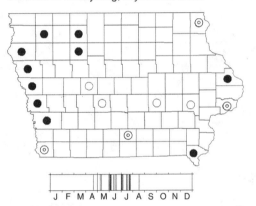

98 Wild Indigo Duskywing, *Erynnis baptisiae*

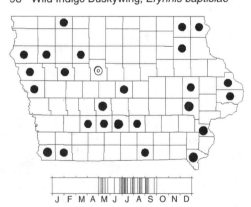

99 Columbine Duskywing, *Erynnis lucilius*

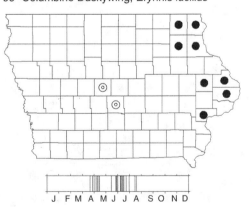

106 Common Checkered-skipper, *Pyrgus communis*

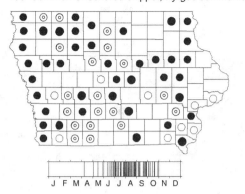

117 Common Sootywing, *Pholisora catullus*

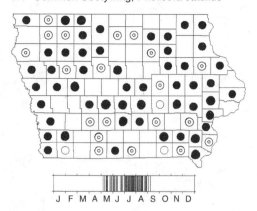

146 Least Skipper, *Ancyloxypha numitor*

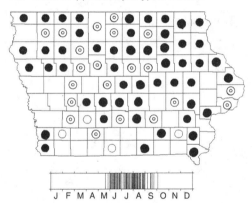

149 Poweshiek Skipperling, *Oarisma poweshiek*

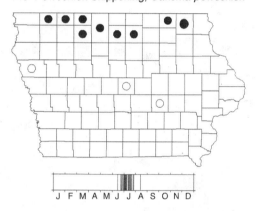

154 European Skipper, *Thymelicus lineola*

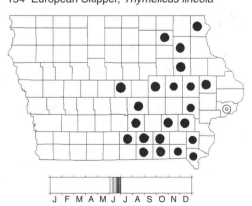

155 Fiery Skipper, *Hylephila phyleus*

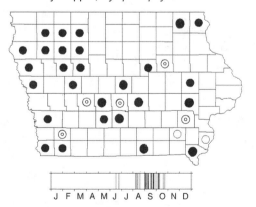

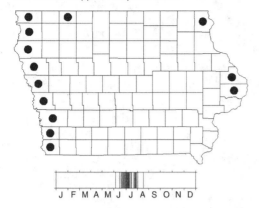

164 Ottoe Skipper, *Hesperia ottoe*

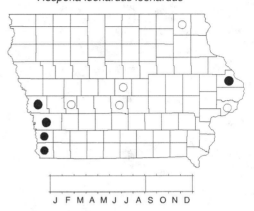

165a Leonard's Skipper,
      Hesperia leonardus leonardus

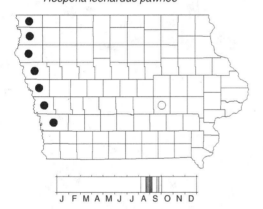

165b Leonard's Skipper,
      Hesperia leonardus pawnee

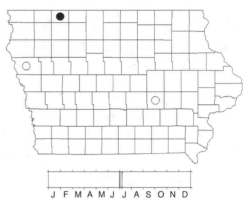

172 Dakota Skipper, *Hesperia dacotae*

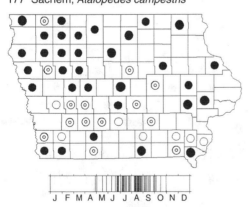

177 Sachem, *Atalopedes campestris*

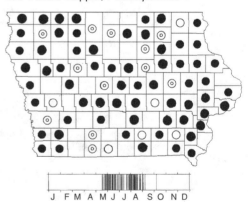

180 Peck's Skipper, *Polites peckius*

184 Tawny-edged Skipper, *Polites themistocles*

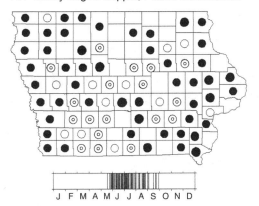

186 Crossline Skipper, *Polites origenes*

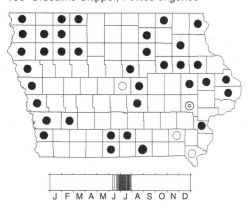

187 Long Dash, *Polites mystic*

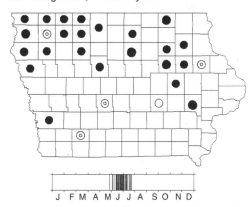

191 Northern Broken-dash, *Wallengrenia egeremet*

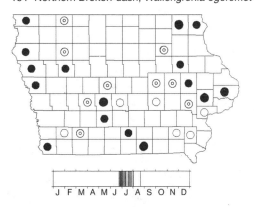

192 Little Glassywing, *Pompeius verna*

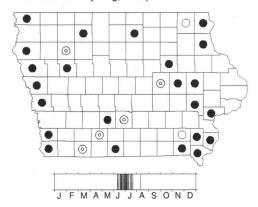

193 Arogos Skipper, *Atrytone arogos*

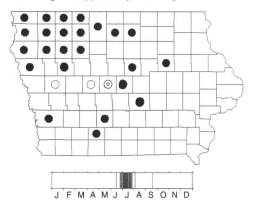

194 Delaware Skipper, *Anatrytone logan*

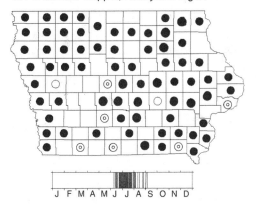

196 Byssus Skipper, *Problema byssus*

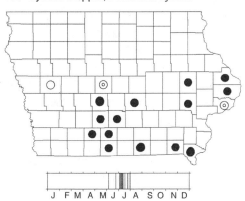

201 Hobomok Skipper, *Poanes hobomok*

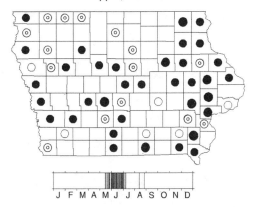

202 Zabulon Skipper, *Poanes zabulon*

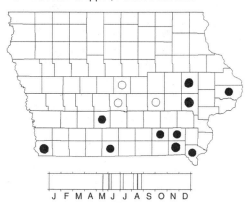

205 Mulberry Wing, *Poanes massasoit*

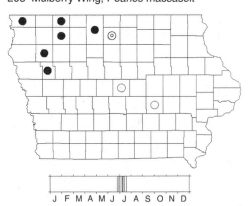

206 Broad-winged Skipper, *Poanes viator*

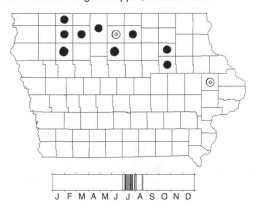

212 Black Dash, *Euphyes conspicua*

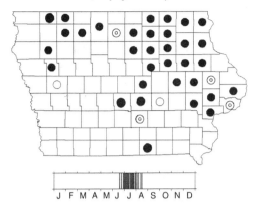

214 Dion Skipper, *Euphyes dion*

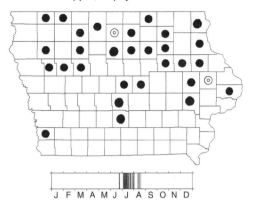

217 Two-spotted Skipper, *Euphyes bimacula*

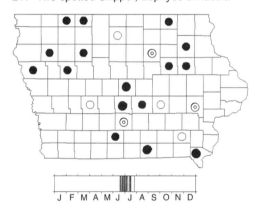

219 Dun Skipper, *Euphyes vestris*

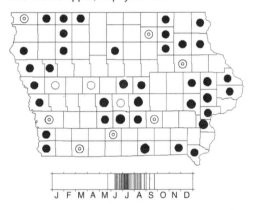

221 Dusted Skipper, *Atrytonopsis hianna*

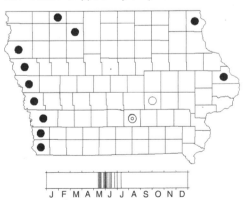

236 Pepper and Salt Skipper, *Amblyscirtes hegon*

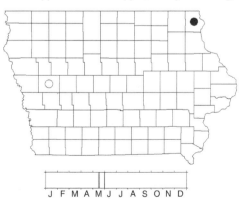

244 Common Roadside-skipper, *Amblyscirtes vialis*

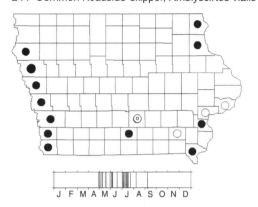

285 Pipevine Swallowtail, *Battus philenor*

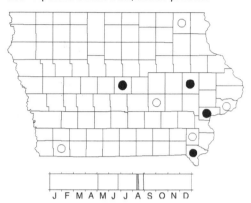

289 Zebra Swallowtail, *Eurytides marcellus*

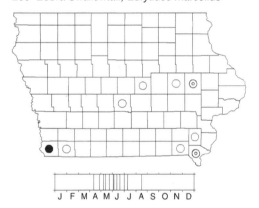

294 Black Swallowtail, *Papilio polyxenes*

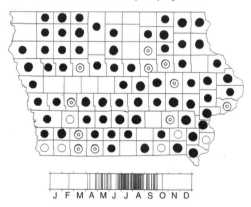

297 Eastern Tiger Swallowtail, *Papilio glaucus*

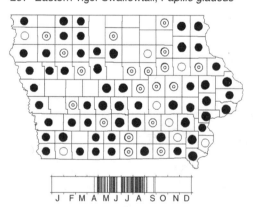

303 Spicebush Swallowtail, *Papilio troilus*

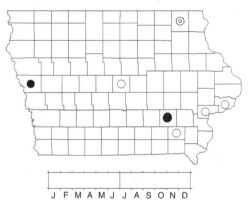

308 Giant Swallowtail, *Papilio cresphontes*

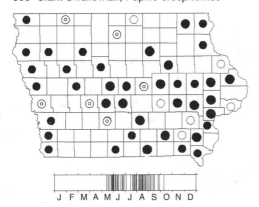

323 Checkered White, *Pontia protodice*

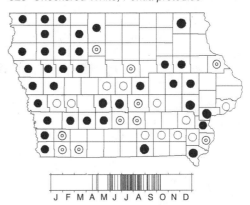

326 Cabbage White, *Pieris rapae*

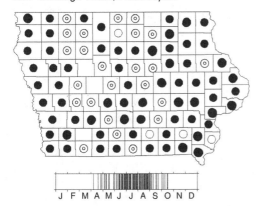

337 Olympia Marble, *Euchloe olympia*

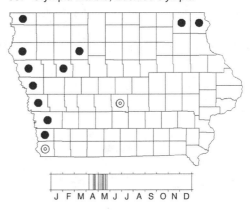

348 Clouded Sulphur, *Colias philodice*

349 Orange Sulphur, *Colias eurytheme*

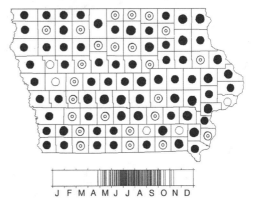

366 Southern Dogface, *Colias cesonia*

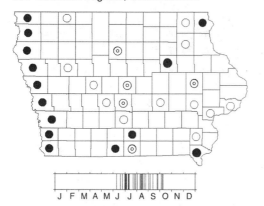

370 Cloudless Sulphur, *Phoebis sennae*

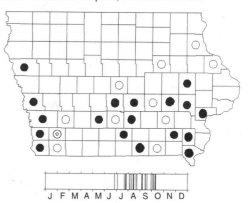

385 Little Yellow, *Eurema lisa*

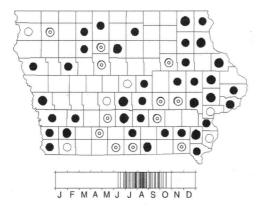

389 Dainty Sulphur, *Nathalis iole*

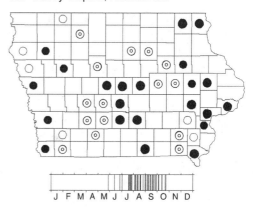

390 Harvester, *Feniseca tarquinius*

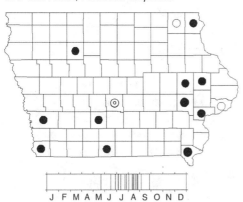

392 American Copper, *Lycaena phlaeas*

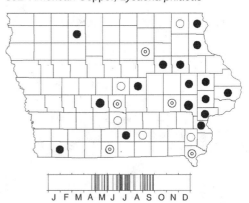

395 Gray Copper, *Lycaena dione*

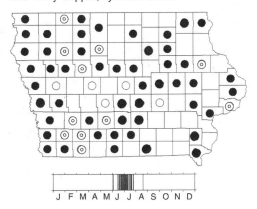

398 Bronze Copper, *Lycaena hyllus*

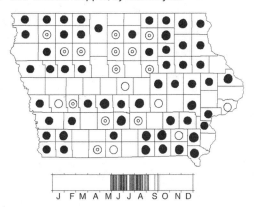

403 Purplish Copper, *Lycaena helloides*

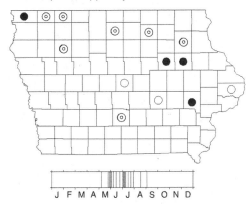

422 Juniper Hairstreak, *Callophrys gryneus*

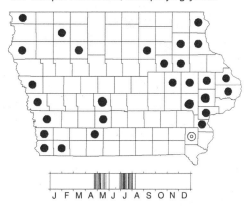

432 Henry's Elfin, *Callophrys henrici*

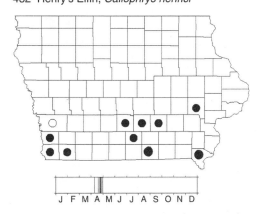

445 Coral Hairstreak, *Satyrium titus*

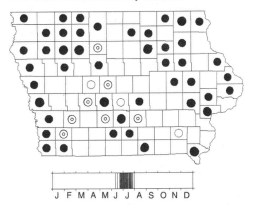

446 Acadian Hairstreak, *Satyrium acadica*

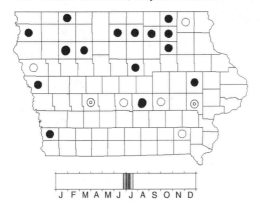

449 Hickory Hairstreak, *Satyrium caryaevorum*

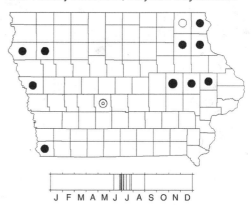

450 Edwards' Hairstreak, *Satyrium edwardsii*

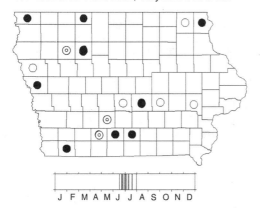

451 Banded Hairstreak, *Satyrium calanus*

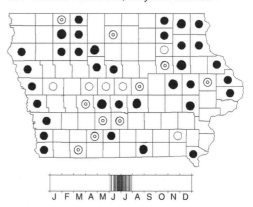

453 Striped Hairstreak, *Satyrium liparops*

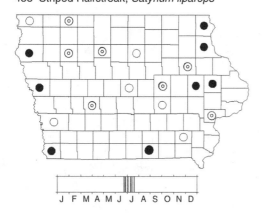

470 Gray Hairstreak, *Strymon melinus*

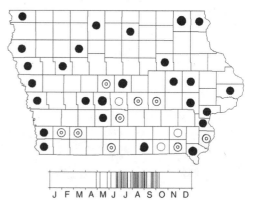

490 White M Hairstreak, *Parrhasius m-album*

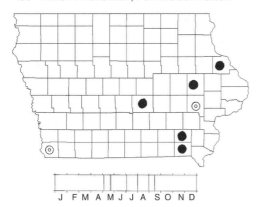

499 Eastern Tailed-blue, *Everes comyntas*

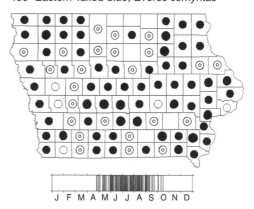

501 Spring Azure, *Celastrina ladon*

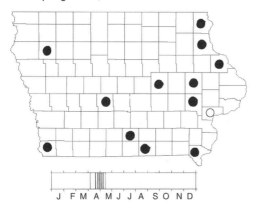

503 Summer Azure, *Celastrina neglecta*

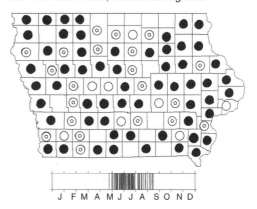

510 Silvery Blue, *Glaucopsyche lygdamus*

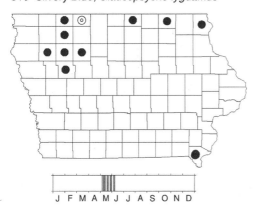

526 Reakirt's Blue, *Echinargus isola*

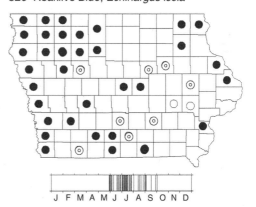

531 Melissa Blue, *Lycaeides melissa*

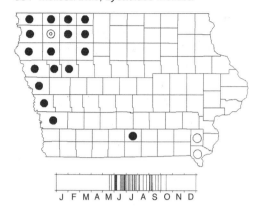

571 American Snout, *Libytheana carinenta*

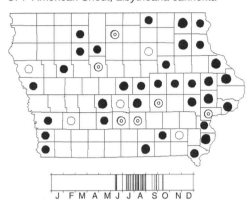

573 Monarch, *Danaus plexippus*

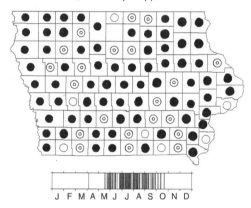

585 Variegated Fritillary, *Euptoieta claudia*

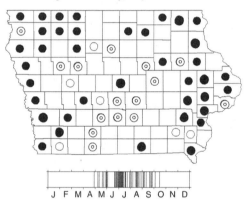

588 Great Spangled Fritillary, *Speyeria cybele*

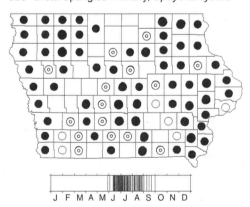

589 Aphrodite Fritillary, *Speyeria aphrodite*

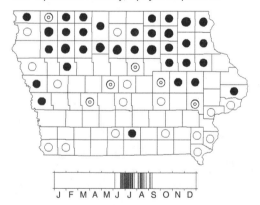

590 Regal Fritillary, *Speyeria idalia*

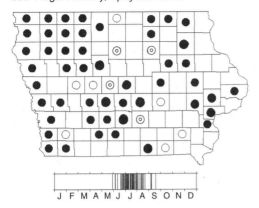

605 Silver-bordered Fritillary, *Boloria selene*

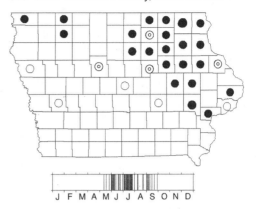

606 Meadow Fritillary, *Boloria bellona*

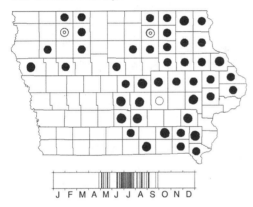

631 Gorgone Checkerspot, *Chlosyne gorgone*

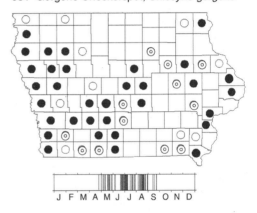

632 Silvery Checkerspot, *Chlosyne nycteis*

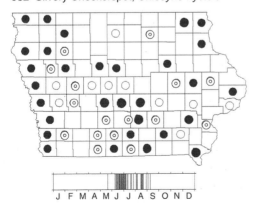

648 Pearl Crescent, *Phyciodes tharos*

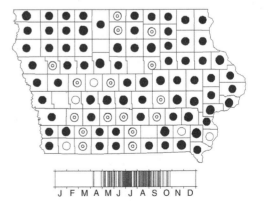

659a Baltimore Checkerspot,
      Euphydryas phaeton phaeton

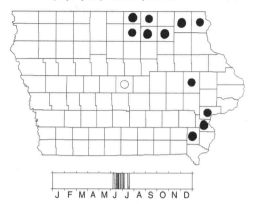

659b "Ozark" Baltimore Checkerspot,
      Euphydryas phaeton ozarkae

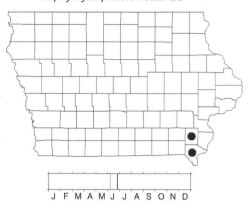

664 Buckeye, *Junonia coenia*

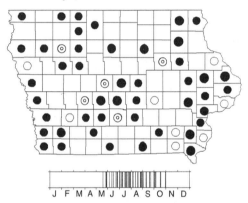

672 Question Mark, *Polygonia interrogationis*

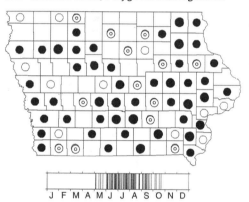

673 Eastern Comma, *Polygonia comma*

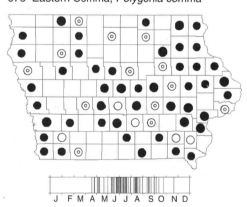

677 Gray Comma, *Polygonia progne*

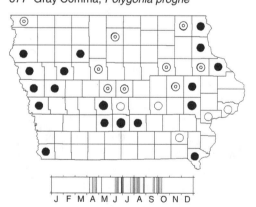

679 Compton Tortoiseshell, *Roddia vaualbum*

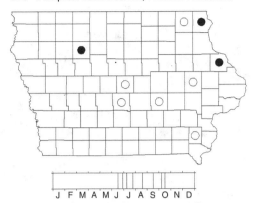

680 Milbert's Tortoiseshell, *Aglais milberti*

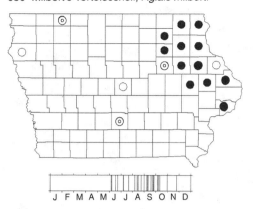

682 Mourning Cloak, *Nymphalis antiopa*

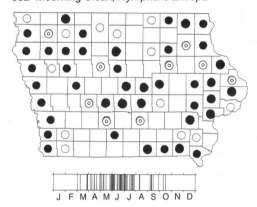

684 Red Admiral, *Vanessa atalanta*

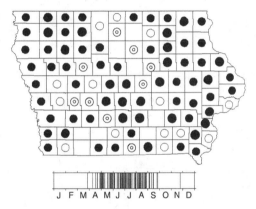

685 Painted Lady, *Vanessa cardui*

687 American Lady, *Vanessa virginiensis*

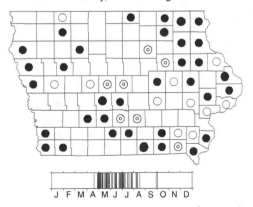

692a White Admiral,
Limenitis arthemis arthemis

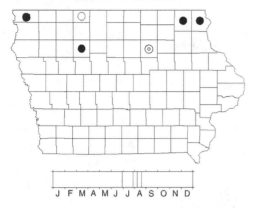

692b Red-spotted Purple,
Limenitis arthemis astyanax

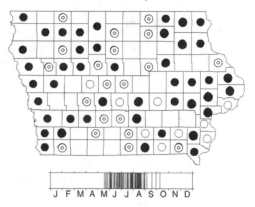

693 Viceroy, *Limenitis archippus*

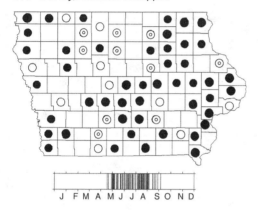

722 Goatweed Leafwing, *Anaea andria*

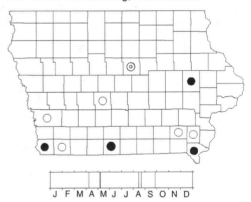

726 Hackberry Emperor, *Asterocampa celtis*

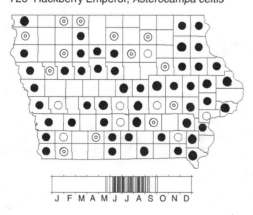

728 Tawny Emperor, *Asterocampa clyton*

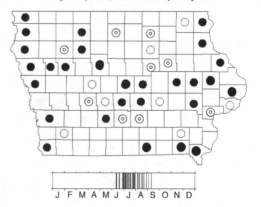

734 Northern Pearly-eye, *Enodia anthedon*

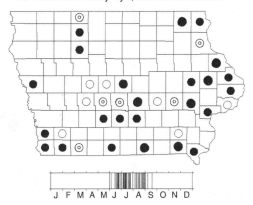

736 Eyed Brown, *Satyrodes eurydice*

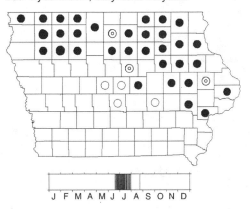

745 Little Wood-satyr, *Megisto cymela*

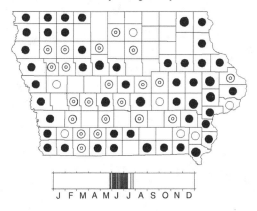

749 Common Ringlet, *Coenonympha tullia*

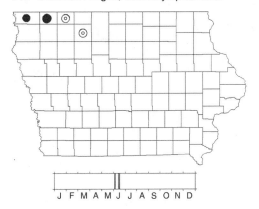

750 Common Wood-nymph, *Cercyonis pegala*

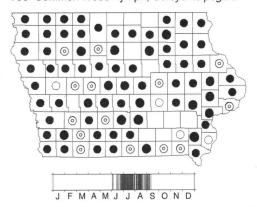

Checklist of Iowa Butterflies

The butterfly numbers follow the order of "Butterflies of North America: 2. Scientific Names List for Butterfly Species of North America, North of Mexico" (Opler and Warren 2003). Each species is assigned a place in the list based on its taxonomic relationships to the others.

Skippers: Family Hesperiidae

- ☐ 5   Silver-spotted Skipper, *Epargyreus clarus*
- ☐ 41   Hoary Edge, *Achalarus lyciades*
- ☐ 47   Southern Cloudywing, *Thorybes bathyllus*
- ☐ 48   Northern Cloudywing, *Thorybes pylades*
- ☐ 70   Hayhurst's Scallopwing, *Staphylus hayhurstii*
- ☐ 85   Dreamy Duskywing, *Erynnis icelus*
- ☐ 86   Sleepy Duskywing, *Erynnis brizo*
- ☐ 87   Juvenal's Duskywing, *Erynnis juvenalis*
- ☐ 92   Horace's Duskywing, *Erynnis horatius*
- ☐ 94   Mottled Duskywing, *Erynnis martialis*
- ☐ 98   Wild Indigo Duskywing, *Erynnis baptisiae*
- ☐ 99   Columbine Duskywing, *Erynnis lucilius*
- ☐ 106   Common Checkered-skipper, *Pyrgus communis*
- ☐ 117   Common Sootywing, *Pholisora catullus*
- ☐ 146   Least Skipper, *Ancyloxypha numitor*
- ☐ 149   Poweshiek Skipperling, *Oarisma poweshiek*
- ☐ 154   European Skipper, *Thymelicus lineola*
- ☐ 155   Fiery Skipper, *Hylephila phyleus*
- ☐ 164   Ottoe Skipper, *Hesperia ottoe*
- ☐ 165   Leonard's Skipper, *Hesperia leonardus leonardus* and *Hesperia leonardus pawnee*

☐ 172 Dakota Skipper, *Hesperia dacotae*

☐ 177 Sachem, *Atalopedes campestris*

☐ 180 Peck's Skipper, *Polites peckius*

☐ 184 Tawny-edged Skipper, *Polites themistocles*

☐ 186 Crossline Skipper, *Polites origenes*

☐ 187 Long Dash, *Polites mystic*

☐ 191 Northern Broken-dash, *Wallengrenia egeremet*

☐ 192 Little Glassywing, *Pompeius verna*

☐ 193 Arogos Skipper, *Atrytone arogos*

☐ 194 Delaware Skipper, *Anatrytone logan*

☐ 196 Byssus Skipper, *Problema byssus*

☐ 201 Hobomok Skipper, *Poanes hobomok*

☐ 202 Zabulon Skipper, *Poanes zabulon*

☐ 205 Mulberry Wing, *Poanes massasoit*

☐ 206 Broad-winged Skipper, *Poanes viator*

☐ 212 Black Dash, *Euphyes conspicua*

☐ 214 Dion Skipper, *Euphyes dion*

☐ 217 Two-spotted Skipper, *Euphyes bimacula*

☐ 219 Dun Skipper, *Euphyes vestris*

☐ 221 Dusted Skipper, *Atrytonopsis hianna*

☐ 236 Pepper and Salt Skipper, *Amblyscirtes hegon*

☐ 244 Common Roadside-skipper, *Amblyscirtes vialis*

Swallowtails: Family Papilionidae

☐ 285 Pipevine Swallowtail, *Battus philenor*

☐ 289 Zebra Swallowtail, *Eurytides marcellus*

☐ 294 Black Swallowtail, *Papilio polyxenes*

☐ 297 Eastern Tiger Swallowtail, *Papilio glaucus*

☐ 303 Spicebush Swallowtail, *Papilio troilus*

☐ 308 Giant Swallowtail, *Papilio cresphontes*

Whites, Sulphurs, and Marbles: Family Pieridae

☐ 323 Checkered White, *Pontia protodice*

☐ 326 Cabbage White, *Pieris rapae*

☐ 337 Olympia Marble, *Euchloe olympia*

- ☐ 348 Clouded Sulphur, *Colias philodice*
- ☐ 349 Orange Sulphur, *Colias eurytheme*
- ☐ 366 Southern Dogface, *Colias cesonia*
- ☐ 370 Cloudless Sulphur, *Phoebis sennae*
- ☐ 385 Little Yellow, *Eurema lisa*
- ☐ 389 Dainty Sulphur, *Nathalis iole*

Coppers, Blues, Hairstreaks, and Harvesters: Family Lycaenidae

- ☐ 390 Harvester, *Feniseca tarquinius*
- ☐ 392 American Copper, *Lycaena phlaeas*
- ☐ 395 Gray Copper, *Lycaena dione*
- ☐ 398 Bronze Copper, *Lycaena hyllus*
- ☐ 403 Purplish Copper, *Lycaena helloides*
- ☐ 422 Juniper Hairstreak, *Callophrys gryneus*
- ☐ 432 Henry's Elfin, *Callophrys henrici*
- ☐ 445 Coral Hairstreak, *Satyrium titus*
- ☐ 446 Acadian Hairstreak, *Satyrium acadica*
- ☐ 449 Hickory Hairstreak, *Satyrium caryaevorum*
- ☐ 450 Edwards' Hairstreak, *Satyrium edwardsii*
- ☐ 451 Banded Hairstreak, *Satyrium calanus*
- ☐ 453 Striped Hairstreak, *Satyrium liparops*
- ☐ 470 Gray Hairstreak, *Strymon melinus*
- ☐ 490 White M Hairstreak, *Parrhasius m-album*
- ☐ 499 Eastern Tailed-blue, *Everes comyntas*
- ☐ 501 Spring Azure, *Celastrina ladon*
- ☐ 503 Summer Azure, *Celastrina neglecta*
- ☐ 510 Silvery Blue, *Glaucopsyche lygdamus*
- ☐ 526 Reakirt's Blue, *Echinargus isola*
- ☐ 531 Melissa Blue, *Lycaeides melissa*

Brush-footed Butterflies: Family Nymphalidae

- ☐ 571 American Snout, *Libytheana carinenta*
- ☐ 573 Monarch, *Danaus plexippus*
- ☐ 585 Variegated Fritillary, *Euptoieta claudia*

☐ 588 Great Spangled Fritillary, *Speyeria cybele*

☐ 589 Aphrodite Fritillary, *Speyeria aphrodite*

☐ 590 Regal Fritillary, *Speyeria idalia*

☐ 605 Silver-bordered Fritillary, *Boloria selene*

☐ 606 Meadow Fritillary, *Boloria bellona*

☐ 631 Gorgone Checkerspot, *Chlosyne gorgone*

☐ 632 Silvery Checkerspot, *Chlosyne nycteis*

☐ 648 Pearl Crescent, *Phyciodes tharos*

☐ 659a Baltimore Checkerspot, *Euphydryas phaeton phaeton*

☐ 659b Ozark Baltimore Checkerspot, *Euphydryas phaeton ozarkae*

☐ 664 Buckeye, *Junonia coenia*

☐ 672 Question Mark, *Polygonia interrogationis*

☐ 673 Eastern Comma, *Polygonia comma*

☐ 677 Gray Comma, *Polygonia progne*

☐ 679 Compton Tortoiseshell, *Roddia vaualbum*

☐ 680 Milbert's Tortoiseshell, *Aglais milberti*

☐ 682 Mourning Cloak, *Nymphalis antiopa*

☐ 684 Red Admiral, *Vanessa atalanta*

☐ 685 Painted Lady, *Vanessa cardui*

☐ 687 American Lady, *Vanessa virginiensis*

☐ 692a White Admiral, *Limenitis arthemis arthemis*

☐ 692b Red-spotted Purple, *Limenitis arthemis astyanax*

☐ 693 Viceroy, *Limenitis archippus*

☐ 722 Goatweed Leafwing, *Anaea andria*

☐ 726 Hackberry Emperor, *Asterocampa celtis*

☐ 728 Tawny Emperor, *Asterocampa clyton*

☐ 734 Northern Pearly-eye, *Enodia anthedon*

☐ 736 Eyed Brown, *Satyrodes eurydice*

☐ 745 Little Wood-satyr, *Megisto cymela*

☐ 749 Common Ringlet, *Coenonympha tullia*

☐ 750 Common Wood-nymph, *Cercyonis pegala*

Strays

☐ 252 Eufala Skipper, *Lerodea eufala*

☐ 380 Mexican Yellow, *Eurema mexicana*

☐ 388   Sleepy Orange, *Eurema nicippe*

☐ 495   Marine Blue, *Leptotes marina*

☐ 574   Queen, *Danaus gilippus*

☐ 579   Gulf Fritillary, *Agraulis vanillae*

Butterfly Collection Data

Skippers: Family Hesperiidae

5 Silver-spotted Skipper, *Epargyreus clarus*
   Wapsipinicon State Park, Anamosa, Jones Co IA, 12 August 1982,
      D. Nauman

41 Hoary Edge, *Achalarus lyciades*
   Lake Ozark, Miller Co MO, 18 August 1990, D. Schlicht

47 Southern Cloudywing, *Thorybes bathyllus*
   Honey Creek Destination State Park, Moravia, Appanoose Co IA,
      27 May 2002, F. Olsen

48 Northern Cloudywing, *Thorybes pylades*
   Clanton Creek Recreation Area, Madison Co IA, 11 June 1976, D. Schlicht

70 Hayhurst's Scallopwing, *Staphylus hayhurstii*
   Big Sand Mound Preserve, Louisa Co IA, 10 July 1987, J. Nekola

85 Dreamy Duskywing, *Erynnis icelus*
   Necedah, Juneau Co WI, 31 May 1987, D. Schlicht

86 Sleepy Duskywing, *Erynnis brizo*
   Roggman Boreal Slopes State Preserve, Clayton Co IA, 14 May 1987, J. Nekola

87 Juvenal's Duskywing, *Erynnis juvenalis*
   Five Ridge Prairie, Plymouth Co IA, 1 May 1988, T. Orwig
   Rock Island Preserve, Linn Co IA, 4 May 2002, D. Schlicht

92 Horace's Duskywing, *Erynnis horatius*
   Croton Unit, Shimek State Forest, Lee Co IA, 16 July 1987, D. Schlicht
   Gilman Terrace, Sioux City, Woodbury Co IA, 17 July 1988, T. Orwig

94 Mottled Duskywing, *Erynnis martialis*
   Stone State Preserve, Sioux City, Woodbury Co IA, 27 April 1989, T. Orwig

98 Wild Indigo Duskywing, *Erynnis baptisiae*
   Honey Creek Destination State Park, Moravia, Appanoose Co IA, 14 August
      2001, D. Schlicht
   Weymiller Prairie, Allamakee Co IA, 14 July 1987, J. Nekola

99 Columbine Duskywing, *Erynnis lucilius*
   Fish Farm Mounds State Preserve, Allamakee Co IA, 14 May 1987, J. Nekola
   Silver Creek Prairie, Allamakee Co IA, 14 May 1987, J. Nekola

106 Common Checkered-skipper, *Pyrgus communis*
Central City, Linn Co IA, 13 September 1981, D. Nauman
Big Sand Mound Preserve, Louisa Co IA, 7 September 1987, D. Schlicht

117 Common Sootywing, *Pholisora catullus*
Motor Mill, Clayton Co IA, 14 August 1984, D. Schlicht
Southwest of Walker, Benton Co IA, 30 June 1981, D. Schlicht

146 Least Skipper, *Ancyloxypha numitor*
Hawker's Fen, Delaware Co IA, 24 June 1986, D. Schlicht
Robinson Bog, Robinson, Delaware Co IA, 14 September 1985, D. Schlicht

149 Poweshiek Skipperling, *Oarisma poweshiek*
Cayler Prairie State Preserve, Dickinson Co IA, July 1989, T. Orwig
Cayler Prairie State Preserve, Dickinson Co IA, 29 June 1980, D. Schlicht

154 European Skipper, *Thymelicus lineola*
Alburnett, Linn Co IA, 27 June 1983, D. Schlicht, male & female

155 Fiery Skipper, *Hylephila phyleus*
Dike, Grundy Co IA, 9 October 1983, D. Schlicht, male & female

164 Ottoe Skipper, *Hesperia ottoe*
Lockwood Place Road Bluff, Council Bluffs, Pottawattamie Co IA, 2 July 1980,
    D. Schlicht
Stone State Park, Sioux City, Woodbury Co IA, 1 July 1988, T. Orwig

165 Leonard's Skipper, *Hesperia leonardus pawnee*
Huser's Prairie, Plymouth Co IA, 20 August 1988, T. Orwig
Plymouth Co IA, 4 September 1988, T. Orwig
Leonard's Skipper, *Hesperia leonardus leonardus*
Mills Co IA, T. Orwig
Mills Co IA, 2 September 1989, T. Orwig

172 Dakota Skipper, *Hesperia dacotae*
Cayler Prairie State Preserve, Dickinson Co IA, 29 June 1980, D. Schlicht
Clay Co MN, 7 July 1996, D. Schlicht

177 Sachem, *Atalopedes campestris*
Bayard, Guthrie Co IA, 10 September 1971, D. Schlicht
Lyon Co IA, 22 August 1992, T. Orwig

180 Peck's Skipper, *Polites peckius*
Coggon Bog/Millard Preserve, Central City, Linn Co IA, 23 May 1985,
    D. Schlicht
Freda Haffner Kettlehole State Preserve, Dickinson Co IA, 2 August 1986,
    J. Nekola

184 Tawny-edged Skipper, *Polites themistocles*
Lake Darling State Park, Brighton, Washington Co IA, 15 August 1990,
    D. Schlicht
Stone State Preserve, Sioux City, Woodbury Co IA, 1 October 1989, T. Orwig

186 Crossline Skipper, *Polites origenes*
Loess Hills Wildlife Area, Monona Co IA, 5 July 1984, D. Schlicht

Peterson, Clay Co IA, 7 July 1986, J. Nekola

187   Long Dash, *Polites mystic*
Sioux City Prairie, Sioux City, Woodbury Co IA, 26 May 1988, T. Orwig
Blazing Star Prairie, Rowley, Buchanan Co IA, 27 June 1984, D. Schlicht

191   Northern Broken-dash, *Wallengrenia egeremet*
Cedar Rapids, Linn Co IA, 21 July 2001, D. Schlicht, male & female

192   Little Glassywing, *Pompeius verna*
Center Point, Linn Co IA, 27 June 1981, D. Schlicht
Urbana, Benton Co IA, 4 July 1983, D. Schlicht

193   Arogos Skipper, *Atrytone arogos*
Kossuth Co IA, 9 July 1986, D. Schlicht, male & female

194   Delaware Skipper, *Anatrytone logan*
Shelburne Wildlife Management Area, Lyon Co MN, 30 June 1994, D. Schlicht
Kossuth Co IA, 4 July 1986, J. Nekola

196   Byssus Skipper, *Problema byssus*
Syslow Prairie, Clinton Co IA, 23 July 1986, D. Schlicht
Cedar Rapids, Linn Co IA, 21 July 2001, D. Schlicht

201   Hobomok Skipper, *Poanes hobomok*
Fish Farm Mounds State Preserve, Allamakee Co IA, 14 May 1987, J. Nekola
Matsell Bridge Natural Area, Viola, Linn Co IA, 27 May 1987, J. Nekola

202   Zabulon Skipper, *Poanes zabulon*
Waubonsie State Park, Fremont Co IA, 7 August 2004, D. Veal, male & female

205   Mulberry Wing, *Poanes massasoit*
Milford Fen, Dickinson Co IA, 9 July 1986, D. Schlicht
Sheldon Seeps, Ransom Co ND, 3 July 1995, T. Orwig

206   Broad-winged Skipper, *Poanes viator*
Hoffman Prairie State Preserve, Cerro Gordo Co IA, 4 July 1986, D. Schlicht
Daubendiek Prairie, Cornelia, Wright Co IA, 8 July 1998, D. Schlicht

212   Black Dash, *Euphyes conspicua*
Loupee Fen, Linn Co IA, 29 June 1985, D. Schlicht
Milford Fen, Dickinson Co IA, 9 July 1986, D. Schlicht

214   Dion Skipper, *Euphyes dion*
Cedar Hills Sand Prairie State Preserve, Black Hawk Co IA, 13 July 1980,
    Rex Schlicht
Clear Lake, Cerro Gordo Co IA, 28 July 1985, D. Schlicht

217   Two-spotted Skipper, *Euphyes bimacula*
Doolittle Prairie State Preserve, Story Co IA, 13 June 2004, F. Olsen
Rowley Fen, Buchanan Co IA, 27 June 1986, J. Nekola

219   Dun Skipper, *Euphyes vestris*
Hensler, Oliver Co ND, 1 July 1994, T. Orwig
Buffalo Creek Wildlife Area, Buchanan Co IA, 8 July 1978, D. Schlicht

221   Dusted Skipper, *Atrytonopsis hianna*
Stone State Preserve, Sioux City, Plymouth Co IA, 15 May 1989, T. Orwig

Sioux City Prairie, Woodbury Co IA, 19 May 1988, T. Orwig

236 Pepper and Salt Skipper, *Amblyscirtes hegon*
Fish Farm Mounds State Preserve, Allamakee Co IA, 14 May 1987, J. Nekola
Fish Farm Mounds State Preserve, Allamakee Co IA, 31 May 1987, D. Schlicht

244 Common Roadside-skipper, *Amblyscirtes vialis*
Big Prairie, Allamakee Co IA, 7 July 1987, J. Nekola
Churdan, Greene Co IA, 29 August 1981, D. Schlicht

Swallowtails: Family Papilionidae

285 Pipevine Swallowtail, *Battus philenor*
Kirksville, Adair Co MO, 28 April 1974, D. Schlicht
Lake Ozark, Miller Co MO, 18 August 1990, D. Schlicht

289 Zebra Swallowtail, *Eurytides marcellus*
Waubonsie State Park, Fremont Co IA, 2 June 1988, T. Orwig

294 Black Swallowtail, *Papilio polyxenes*
Donnan Prairie, Fayette Co IA, 24 June 1986, J. Nekola
Onslow, Jones Co IA, 3 August 1988, J. Nekola

297 Eastern Tiger Swallowtail, *Papilio glaucus*
Five Ridge Prairie, Westfield, Plymouth Co IA, 30 April 1987, T. Orwig
Sioux City, Woodbury Co IA, 11 May 1987, K. Arnburg
Bucklin, Linn Co MO, 3 June 1977, D. Schlicht

303 Spicebush Swallowtail, *Papilio troilus*
Kissimmee, Osceola Co FL, 5 July 1986, G. Sutton
Lake Ozark, Miller Co MO, 17 August 1990, D. Schlicht

308 Giant Swallowtail, *Papilio cresphontes*
Wyalusing, Grant Co WI, 30 July 1984, M. Schlicht

Whites, Sulphurs, and Marbles: Family Pieridae

323 Checkered White, *Pontia protodice*
Sioux City Prairie, Woodbury Co IA, 10 September 1988, T. Orwig
Waterloo, Black Hawk Co IA, 22 September 1979, D. Schlicht

326 Cabbage White, *Pieris rapae*
Pine Lake State Park, Hardin Co IA, 20 August 1977, D. Schlicht
Big Sand Mound Preserve, Louisa Co IA, 27 June 1987, D. Schlicht

337 Olympia Marble, *Euchloe olympia*
Stone State Preserve, Sioux City, Woodbury Co IA, 2 May 1989, T. Orwig
Sgt. Floyd Monument, Sioux City, Woodbury Co IA, 28 April 1992, T. Orwig

348 Clouded Sulphur, *Colias philodice*
Indianola, Warren Co IA, 18 August 1975, D. Schlicht
Osborne, Clayton Co IA, 22 July 1986, D. Schlicht
Indianola, Warren Co IA, 16 June 1976, D. Schlicht

349 Orange Sulphur, *Colias eurytheme*

Bayard, Guthrie Co IA, 2 September 1971, D. Schlicht
Swan Lake Refuge, Chariton Co MO, 24 September 1972, D. Schlicht
Broken Kettle Grassland, Plymouth Co IA, 17 August 1992, T. Orwig

366   Southern Dogface, *Colias cesonia*
Huser's Prairie, Sioux City, Plymouth Co IA, 1 October 1989, T. Orwig
Sioux City Prairie, Woodbury Co IA, 23 September 1986, T. Orwig

370   Cloudless Sulphur, *Phoebis sennae*
Sioux City Prairie, Woodbury Co IA, 13 September 1987, T. Orwig
Bucklin, Linn Co MO, 24 September 1972, D. Schlicht

385   Little Yellow, *Eurema lisa*
Rochester Twp, Cedar Co IA, 22 July 1996, D. Schlicht
Bucklin, Linn Co MO, 11 September 1972, D. Schlicht
Honey Creek Destination State Park, Moravia, Appanoose Co IA,
    5 August 2001, D. Schlicht

389   Dainty Sulphur, *Nathalis iole*
Vinton, Benton Co IA, 24 July 1981, D. Schlicht
Indianola, Warren Co IA, 17 August 1975, D. Schlicht

Coppers, Blues, Hairstreaks, and Harvesters: Family Lycaenidae

390   Harvester, *Feniseca tarquinius*
Cota Creek, Allamakee Co IA, 16 June 1987, J. Nekola

392   American Copper, *Lycaena phlaeas*
Wendy Oaks Road Sand Prairie, Linn Co IA, 1 May 1987, D. Schlicht

395   Gray Copper, *Lycaena dione*
Indianola, Warren Co IA, 16 June 1976, D. Schlicht
Big Sand Mound Preserve, Louisa Co IA, 15 June 1991, D. Schlicht

398   Bronze Copper, *Lycaena hyllus*
Central City, Linn Co IA, 15 August 1984, D. Nauman
Salisbury Bridge Recreation Area, Muscatine Co IA, 9 July 2004, E. Freese

403   Purplish Copper, *Lycaena helloides*
Williams Prairie, Johnson Co IA, 31 May 1989, J. Nekola
Hankinson, Richland Co ND, 9 July 1997, T. Orwig

422   Juniper Hairstreak, *Callophrys gryneus*
Hitchcock Nature Area, Pottawattamie Co IA, 4 July 2004, D. Veal
Wendy Oaks Road Sand Prairie, Linn Co IA, 1 May 1987, D. Schlicht

432   Henry's Elfin, *Callophrys henrici*
Honey Creek Destination State Park, Moravia, Appanoose Co IA, 23
    April 2003, F. Olsen

445   Coral Hairstreak, *Satyrium titus*
Hamilton's Prairie, Maquoketa, Jackson Co IA, 24 June 1985, D. Schlicht
Southwest of Walker, Benton Co IA, 30 June 1981, D. Schlicht

446   Acadian Hairstreak, *Satyrium acadica*

Kliess Fen, Chickasaw Co IA, 24 June 1986, D. Schlicht
Hankinson, Richland Co ND, 9 July 1997, T. Orwig

449 Hickory Hairstreak, *Satyrium caryaevorum*
Pleasant Creek State Park, Linn Co IA, 22 July 1978, D. Schlicht
Bucklin, Linn Co MO, 3 June 1977, D. Schlicht

450 Edwards' Hairstreak, *Satyrium edwardsii*
Gitchie Manitou State Preserve, Lyon Co IA, 3 July 1989, T. Orwig
Clanton Wildlife Area, Madison Co IA, 30 June 1976, D. Schlicht

451 Banded Hairstreak, *Satyrium calanus*
Fish Farm Mounds State Preserve, Allamakee Co IA, 25 June 1985, D. Schlicht
Clanton Wildlife Area, Madison Co IA, 30 June 1976, D. Schlicht

453 Striped Hairstreak, *Satryium liparops*
Coggon Bog/Millard Preserve, Central City, Linn Co IA, 21 June 1985,
    D. Schlicht

470 Gray Hairstreak, *Strymon melinus*
Broken Kettle Grassland, Plymouth Co IA, 5 July 1984, D. Schlicht
Honey Creek Destination State Park, Moravia, Appanoose Co IA, 23 April 2002,
    F. Olsen

490 White M Hairstreak, *Parrhasius m-album*
Rock Island Preserve, Linn Co IA, 31 August 2000, F. Olsen

499 Eastern Tailed-blue, *Everes comyntas*
Hoffman Prairie State Preserve, Cerro Gordo Co IA, 26 July 1986, L. Schlicht
Pinicon Ridge Park, Central City, Linn Co IA, 22 August 1978, D. Schlicht

501 Spring Azure, *Celastrina ladon*
Bucklin, Linn Co MO, 13 April 19 1986, D. Schlicht
Lick Creek Unit, Shimek State Forest, Lee Co IA, 18 April 1987, J. Nekola

503 Summer Azure, *Celastrina neglecta*
Clay Prairie Preserve, Butler Co IA, 27 July 2004, F. Olsen
Rock Island Preserve, Linn Co IA, 17 June 1985, D. Schlicht

510 Silvery Blue, *Glaucopsyche lygdamus*
Rice Lake State Park, Worth Co IA, 14 May 1989, T. Orwig

526 Reakirt's Blue, *Echinargus isola*
Weymiller Prairie, Allamakee Co IA, 14, July 1987, D. Schlicht
Johnson's Ridge Prairie, Monona Co IA, 30 May 1987, J. Nekola

531 Melissa Blue, *Lycaeides melissa*
Broken Kettle Grassland, Plymouth Co IA, 17 August 1992, T. Orwig
Oak Grove State Park, Sioux Co IA, 8 June 1989, T. Orwig

Brush-footed Butterflies: Family Nymphalidae

571 American Snout, *Libytheana carinenta*
Pleasant Creek State Park, Linn Co IA, 22 July 1978, D. Schlicht

573 Monarch, *Danaus plexippus*
Sac City, Sac Co IA, 29 August 1981, D. Schlicht

Bayard, Guthrie Co IA, 26 August 1971, D. Schlicht
585 Variegated Fritillary, *Euptoieta claudia*
Bokelman Prairie, Cerro Gordo Co IA, 4 July 1986, J. Nekola
588 Great Spangled Fritillary, *Speyeria cybele*
Urbana, Benton Co IA, 29 June 1978, D. Schlicht
Waubonsie State Park, Fremont Co IA, 30 June 1980, D. Schlicht
589 Aphrodite Fritillary, *Speyeria aphrodite*
Robinson Bog, Buchanan Co IA, 24 June 1986, D. Schlicht
Steele Prairie State Preserve, Cherokee Co IA, 6 July 2004, F. Olsen
590 Regal Fritillary, *Speyeria idalia*
Kalsow Prairie State Preserve, Pocahontas Co IA, 5 July 1985, M. Schlicht
Stone State Park, Woodbury Co IA, 1 July 1988, T. Orwig
605 Silver-bordered Fritillary, *Boloria selene*
Chickasaw Fen, Chickasaw Co IA, 13 July 1990, D. Schlicht
606 Meadow Fritillary, *Boloria bellona*
Chipera Prairie, Winneshiek Co IA, 18 July 1997, E. Freese
631 Gorgone Checkerspot, *Chlosyne gorgone*
North of Manikowski Prairie State Preserve, Clinton Co IA, 17 May 2003,
    F. Olsen
632 Silvery Checkerspot, *Chlosyne nycteis*
Honey Creek Destination State Park, Moravia, Appanoose Co IA, 16 June 2002,
    F. Olsen
648 Pearl Crescent, *Phyciodes tharos*
Rowley Fen, Buchanan Co IA, 15 June 1985, D. Schlicht
North Cedar Creek, Clayton Co IA, 23 August 1986, D. Schlicht
659a Baltimore Checkerspot, *Euphydryas phaeton phaeton*
Buffalo Slough, Mason City, Cerro Gordo Co IA, 3 July 1987, D. Schlicht
Conesville Fen, Muscatine Co IA, 18 June 1989, J. Nekola
659b Ozark Baltimore Checkerspot, *Euphydryas phaeton ozarkae*
Croton Unit, Shimek State Forest, Lee Co IA, 10 June 1987, R. Cecil
664 Buckeye, *Junonia coenia*
Sioux City Prairie, Woodbury Co IA, 23 August 1991, T. Orwig
Bucklin, Linn Co MO, 13 September 1975, D. Schlicht
Bucklin, Linn Co MO, 4 October 1980 (form *rosa*), D. Schlicht
672 Question Mark, *Polygonia interrogationis*
Atlanta, Macon Co MO, 31 July 1978, D. Schlicht
Sioux City, Woodbury Co IA, 1 September 1987, T. Orwig
673 Eastern Comma, *Polygonia comma*
Pike's Peak State Park, Clayton Co IA, 23 August 1986, D. Schlicht
Wapsipinicon State Park, Anamosa, Jones Co IA, 12 August 1982, D. Schlicht
677 Gray Comma, *Polygonia progne*
Urbana, Benton Co IA, 29 June 1978, D. Schlicht
Bucklin, Linn Co MO, 5 June 1977, D. Schlicht
679 Compton Tortoiseshell, *Roddia vaualbum*

Cota Creek, Allamakee Co IA, 6 June 1987, J. Nekola
680 Milbert's Tortoiseshell, *Aglais milberti*
Center Point, Linn Co IA, 31 August 1984, D. Schlicht
682 Mourning Cloak, *Nymphalis antiopa*
Bayard, Guthrie Co IA, 10 October 1971, D. Schlicht
684 Red Admiral, *Vanessa atalanta*
Chipera Prairie, Winneshiek Co IA, 1 September 1997, E. Freese
685 Painted Lady, *Vanessa cardui*
Troy Mills Access, Buchanan Co IA, 30 June 1981, D. Schlicht
687 American Lady, *Vanessa virginiensis*
Osage Beach, Camden Co MO, 3 June 1981, D. Nauman
692a White Admiral, *Limenitis arthemis arthemis*
Sheldon Seeps, Anselm, Ransom Co ND, 3 July 1995, T. Orwig
692b Red-spotted Purple, *Limenitis arthemis astyanax*
Central City, Linn Co IA, 11 August 1982, D. Nauman
693 Viceroy, *Limenitis archippus*
Worthington, Dubuque Co IA, 15 August 1977, D. Schlicht
722 Goatweed Leafwing, *Anaea andria*
Bucklin, Linn Co MO, 8 September 1973, D. Schlicht
Bucklin, Linn Co MO, 16 September 1973, D. Schlicht
726 Hackberry Emperor, *Asterocampa celtis*
Osage Beach, Camden Co MO, 3 June 1981, D. Schlicht
Brown's Bluff, Marion Co IA, 1 July 1975, D. Schlicht
728 Tawny Emperor, *Asterocampa clyton*
Troy Mills Access, Buchanan Co IA, 30 June 1981, D. Schlicht
Center Point, Linn Co IA, 25 July 1977, D. Schlicht
734 Northern Pearly-eye, *Enodia anthedon*
Pinicon Ridge Park, Central City, Linn Co IA, 5 July 1981, D. Schlicht
736 Eyed Brown, *Satyrodes eurydice*
Cedar Hills Sand Prairie State Preserve, Black Hawk Co IA, 3 July 1980,
D. Schlicht
Kirchner Prairie, Clay Co IA, 8 July 1986, D. Schlicht
745 Little Wood-satyr, *Megisto cymela*
Clanton Wildlife Area, Madison Co IA, 30 June 1976, D. Schlicht
Central City, Linn Co IA, 14 June 1982, D. Schlicht
749 Common Ringlet, *Coenonympha tullia*
Snyder's Prairie, Lyon Co IA, 4 June 1989, T. Orwig
Blood Run National Historic Landmark, Lyon Co IA, 13 June 1992, T. Orwig
750 Common Wood-nymph, *Cercyonis pegala*
Buffalo Creek Wildlife Area, Buchanan Co IA, 8 July 1978, D. Schlicht
Rowley, Buchanan Co IA, 30 July 1982, D. Schlicht

GLOSSARY

The following words represent a very select assortment judged to be most helpful in building a vocabulary of technical knowledge about butterflies. Most of the words are not restricted to the discipline. Just as the species name is an index to published information, a word may also be a clue to additional data.

adaptation. Genetic feature which imparts to individuals greater reproductive success under specific environmental conditions. Adaptations occur in a population or species as a result of natural selection.

albinism. Hereditary trait characterized by the inability to form pigments.

androconium (pl. androconia). Modified scale which produces a sexual attractant in certain male butterflies.

antenna (pl. antennae). Paired, segmented, movable sensory appendage on the head of larvae and adults.

apical. Toward or on the tip of a wing.

basking. Behavior where the wings are positioned to obtain heat from a light source or by conduction through the substrate.

blending zone. Area where individuals show an intermix of characters diagnostic of two or more populations elsewhere; morphological intergrade zone between two distinctive populations.

caterpillar. The larval stage of a butterfly or moth.

caudal. Toward the tail end of an animal.

chrysalis (pl. chrysalides). Another name for the pupal stage of butterflies.

cline. Gradual and more or less continuous change in a character in a series of continuous populations from the individuals at the two extremes, who differ markedly.

competition. Struggle between organisms for a limiting environmental resource, such as larval or adult food, space, mates, or other necessities.

copula. Linking of male and female during which sperm is introduced into the female; sometimes called pairing.

costa (pl. costae). Vein in the anterior marginal area of the wing; the front margins of the wings are also called costal margins.

cremaster. Arrangement of hooks at the back end of the pupal body by means of which it is attached to its support; hooklets on the cremaster entangle in a pad of silk spun for that purpose by the mature larva.

cryptic coloration. Camouflage patterns which conceal the butterfly by making it resemble the background on which it rests.

diapause. Process or action of being arrested in growth.

dicotyledonous. Type of flowering plant whose sprout has a pair of leaves with branched veins (such as a bean).

dimorphism. Existence in two distinct forms; for example, sexual dimorphism, when male and female are obviously different (in color, size, wing shape, etc.).

distal. Positioned farther from the body.

dorsal. Pertaining to the top, back, or upper side.

endemic. Occurring only in a peculiar locality.

exoskeleton. Skeleton or shell supporting the body on the outside.

extinction. Loss of an evolutionary lineage or species from the planet.

extirpation. Loss of a species from a defined area of its range.

eyespot. Wing pattern consisting of concentric circles of different colors, giving the appearance of eyes (believed to deflect the attention of predators to nonvital areas).

family. Taxonomic grouping that contains genera.

fauna. Animal life of any given region or habitat; butterflies are part of the local fauna.

fen. Peatland whose water comes out of the ground (as opposed to bogs, whose water comes from precipitation).

flora. The plants of a given area.

gene flow. Movement of genetic characteristics in a population.

gene pool. All the genes in a given population of a species.

genitalia. External organs of reproduction.

genus (pl. genera). Taxonomic category that includes (usually) several closely related species; "related" genera are placed in a single family.

habitat. The natural home or environment of an organism.

hibernaculum. Winter shelter of leaves, silk, and/or other detritus constructed to protect larvae or pupae.

hibernation. Period of prolonged inactivity or dormancy (diapause) accompanied by lowered metabolic activity and functioning to withstand winter cold.

honeydew glands. Glands on the abdomens of Lycaenid larvae that produce a sugary solution called honeydew.

host plant. Food source of the larvae or adult.

hyaline spot. Shiny or glassy and transparent spot.

hybrid. Organism produced by genetically dissimilar parents; the result of a cross between unlike individuals, sometimes showing characters of both.

instar. Individual during a period between apolyses (molting processes); initially each instar is concealed by an egg shell, an old larval skin, or a pupal case.

larva (pl. larvae). Caterpillar, the immature stage of butterflies between the egg and pupal stage.

limbal. On the outer quarter of the hind wing (the opposite of basal).

maculation. The arrangement, degree, and pattern of the spots or pupils (macules) on the wing.

melanism. Condition of having increased amounts of black or brownish pigments (melanins) so that the individual looks darker than typical.

mesic. Having moderate water availability, as opposed to hydric (wet) or xeric (dry).

microandroconia. Scales involved in the production of scent, as found in the stigma of members of the genus *Hesperia*.

migration. Dispersal and movement of individuals from place to place; periodic movement of individuals in or out of one area.

mimicry. Superficial resemblance in form, color, sound, smell, or behavior of certain organisms (mimics) to other more powerful or protected ones (models), resulting in protection, concealment, or some other advantage for the mimic.

molt. The process of shedding the exoskeleton.

monocotyledonous. Type of flowering plant whose sprout has only a single seedling leaf with parallel veins (such as corn).

morphology. Study of the structure or form of organisms.

morphotype. Physical-type of an organism (for example, tailed wings).

Müllerian mimicry. Type of biological advertising wherein two or more distasteful or protected species share a warning (aposomatic) color. They thus share a mutual characteristic which renders them somewhat more protected from vertebrate predators.

nectaring. Acquiring nectar from a flower.

niche. Way in which an organism uses the factors of its environment; the ecological range of a species.

nominate. Typical of the species.

ocellus (pl. ocelli). Small, simple eyelike spot or color.

olfactory. Pertaining to the sense of smell.

osmeterium. Fleshy forked organ on the dorsal part of the caterpillars of some swallowtails. It emits an unpleasant odor.

overscaling. Appearance of a layer of wing scales on top of another layer.

overwintering. Surviving the winter inactively (as in hibernation) in the habitat where the active stage occurs, as opposed to migration.

oviposition. Laying eggs or ova.

paha. Elongated ridge capped with wind-blown loess and sand.

Paleozoic Plateau. Topographic area in northeast Iowa characterized by deeply cut stream courses.

palp (pl. palpi). Feeding and sensory appendage on the head of larvae; also an olfactory and cleaning appendage on the head of adults.

parasite. Organism living on, in, or around another organism of a different species, killing it during its immature stages; because only one host is usually destroyed, use of the term "predator" seems inappropriate.

parasitoid. Parasite that lives within its host only during its larval development, killing the host.

perching. Act of alighting on a spot (often an elevated twig or prominence), from which short circling or "territorial" flights are made; perhaps a mate-seeking behavior preceding courtship, particularly in males.

phenology. Time of recurrence of annual events, such as the first and last appearance of a butterfly in the year.

phenotype. Appearance of an individual resulting from the interaction of its genes and the environment.

pheromone. Chemical compound secreted by an individual which influences the behavior or development of other individuals of the same species.

phylogeny. Evolutionary history of a species.

polymorphism. Occurrence of several distinct forms (phenotypes) in a population.

poor fen. Fen whose water source is very low in nutrients and cations.

proboscis. Paired, coiled, siphonlike tongue (maxilla) on the adult head.

proximal. Positioned closer to the body.

puddling. Behavior whereby butterflies go to a mud puddle for water and/or minerals. Gatherings of butterflies at a puddle are often called "puddle clubs."

pupa (pl. pupae). Stage between the larva and the adult characterized in butterflies by having the appendages and the body relatively fused, with any movement limited to the fourth, fifth, and sixth abdominal segments.

race. Population within a species with a degree of constant characters; used synonymously with "subspecies."

roosting. Remaining inactive on a substrate at night or in adverse conditions, sometimes in groups called communal roosting.

sampling. Selection of a representative series from a larger series.

scent patch. Specialized cluster of scales or setae which produces an odor often involved in courtship activity; see *androconium, stigma*.

sex-patch. Patch of wing scales that produce pheromones.

species (pl. also species). Taxonomic category below genus; populations that are reproductively or morphologically isolated from others.

stigma (pl. stigmata). Specialized patch of scales on the dorsal fore wing of Hesperidae (see *scent patch*); it may also refer to a spiracle (opening through which air enters the abdomen).

stimulus. Factor or change in the environment of an organism that initiates a response.

stridulation. Type of noise produced by rubbing two body parts together; Lycaenid pupae produce sound in this manner.

subapical. Adjacent to the apex of the wing.

subfamily. Taxonomic group which is a division of a family. Individuals in a subfamily share more characters than individuals in a family.

subspecies. Local population or group within a species which exhibits recognizable consistent characters and is distinguishable.

substrate. Solid material on which an organism lives.

survivia. Place where a species survives within its original range, as opposed to refugia, which may not be within the range.

sympatric. Referring to species which live in the same geographical region.

tarsal claw. Claw on the last segment of a walking leg.

taxon. Any designated taxonomic group or entity.

territoriality. Type of behavior whereby an individual "guards" an area or space and reacts aggressively toward intruders; may be part of mate-locating behaviors.

transgenic. Organism made by artificially combining genes of two or more species in a laboratory.

type. The museum specimen on which a species or subspecies name is based.

type locality. Geographical site from which the type specimen came.

ventral. Pertaining to the bottom or underside of the body.

xeric. Dry.

PLANT NAMES

Nomenclature generally follows Swink and Wilhelm (1994) and Eilers and Roosa (1994).

alder: *Alnus rugosa*
alfalfa: *Medicago sativa*
alyssum: *Alyssum* spp.
arrow-grass, common: *Triglochin maritimum*
   small: *Triglochin palustris*
artichoke, Jerusalem: *Helianthus tuberosus*
ash: *Fraxinus* spp.
   prickly: *Zanthoxylum americanum*
   wafer: *Ptelea trifoliata*
aspen: *Populus tremuloides*
aster: *Aster* spp.
   flat-topped: *Aster umbellatus*
   flax-leaved: *Aster linariifolius*
   golden: *Chrysopsis villosa*
   New England: *Aster novae-angliae*
   silky: *Aster sericeus*

bean, wild: *Strophostyles* spp.
bee-balm: *Monarda didyma*
berry, buffalo: *Shepherdia argentea*
birch, paper: *Betula papyrifera*
   river: *Betula nigra*
biscuitroot: *Lomatium foeniculaceum*
   eastern: *Lomatium orientale*
black-eyed Susan: *Rudbeckia hirta*
bladderwort, small: *Utricularia minor*
blazing star, dotted: *Liatris punctata*
   rough: *Liatris aspera*
blueberry: *Vaccinium angustifolium,*
   V. myrtilloides
bluegrass: *Poa* spp.
   Kentucky: *Poa pratensis*
bluestem, big: *Andropogon gerardii*
   little: *Andropogon (Schizachyrium)*
    scoparium

buckeye: *Aesculus* spp.
buddleia: *Buddleia* spp.

cabbage: *Brassica oleracea*
cardinal flower: *Lobelia cardinalis*
carrot: *Daucus carota*
cattail: *Typha* spp.
cedar, red: *Juniperus virginiana*
cherry, choke: *Prunus virginiana*
   sand: *Prunus pumila*
   wild: *Prunus serotina, P. virginiana*
chickweed: *Cerastium vulgatum*
chive: *Allium schoenoprasum*
chrysanthemum: *Chrysanthemum* spp.
cinquefoil, Pennsylvania: *Potentilla*
    pensylvanica
clover: *Trifolium* spp.
   bush: *Lespedeza* spp.
   prairie: *Petalostemon* spp.
   prairie bush: *Lespedeza leptostachya*
   red: *Trifolium pratense*
   white: *Trifolium repens*
columbine: *Aquilegia canadensis*
coneflower, gray-headed: *Ratibida*
    columnifera
   pale purple: *Echinacea pallida*
   purple: *Echinacea purpurea*
   yellow: *Ratibida pinnata*
coreopsis: *Coreopsis* spp.
cosmos: *Cosmos bipinnatus*
cottonwood: *Populus deltoides*
crabgrass: *Digitaria* spp.
cress: *Lepidium* spp.
   hairy rock: *Arabis hirsuta*
   rock: *Arabis lyrata*
croton: *Croton* spp.
currant: *Ribes* spp.
cut-grass, rice: *Leersia oryzoides*

daisy, ox-eye: *Chrysanthemum leucanthemum*
    Shasta: *Chrysanthemum maximum*
dandelion: *Taraxacum officinale*
    dwarf: *Krigia virginica*
day-flower, erect: *Commelina erecta*
dill: *Anethum graveolens*
dock, curly: *Rumex crispus*
    yard: *Rumex longifolius*
dogbane: *Apocynum* spp.
dogwood: *Cornus* spp.

elm: *Ulmus* spp.

fameflower: *Talinum parviflorum*
    rough-seeded: *Talinum rugospermum*
flax, stiff: *Linum rigidum*

gaillardia: *Gaillardia aristata*
gentian, downy: *Gentiana puberulenta*
    small fringed: *Gentianopsis procera*
goat's-rue: *Tephrosia virginiana*
goldenrod: *Solidago* spp.
gooseberry: *Ribes* spp.
grama, blue: *Bouteloua gracilis*
grass, Bermuda: *Cynodon dactylon*
    bottlebrush: *Hystrix patula*
    buffalo: *Buchloe dactyloides*
    gama: *Tripsacum dactyloides*
    Indian: *Sorghastrum nutans*
    Johnson: *Sorghum halepense*
    orchard: *Dactylis glomerata*
    pampas: *Miscanthus sacchariflorus*
    panic: *Panicum* spp.
    reed canary: *Phalaris arundinacea*
    yellow-eyed: *Xyris torta*
grass of Parnassus: *Parnassia glauca*

hackberry: *Celtis occidentalis*
hawthorn: *Crataegus* spp.
heather, false: *Hudsonia tomentosa*
heliotrope: *Heliotropum* spp.
hickory: *Carya* spp.
    shagbark: *Carya ovata*
hollyhock: *Alcea rosea*
hops: *Humulus lupulus*
hoptree: *Ptelea trifoliata*
huckleberry: *Gaylussacia baccata*

Indian paintbrush, yellow: *Castilleja sessiliflora*
indigo, cream wild: *Baptisia leucophaea*
    false: *Amorpha fruticosa*
    wild: *Baptisia* spp.
ironwood: *Ostrya virginiana*

Joe-pye-weed, spotted: *Eupatorium maculatum*

kittentails: *Besseya bullii*
knapweed: *Centaurea maculosa*
knotweed: *Polygonum* spp.

ladies'-tresses, early: *Spiranthes vernalis*
    hooded: *Spiranthes romanzoffiana*
lamb's quarters: *Chenopodium album*
lavender: *Lavandula angustifolia*
lead plant: *Amorpha canescens*
lilac: *Syringa vulgaris*
lily, common day: *Hemerocallis fulva*
    sand: *Mentzelia decapetala*
lobelia, Kalm's: *Lobelia kalmii*
locust, black: *Robinia pseudoacacia*
    honey: *Gleditsia triacanthos*
loosestrife, purple: *Lythrum salicaria*
lungwort, northern: *Mertensia paniculata*
lupine: *Lupinus* spp.
    wild: *Lupinus perennis*

mallow, poppy: *Callirhoe triangulata*
marigold, African: *Tagetes erecta*
    gem: *Tagetes signata*
mayflower, Canada: *Maianthemum canadense*
meadowsweet: *Spiraea alba*
milkweed: *Asclepias* spp.
    butterfly: *Asclepias tuberosa*
    common: *Asclepias syriaca*
    eared: *Asclepias auriculata*
    wooly: *Asclepias lanuginosa*
milkwort, cross-leaved: *Polygala cruciata*
mock orange: *Philadelphus* spp.
monkshood, northern wild: *Aconitum noveboracense*
morning glory, Pickering's: *Stylisma pickeringii* var. *pattersonii*

moss-pink: *Phlox subulata*
mullein foxglove: *Dasistoma macrophylla*
mustard, wild: *Brassica* spp.

nettle: *Urtica dioica*
    wood: *Laportea canadensis*
New Jersey tea: *Ceanothus* spp.

oak: *Quercus* spp.
    black: *Quercus velutina*
    bur: *Quercus macrocarpa*
obedient plant: *Physostegia virginiana*
orchid, leafy northern green: *Platanthera*
    hyperborea

parsley: *Petroselinum crispum*
pasque flower: *Anemone patens*
paw paw: *Asimina triloba*
pea, partridge: *Cassia fasciculata*
peanut, hog: *Amphicarpaea bracteata*
pearly everlasting: *Anaphalis margaritacea*
penstemon, cobaea: *Penstemon cobaea*
    large-flowered: *Penstemon grandiflorus*
    slender: *Penstemon gracilis*
petunia, wild: *Ruellia humilis*
phlox, cleft: *Phlox bifida*
    summer: *Phlox paniculata*
    sweet William: *Phlox maculata*
pineweed: *Hypericum gentianoides*
plantain: *Plantago* spp.
plum, ground: *Astragalus crassicarpus*
    wild: *Prunus americana*
poplar: *Populus* spp.
prickly pear: *Opuntia humifusa*
    big-rooted: *Opuntia macrorhiza*
    fragile: *Opuntia fragilis*
primrose, toothed evening: *Oenothera*
    serrulatus
privet: *Ligustrum* spp.
purple top: *Tridens flavus*
pussytoes: *Antennaria* spp.

Queen Anne's lace: *Daucus carota*

redbud: *Cercis canadensis*
rose, multiflora: *Rosa multiflora*
rush, beaked: *Rhynchospora capillacea*

sagewort, prairie: *Artemisia frigida*
salvia, blue: *Salvia farinacea*
sassafras: *Sassafras albidum*
saxifrage, Iowa golden: *Chrysosplenium*
    iowense
scabiosa: *Scabiosa* spp.
sedge, deep green: *Carex tonsa*
    lake: *Carex lacustris*
    nut: *Scleria verticillata*
    tussock: *Carex stricta*
    woolly: *Carex trichocarpa*
shinleaf, one-sided: *Pyrola secunda*
shorthusk, bearded: *Brachyelytrum*
    erectum
skeletonweed: *Lygodesmia juncea*
snakeroot, Virginia: *Aristolochia*
    serpentaria
snapdragon: *Antirrhinum majus*
sorrel, red: *Rumex acetosella*
spearmint: *Mentha spicata*
spicebush: *Lindera benzoin*
spikemoss: *Selaginella rupestris*
spurge, leafy: *Euphorbia esula*
strawberry, wild: *Fragaria virginiana*
sumac: *Rhus* spp.
sunflower: *Helianthus* spp.
    Mexican: *Tithonia rotundiflora*
    western: *Helianthus occidentalis*
switchgrass: *Panicum virgatum*

tansy: *Tanacetum vulgare*
thistle: *Cirsium* spp.
    wavy-leaved: *Cirsium undulatum*
tickseed: *Bidens* spp.
tick-trefoil: *Desmodium* spp.
timothy: *Phleum pratense*
toadflax: *Linaria vulgaris*
tobacco, flowering: *Nicotiana sylvestris*
trefoil, bird's-foot: *Lotus corniculatus*
turtlehead: *Chelone glabra*
twinflower: *Linnaea borealis*
twisted stalk, rosy: *Streptopus roseus*

vervain: *Verbena* spp.
vetch: *Vicia* spp.
    bent milk: *Astragalus distortus*
    crown: *Coronilla varia*
    lotus-flowered milk: *Astragalus lotiflorus*

viburnum: *Viburnum* spp.
vine, silver lace: *Polygonum auberti*
violet: *Viola* spp.
   bird's-foot: *Viola pedata*
   bog: *Viola nephrophylla*
   lance-leaved: *Viola lanceolata*

walnut: *Juglans* spp.
water-clover, hairy: *Marsilea vestita*

willow: *Salix* spp.
   shining: *Salix lucida*

yarrow: *Achillea millefolium*
yucca: *Yucca glauca*

zinnia: *Zinnia elegans*

LITERATURE CITED

In the citations of original descriptions, we list the true date of publication; we trust that the reader will be able to identify the publication referred to, because its publication date will encompass the date quoted. In the case of authors whose works appeared in overlapping years, we give first the initial year of the reference in quotation marks, followed by the true date of publication of the name in brackets. For multivolume publications in which more than one volume had pages starting with the number 1 (instead of being numbered consecutively), we give the volume number in parentheses following the year of description: for example, "Cramer 1777(2):4."

Some names proposed by Cramer, Stoll, and Drury were dated from the appearance of the indexes to their works. For brevity, we give the page references to the text descriptions in each case but date the names from the indexes.

References preceded by an asterisk have not been examined by the authors.

Anderson, W. I. 1982. Recorded in rocks. Pp. 10–41 in T. C. Cooper, ed., Iowa's natural history. Iowa Natural Heritage Foundation and the Iowa Academy of Science, Des Moines.

Arnold, R. A. 1983. Ecological studies of six endangered butterflies (Lepidoptera, Lycaenidae): Island biogeography, patch dynamics, and design of habitat preserves. University of California Publications in Entomology, Volume 99. Berkeley, California.

Berry, George H. 1914. A list of the Lepidoptera of Linn County, Iowa. Proc. Iowa Acad. Sci. 21:279–316.

Berry, Lulu M. 1934. Larvae of *Natholis iole* Boisd. (Lepid.: Pieridae). Ent. News 45(9):252–253.

Boisduval, Jean A. 1836. Histoire naturelle des insectes: Spécies general des lepidoptères. Vol. 1. Papillons diurnes. Roret, Paris.

———. 1852. Lepidoptères de la Californie. Ann. Soc. Ent. France, ser. 2, 10:275–324.

*———, and John M. LeConte. "1833" [1829–1834]. Histoire générale et iconographie des lepidoptères et des chenilles de l'Amérique septentrionale. Roret, Paris.

———. 1835. Hist. Gen. Iconogr. Lep. Amer. Sept.:210.

Borkin, Susan. 1994 and 1995. Ecological studies of the Poweshiek Skipper (*Oarisma poweshiek*) in Wisconsin. Milwaukee Public Museum.

Burns, John. 1964. Evolution in skipper butterflies of the genus *Erynnis*. Univ. Calif. Pub. in Ent. Vol. 37.

Butterfly gardening: Creating summer magic in your garden. 1990. Xerces Society/Smithsonian Institution. Sierra Club Books, San Francisco.

Calvin, S. 1897. Geology of Buchanan County. Annual Rep. Iowa Geol. Surv. 8:291–339.

———. 1902. Geology of Chickasaw County. Annual Rep. Iowa Geol. Surv. 13:257–292.

Carde, Ring T., Arthur M. Shapiro, and Harry K. Clench. 1970. Sibling species in the *Eurydice* group of Lethe (Lepidoptera: Satyridae). Psyche 77:70–103.

Christenson, Michael C. 1971. An annotated checklist of the butterflies of Iowa. Master's thesis, University of Northern Iowa, Cedar Falls.

Clark, Austin H. 1936. Notes on the butterflies of the genus *Enodia* and description of a new fritillary from Peru. U.S. Nat. Mus. Proceedings 83:251–259.

Clench, Harry K. 1976. Fugitive color in the males of certain Pieridae. J. Lepid. Soc. 30(2):88–90.

Cramer, Pierre. [1776]. Uitl. Kapellen 1:24.

———. 1777. Uitl. Kapellen 2:18.

———. [1779]. Uitl. Kapellen 3:31.

———. "1779" [1775]–1782. Papillons exotiques des trois parties du monde, l'Asie, l'Afrique et l'Amérique. [Title and text in Dutch and French.] S. J. Baalde, Amsterdam.

Dana, R. F. 1985. Effects of prescribed burning on two prairie-obligate skippers, *Hesperia dacotae* Skinner and *H. ottoe* Edwards (Lepidoptera, Hesperidae). P. 15 in Ninth North American prairie conference abstracts of contributed papers. Moorhead State University, Moorhead, Minnesota.

———. 1991. Conservation management of the prairie skippers *Hesperia dacotae* and *Hesperia ottoe*. University of Minnesota, St. Paul.

Denis and Schiffermuller. 1775. Ankundung eines syst. Werkes Schmett. Wiener Gerend:321.

Dodge, G. M. 1874. *Hesperia pawnee* n. sp. Canad. Ent. 6(3):44–45.

dos Passos, Cyril F. 1935. Some butterflies of southern Newfoundland with descriptions of new subspecies (Lepid, Rhopal.). Canad. Ent. 67:82–88.

Doubleday, Edward. 1841. Entomologist 1:209.

———. 1846–1850. The genera of diurnal Lepidoptera: Comprising their generic characters, a notice of their habits and transformations, and a catalogue of the species of each genus. Vol. 1. Longman, Brown, Green and Longmans, London.

———, and William C. Hewitson. [1847]. The genera of diurnal Lepidoptera. Longman, Brown, Green and Longmans, London.

Downey, John C. 1962. Inter-specific pairing in Lycaenidae. J. Lepid. Soc. 16(4):235–237.

———. 1966. Sound production in pupae of Lycaenidae. J. Lepid. Soc. 20:129–155.

———. 1975. Two new Iowa records. J. Lepid. Soc. 29(2):94.

———. 1978. The butterflies of Fremont County, Iowa, and the cabbage principle. Iowa Bird Life, 48(1):20–24.

Drury, Dru. 1773–1782. Illustrations of natural history . . . To which is added, a translation into French. 3 vols. B. White, London.

Ebner, James A. 1970. The butterflies of Wisconsin. Pop. Sci. Handbook No. 12. Milwaukee Public Museum.

Edwards, William H. 1862a. Descriptions of certain species of diurnal Lepidoptera found within the limits of the United States and British America. No. 2. Proc. Acad. of Nat. Sci. Philad. 14:54–58.

———. 1862b. Descriptions of certain species of diurnal Lepidoptera found within the limits of the United States and British America. No. 3. Proc. Acad. of Nat. Sci. Philad. 14:221–226.

———. 1863. Descriptions of certain species of diurnal Lepidoptera found within the limits of the United States and British America. No. 1. Proc. Ent. Soc. Philad. 2:14–22.

———. 1865. Descriptions of certain species of diurnal Lepidoptera found within the limits of the United States and British America. No. 4. Proc. Ent. Soc. Philad. 4:201–204.

———. "1866" [1867]. Descriptions of certain species of diurnal Lepidoptera found within the limits of the United States and British America. No. 5. Proc. Ent. Soc. Philad. 6:200–208.

———. 1869. Descriptions of certain species of diurnal Lepidoptera found in the United States. Trans. Amer. Ent. Soc. 2:311–312.

———. 1870. Descriptions of new species of diurnal Lepidoptera found in the United States. Trans. Amer. Ent. Soc. 3:10–22.

———. "1871" [1872]. Descriptions of new species of North American butterflies. Trans. Amer. Ent. Soc. 3:266–277.

———. 1873. Trans. American Ent. Soc. 4:346–348.

———. 1879. Description of a new species of *Amphila*. Canad. Ent. 11:238–239.

———. 1880. On certain species of *Satyrus*. Canad. Ent. 12:21–32, 51–55, 90–94, 109–115, 147.

Eilers L. J. 1982. Iowa as it was. Pp. 122–125 in T. C. Cooper, ed., Iowa's natural history. Iowa Natural Heritage Foundation and the Iowa Academy of Science, Des Moines.

Eilers, Lawrence J., and Dean M. Roosa. 1994. The vascular plants of Iowa: An annotated checklist and natural history. University of Iowa Press, Iowa City.

Fabricius, Johann C. 1775. Systema entomologiae, sistens insectorum classes, ordines, genera, species, adiectis synonymis, locis, descriptionibus, observationibus. Kortii, Flensburg and Leipzig.

———. 1787. Mantissa insectorum, sistens eorum species nuper detectae adiectis characteribus genericis, differentiis specificis, emendationibus, observationibus. Vol. 2. Christ. Gottl. Proft, Copenhagen.

———. 1793. Entomologia systematica emendata et aucta, secundum classes, ordines, genera, species, ajectis synonimis, locis, observationibus, descriptionibus. Vol. 3, part 1. C. G. Proft, fil, et soc., Copenhagen.

———. 1798. Supplementum entomologiae systematicae. Proft et Storch, Copenhagen.

Field, William D. 1938. A manual of the butterflies and skippers of Kansas (Lepidoptera, Rhopalocera). Bull. Univ. of Kansas 39(10):1–328.

Forbes, William T. M. 1936. The *persius* group of *Thanaos* (Lepidoptera, Hesperiidae). Psyche 43:104–113.

French, George H. 1897. Preparatory stages of *Pyrus* [*sic*] *tessellata*. Scud. Canad. Ent. 29(12):283–285.

Gatrelle, Ronald R. 1975. *Thymelicus lineola* in Iowa. News Lepid. Soc. No. 6.

Geyer, Carl. 1832–1837. In Jacob Hubner, 1818–1837, pl. 104–172.

Glassberg, Jeffrey. 1999. Butterflies through binoculars: The East. Oxford University Press, New York.

Godart, Jean B. 1819. Encyclopédie méthodique. Histoire naturelle. Entomologie, ou histoire naturelle des crustaces, des arachnides et des insectes. Vol. 9, Part 1. Agasse, Paris.

———. "1819" [1824]. Encyclopédie méthodique: Histoire naturelle—Entomologie, ou histoire naturelle des crustaces, des arachnides et des insectes. Vol. 9, Part 2. Agasse, Paris.

Grote, Augustus R. 1872. On a new checkered *Hesperia*. Canad. Ent. 4:69–70.

———. 1874. On the butterflies of Anticosti. Bull. Buffalo Soc. Nat. Sci. 1:185.

*———, and Coleman T. Robinson. 1867a. Descriptions of American Lepidoptera. Trans. Amer. Ent. Soc. 1:171–192, pl. 4.

———. 1867b. Notes on the Lepidoptera of America. Ann. Lyceum of Nat. His. (New York) 8:432–466.

Hallberg, G. R., E. A. Bettis III, and J. C. Prior. 1984. A geologic overview of the Paleozoic Plateau region of northeastern Iowa. Proc. Iowa Acad. Sci. 91(1):5–11.

Hallberg, G. R., T. E. Fenton, G. A. Miller, and A. J. Luttenbergger. 1978. The Iowan erosion surface: An old story, an important lesson, and some new wrinkles. Pp. 2–94 in Raymond Anderson ed., 42nd Annual Tri-State Geological Field Conference on Geology of East-Central Iowa. Iowa City.

Harris, Thaddeus W. 1842. Report ins. inj. veg., 1st ed.:221.

———. 1862a. P. 101 in John G. Morris, 1862.

———. 1862b. A treatise on some of the insects injurious to vegetation. New ed., edited by C. L. Flint. Crosby and Nichols, Boston.

Heitzman, J. Richard. 1969. Nocturnal copulation of Rhopalocera. J. Lepid. Soc. 23(2):105–106.

———, and Joan E. Heitzman. 1987. Butterflies and moths of Missouri. Missouri Department of Conservation, Jefferson City.

Hendrickson, George O. 1928. Some notes on the insect fauna of an Iowa prairie. Ann. Ent. Soc. Amer. 21(1):132–138.

———. 1930. Studies on the insect fauna of Iowa prairies, Iowa State College J. Sci. 4(2):49–179.

Hoffmeister, A. W. 1881. [*Melitaea phaeton, Callidryas eubule* and *Terias mexicana* in Lee County, Iowa.] Canad. Ent. 13(9):196.

Holland, William J. 1940 (1931). The butterfly book. New and thoroughly revised edition. Doubleday, Doran and Company, Garden City, N.Y.

Hovanitz, William. 1962. The distribution of the species of the genus *Pieris* in North America. J. Res. Lepid. 1(1):73–83.

Howe, William H. 1975. The butterflies of North America. Doubleday and Co., Garden City, N.Y.

Huber, Ronald L., J. S. Nordin, and O. R. Taylor. 1966. A systematic checklist of Minnesota Rhopalocera (butterflies and skippers). Science Museum, St. Paul.

Hubner, Jacob. 1806–1824. Sammlung exotischer Schmetterlinge. Published by the author, Augsburg.

———. 1816 [1819]–1826. Verzeichniss bekannter Schmettlinge [*sic*]. Published by the author, Augsburg.

———. 1818–1837. Zutrage zur sammlung exotischer Schmetterlinge, bestehend in bekundigung einzelner Fliegmuster neuer oder rarer nicht europäischer Gattungen. Published by the author, Augsburg. [Pl. 1–103 by Hubner; pl. 104–172 by Carl Geyer.]

Irwin, Roderick R., and John C. Downey. 1973. Annotated checklist of the butterflies of Illinois. Biol. Notes No. 81. Illinois Nat. Hist. Survey, Urbana.

Johnson, Kurt. 1973. The butterflies of Nebraska. J. Res. Lepid. 11(1):1–64.

*Kirby, William. 1837. Fauna boreali-americana, or the zoology of the northern parts of British America, containing descriptions of the objects of natural history collected on the late northern land expeditions, under command of Captain Sir John Franklin by John Richardson. Part 4. The insects, by W. Kirby. Longman, etc., London.

Klots, Alexander B. 1951. A field guide to the butterflies of North America, east of the Great Plains. Houghton Mifflin Company, Boston.

Lammers, T. G., and A. G. Van der Valk. 1979. A checklist of the aquatic and wetland vascular plants of Iowa: II. Monocotyledons. Proc. Iowa Acad. Sci. 85:121–163.

Latreille, Pierre A. "1819" [1824]. Pp. 769, 777 in Jean B. Godart, "1819" [1824].

LeConte, John M. 1833. In Jean A. Boisduval and John M. LeConte, Hist. Lepid. Amerique (Sept.):99.

Leussler, Richard A. 1921. *Pamphila ottoe* Edw. and *pawnee* Dodge, with description of a new form (Lep., Rhop). Ent. News 32(7):206–207.

Lindsay (for Lindsey), Arthur W. 1917. A list of butterflies of Iowa. Ent. News 28:327–353.

Lindsey, Arthur W. 1915. The butterflies of Woodbury County. Proc. Iowa Acad. Sci. 21:341–346.

———. 1921. The Hesperioidea of America north of Mexico. Univ. Iowa Stud. Nat. Hist. 9(4):1–114.

———. 1922. Some Iowa records of Lepidoptera. Proc. Iowa Acad. Sci. 27:319–335.

———. 1931 (1932). The Hesperioidea of North America. Denison University Bulletin. J. American Laboratories. 26(1):87–91.

———. 1942. A primary revision of *Hesperia*. Scientific Laboratories of Denison University 37:1–50.

Linnaeus, Carolus. 1758. Systema nataurae per regna tria naturae secundum classes, ordines, genera, species, cum characteribus, differentiis, synonymis, locis. Editio decima, reformata. Vol. 1. Salvius, Stockholm.

———. 1761. Fauna Sveccia, 2:285.

———. 1763. In Johansson, Amoen. Acad. (1763) 6:406.

———. 1771. Mantissa plantarum, altera generum editionis VI & specierum editionis II. Vol. 2. Salvius, Stockholm.

Macy, R. W., and H. H. Shepard. 1941. Butterflies: A handbook of the butterflies of the United States, complete for the region north of the Potomac and Ohio rivers and east of the Dakotas. University of Minnesota Press, Minneapolis.

Masters, John H. 1968. Butterflies of Lynch Hollow, Camden County, Missouri. J. Kansas Ent. Soc. 42(2):133–141.

McAlpine, Wilbur S. 1973. Observations on life history of *Oarisma powesheik* (Parker) 1870. J. Res. on the Lepid. 11(2):82–93.

McDunnough, James. 1942. A new Canadian *Strymon* (Lycaenidae, Lepidoptera). Canad. Ent. 74:1.

*Menetries, E. 1857. Enumeratio corporum animalium Musei imperialis academiae scientiarum Petropolitaniae, Petropoli [St. Petersburg]. 1 (1855)–3 (1863).

Miller, Lee D. 1961. Notes on nine Iowa butterfly species, including four new to the state. J. Lepid. Soc. 15(2):97–98.

———, and F. Martin Brown. 1981. A catalogue/checklist of the butterflies of America north of Mexico. Memoir No. 2, Lepidopterists' Society. Sarasota, Fla.

Miller, Stephen. 1972. Observations and new records of Iowa Rhopalocera. J. Lepid. Soc. 26(4):229–234.

Moore, P. D., and D. J. Bellamy. 1974. Peatlands. Springer-Verlag, New York.

Morris, John G. 1862. Synopsis of the described Lepidoptera of North America. Part I: Diurnal and crepuscular Lepidoptera. Smithsonian Misc. Coll. Smithsonian Institution, Washington, D.C.

Muller. 1764. Faun. Fridrichsdalinae Nov:36.

Nabokov, Vladimir. 1943. The nearctic forms of *Lycaeides* Hubner. (Lycaenidae, Lepidoptera). Psyche 50:87–99.

———. 1944. Notes on the morphology of the genus *Lycaeides* (Lycaeides, Lepidoptera), Psyche 51:104–138.

Nekola, J. C. 1988a. Final report, Fayette County fen survey: 1986–1988. Unpublished manuscript submitted to the Fayette County Conservation Board.

———. 1988b. Final report, 1988 fen survey. Unpublished manuscript submitted to Dean M. Roosa and Terrance J. Frest.

———. 1993. Ecology and biogeography of isolated habitats: Fens and algific talus slopes in northeastern Iowa. Doctoral thesis in ecology, University of North Carolina, Chapel Hill.

*Ochsenheimer, Ferdinand. 1808. Die Schmetterlinge von Europa. Vol. 1, part 2. Gerhard Fleischer, Leipzig.

Olsen, Franklin L. 1990. A study of the butterflies and skippers at Rock Island Preserve. Report to the Linn County Conservation Board.

Opler, Paul A., and George O. Krizek. 1984. Butterflies east of the Great Plains. Johns Hopkins University Press, Baltimore.

Opler, Paul A., and Vichai Malikul. 1998. A field guide to eastern butterflies. Houghton Mifflin, Boston.

Opler, Paul A., and Andrew D. Warren. 2003. Butterflies of North America: 2. Scientific names list for butterfly species of North America, north of Mexico. http://www.biology.ualberta .ca/old_site/uasm// Opler&Warren.pdf.

Orwig, Timothy T. 1992. Loess Hills prairies as butterfly survivia: Opportunities and challenges. Pp. 131–135 in D. C. Smith and C. A. Jacobs, eds., Proceedings of the Twelfth North American Prairie Conference. University of Northern Iowa, Cedar Falls.

———. 1994. Morningside College: A centennial history. Morningside College, Sioux City.

Osborn, Herbert. 1890. Butterflies in Iowa. Amer. Ent. and Bot. 1 (new series):226.

———. 1891. A partial catalogue of the animals of Iowa, represented in the collections of the Department of Zoology and Entomology of the Iowa Agriculture College, Ames. Iowa Agriculture College, Ames.

Parker, H. W. 1870a. Iowa butterflies. Amer. Ent. & Bot. 2:175.

———. 1870b. A new hesperian. Amer. Ent. & Bot. 2:271–272.

Pellett, Frank C. 1915. Butterflies of chance occurrence in Cass Co., Iowa. Proc. Iowa Acad. Sci. 21:347–348, pl. 36.

Platt, Austin P., and Joseph C. Greenfield, Jr. 1971. Inter-specific hybridization between *Limenitis arthemis astyanax* and *L. archippus* (Nymphalidae). J. Lepid. Soc. 25(4):278–284.

Porter, A. F. 1908. A list of local Lepidoptera found at Decorah, Iowa. Ent. News 19:369–372.

Prior, J. C. 1976. A regional guide to Iowa landforms. Iowa Geological Survey Educ. Series No.3. Iowa Geological Survey, Iowa City.

———. 1991. Landforms of Iowa. University of Iowa Press, Iowa City.

———, R. G. Baker, G. R. Hallberg, and H. A. Semken. 1982. Glaciation. Pp. 44–61 in T. C. Cooper, ed., Iowa's Natural History. Iowa Natural Heritage Foundation and the Iowa Academy of Science, Des Moines.

Putnam, Joseph D. 1876. List of Lepidoptera collected in the vicinity of Davenport, Iowa. Proc. Davenport Acad. Sci. 1:174–177.

Pyle, Robert Michael. 1981. The Audubon Society field guide to North American butterflies. Knopf, New York.

Pyle, R., M. Bentzien, and P. Opler. 1981. Insect conservation. Ann. Rev. Entomology 26:233–258.

Reakirt, Tyson. "1865" [1866]. Descriptions of some new species of *Eresia*. Proc. Ent. Soc. Philad. 5:224–227.

———. 1868 [1867]. Proc. Acad. Nat. Sci. Philad. 20:87.

Roosa, D. M. 1982. Natural regions of Iowa. Pp. 126–135 in T. C. Cooper, ed., Iowa's Natural History. Iowa Natural Heritage Foundation and the Iowa Academy of Science, Des Moines.

Schlicht, D. W., and T. T. Orwig. 1992. Sequential use of niche by prairie obligate Skipper butterflies (Lepidoptera: Hesperidae) with implications for management. Pp. 137–139 in D. C. Smith and C. A. Jacobs, eds., Proceedings of the Twelfth North American Prairie Conference. University of Northern Iowa, Cedar Falls.

———. 1998. The status of Iowa's Lepidoptera. Iowa Acad. Sci. 105(2):82–88.

Scott, James A. 1986. The butterflies of North America: A natural history and field guide. Stanford University Press, Stanford.

Scudder, Samuel H. 1864. A list of the butterflies of New England. Proc. Essex Institute 3:161–179.

———. 1868a. Supplement to a list of the butterflies of New England. Proc. Bost. Soc. Nat. Hist. 11:375–384.

———. 1868b. [Untitled notes on three Iowa butterflies.] Proc. Bost. Soc. Nat. Hist. 11:401.

———. 1869. A preliminary list of the butterflies of Iowa. Chicago Academy of Science Transactions 1:326–337.

———. 1870. In Minutes of the section of entomology, January 26, 1870. Proc. Bost. Soc. Nat. Hist. 13:205–208.

———. 1875. Synonymie list of the butterflies of North America, North of Mexico. Bull. Buff. Soc. Nat. Sci. 2:233–269.

———. 1887. *Limochores pontiac* and *Atrytone kumskaka*. Canad. Ent. 19(3):45–48.

————. 1889. The butterflies of the eastern United States and Canada, with special reference to New England. 3 vols. Published by the author, Cambridge, Mass.

————, and Edward Burgess. 1870. On asymmetry in the appendages of hexapod insects, especially as illustrated in the Lepidopterous genus *Nisoniades*. Proc. Bost. Soc. Nat. Hist. 13:282–306.

Shimek, B. 1948. The plant geography of Iowa. U. Iowa Stud. Nat. Hist. 18(4):1–178.

Skinner, Henry. 1893. The larvae and chrysalis of *Chrysophanus dione*. Canad. Ent. 25(1):22.

————. 1911. New species or subspecies of North American butterflies (Lepid.). Ent. News 22:412–413.

Smith, D. D. and P. Christiansen. 1982. Prairies. Pp. 160–179 in T. C. Cooper, ed., Iowa's Natural History. Iowa Natural Heritage Foundation and the Iowa Academy of Science, Des Moines.

Smith, James E. 1797. The natural history of the rarer lepidopterous insects of Georgia, including their systematic characters, the particulars of their several metamorphoses, and the plants on which they feed, collected from the observations of Mr. John Abbott, many years resident in that country. T. Bensley for J. Edwards, London.

Spomer, S. M., L. G. Higley, T. T. Orwig, G. L. Selby, and L. J. Young. 1993. Clinal variation in *Hesperia leonardus* (Hesperiidae) in the Loess Hills of the Missouri River Valley. J. Lep. Soc. 47(4):291–302.

Stoll, Caspar. 1782. P. 194 in Pierre Cramer, "1779" [1775]–1782.

————. "1791" [1790]. Supplement à l'ouvrage, intitulé les papillons exotiques, des trois parties du monde l'Asie, l'Afrique et l'Amerique; par Mr. Pierre Cramer, contenant les figures exactes des chenilles et des chrysalides de Suriname; comme celles des plusieurs rares et nouvellement découvertes papillons et phalènes rassemblies et décrits par Mr. C. Stoll. Nic. Th. Gravius, Amsterdam.

Succow, M., and E. Lange. 1984. The mire types of the German Democratic Republic. Pp. 149–175 in P. D. Moore, ed., European Mires. Academic Press, New York.

Swengel, Ann B. 1998. Effects of management on butterfly abundance in tallgrass prairie and pine barrens. Biological Conservation 81(1):77–89.

Swink, Floyd, and Gerould Wilhelm. 1994. Plants of the Chicago region. 4th ed. Indiana Academy of Science, Morton Arboretum, Lisle, Ill.

Tilden, J. W., and A. C. Smith. 1986. A field guide to western butterflies. Houghton Mifflin Co., Boston.

Urquhart, F. A. 1960. The monarch butterfly. University of Toronto Press, Toronto.

Van Winkle, A. S. 1893a. A black male of *Papilio turnus*. Canad. Ent. 25(8):212.

————. 1893b. *Callidryas eubule*. Canad. Ent. 25(11):296.

Walton, Alice B. 1879. Entomology. Pp. 334–338 in The history of Muscatine County, Iowa. Western Historical Soc., Chicago.

————. 1880. List of the Lepidoptera of Muscatine County, Iowa. Proc. Davenport Acad. Nat. Sci. 2:191–192.

White, C. A. 1870. Report on the geological survey of the state of Iowa to the Thirteenth General Assembly. Vol. 2. Mills, State Printer, Des Moines.

Willard, H. G. 1892. *Thy. poweshiek*. Ent. News 3:232.

————. 1893. [Notes on the biology of *C. dione*]. Ent. News 4:126–127.

Winter, William D., Jr. 2000. Basic techniques for observing and studying moths and butterflies. Memoir of the Lep. Soc. No. 5. Los Angeles.

Wolden, B. O. 1917. The White Admiral or Banded Purple butterfly in Iowa. Proc. Iowa Acad. Sci. 23:269.

INDEX

The first page number indicates the species account; the second number indicates the photographs; the third indicates the maps and flight diagrams.

BUR OAK NATURE GUIDES

Birds at Your Feeder:
A Guide to Winter Birds of the Great Plains
By Dana Gardner and Nancy Overcott

Birds of an Iowa Dooryard
By Althea R. Sherman

Butterflies in Your Pocket:
A Guide to the Butterflies of the Upper
Midwest
By Steve Hendrix and Diane Debinski

A Country So Full of Game:
The Story of Wildlife in Iowa
By James J. Dinsmore

Gardening in Iowa and Surrounding Areas
By Veronica Lorson Fowler

An Illustrated Guide to Iowa Prairie Plants
By Paul Christiansen and
Mark Müller

Iowa Birdlife
Gladys Black

The Iowa Breeding Bird Atlas
By Laura Spess Jackson, Carol A. Thompson,
and James J. Dinsmore

Mushrooms in Your Pocket:
A Guide to the Mushrooms of Iowa
By Donald M. Huffman and Lois H. Tiffany

Orchids in Your Pocket:
A Guide to Native Orchids of Iowa
By Bill Witt

A Practical Guide to Prairie Reconstruction
By Carl Kurtz

Prairie:
A North American Guide
By Suzanne Winckler

Prairie in Your Pocket:
A Guide to Plants of the Tallgrass Prairie
By Mark Müller

Prairies, Forests, and Wetlands:
The Restoration of Natural Landscape
Communities in Iowa
By Janette R. Thompson

Raptors in Your Pocket:
A Great Plains Guide
By Dana Gardner

Restoring the Tallgrass Prairie:
An Illustrated Manual for Iowa
and the Upper Midwest
By Shirley Shirley

The Vascular Plants of Iowa:
An Annotated Checklist and
Natural History
By Lawrence J. Eilers and Dean M. Roosa

Wetlands in Your Pocket:
A Guide to Common Plants and
Animals of Midwestern Wetlands
By Mark Müller

Where the Sky Began:
Land of the Tallgrass Prairie
By John Madson

Woodland in Your Pocket:
A Guide to Common Woodland Plants
of the Midwest
By Mark Müller